From
WORD
to LIFE

From WORD to LIFE

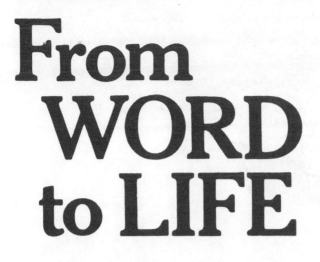

A Guide to the Art of Bible Study

Perry Yoder

Foreword by Willard M. Swartley

HERALD PRESS
Scottdale, Pennsylvania
Kitchener, Ontario
1982

Library of Congress Cataloging in Publication Data

Yoder, Perry B.
    From word to life.

    (The Conrad Grebel lectures; 1980)
    Bibliography: p.
    Includes index.
    1. Bible—Study. I. Title. II. Series.
    BS600.2.Y62   220.6'01   81-20071
    ISBN 0-8361-1249-0 (pbk.)   AACR2

FROM WORD TO LIFE
Copyright © 1982 by Herald Press, Scottdale, Pa. 15683
    Published simultaneously in Canada by Herald Press,
    Kitchener, Ont. N2G 4M5
Library of Congress Catalog Card Number: 81-20071
International Standard Book Number: 0-8361-1249-0
Printed in the United States of America
Design: Alice B. Shetler

82 83 84 85 86 87 88 10 9 8 7 6 5 4 3 2 1

To my parents

Contents

Chapter 3. From Structure to Type: Form Analysis

Chapter 4. From Form to Content: Lexical Analysis

PART II. THE CONTEXT

Chapter 5: From Context to Composition: Tradition Analysis

Chapter 6: From Composition to Collection: Transmission and Redaction Analysis

Chapter 7: From Author to Audience: Historical Analysis

PART III. THE APPLICATION

Chapter 8: From Text to Practice: Making Application

Foreword

Few books on Bible study method both explain how and show how. Fewer still seek to do this by utilizing current biblical scholarship while writing for informed lay people. Virtually no books with this objective demonstrate a competent grasp of both the linguistic and historical schools of biblical interpretation. This volume, *From Word to Life*, fills the gap with this distinctive contribution. Written clearly, it should enjoy wide usage especially in the classroom setting.

Perry Yoder's experience and study have prepared him well for the task. He has studied widely in the linguistic backgrounds for biblical interpretation, mastered the historical-critical method, and has taught the Bible to lay people in congregational settings within the context of a two-year-long voluntary service assignment. His earlier book *Toward Understanding the Bible: Hermeneutics for Lay People* resulted directly from this experience.

Of the many features meriting commendation in this volume, *From Word to Life*, I identify two especially. First, Yoder presents a method in eight clear steps: the first and last are translation and application of the text respectively. Steps two, three, and four deal with the linguistic conventions of the text: its structure, genre, and word (grammar). Steps five, six, and seven focus upon the context of the text: its tradition-history, its transmission and redaction, and its historical-cultural setting. This comprehensive treatment, described and illustrated well, qualifies the book to become a gold mine for teachers and students of biblical hermeneutics.

Second, Yoder uses the same four biblical texts in each chapter to illustrate the contribution of each phase of study. Hence the book contains a valuable exegesis of four important biblical texts (Gen. 12:10-20; Amos 2:6-16; Mt. 5:38-42; Rom. 13:1-7) selected two each from the Old and New Testaments and representing four different types of literature.

The book is not written for the beginner in Bible study; its best use will be by those who, having already started on the pilgrimage of Bible study, are at least minimally acquainted with the historical-critical method and have thought some about how language works. Because of its clarity and scope, it will reward both the serious student and the seasoned professor of biblical studies.

As a contribution of the Conrad Grebel Projects Committee, this lectureship was commissioned to assist informed lay people in one of the most crucial tasks facing the church: the systematic, serious, and responsible study of the Bible. To this end I am happy to commend the volume.

Willard M. Swartley
Executive Secretary
Conrad Grebel Projects Committee

Author's Preface

The inductive Bible study method presented in this book is motivated by three objectives. The first is to show the reasonableness of the way biblical scholars work with the Bible. Through the explanation and illustration of the methods of biblical scholarship, it will become evident that to a large extent scholars are asking questions which the biblical texts themselves, so to speak, force upon them. Contrary to popular stereotypes, scholars by and large do not bring irrelevant questions which are the result of their own ingenuity. Instead, the methods that scholars have developed over the years have remained because they have proven to be useful in understanding the text.

In addition, many of the resources which are available to help understand the Bible, such as commentaries and Bible dictionaries, are the result of scholarship using these methods. This makes it difficult at times for those unacquainted with this type of study to use these resources as well as they might. By gaining some knowledge of the methods used and how to use the information gotten from these methods one should be able to use these valuable tools more effectively.

A second motive is to present these methods or ways of study in such a manner that others can also appropriate them for their own use. Because of the importance of these study tools, they should not be the property of any one group. While the present book is not a Bible study workbook, it should help persons become better students of the Bible. Not everyone can do all the various stages of study equally well. For some the whole method may appear to be quite overwhelming. Yet for others, the various steps of study will prove to be helpful, and will lead them to a deeper and surer understanding of Scripture. It is not necessary to be able to read to understand the Bible—someone may read it to you. Yet it is obviously of great benefit to be able to read the Scriptures in order to understand them better. Likewise it may not be to everyone's taste to study the Bible carefully and inductively, yet it is of great importance for those who will to do so.

Third, and perhaps most importantly, it is hoped that through an acquaintance with good Bible study methodology, discernment may be gained as to what constitutes valid and invalid uses and interpretations of Scripture. At present there is such a variety of competing voices claiming a biblical base that interpretation seems to by synonymous with opinion. In such a situation, the unconscious temptation is to choose those voices which best suit our own views. One of the major gifts of using or following a proper inductive method as presented below is that it gives reliable and valid results. This means that if we want to have "objective, valid" interpretations rather than the expression of personal prejudices, we need to follow an "objective" method in the study of the Bible. From this it is hoped that the church will see that it is in her own best interest to allow, indeed, even promote the scholarly study of the Bible. This means that although everyone may not have the time and the gifts to undertake such study, all should have some knowledge of how the results of such study are gained and why they are valid. By understanding what constitutes such inductive Bible study, and how this relates to validity in interpretation, congregations may come to appreciate and feel a greater need for inductive Bible study.

This present book is a sequel to my earlier work, *Toward Understanding the Bible* (Faith and Life, 1978). There in simplified form I attempted to lay out a *theory* of interpretation. Here I am attempting to outline the *practice* of interpretation. To do this I have tried to arrange into a logical sequence the major approaches used by scholars to study the text.

The methods used by scholars are sometimes grouped under the title the historical-critical method. The use of historical in this title indicates an influence by historical method on biblical studies, for historical questions and the writing of history has been a major preoccupation of students of the Bible. However in the decade of the seventies a shift has taken place in biblical studies—a shift from history and historical method as the handmaiden of biblical scholarship to linguistics and literary method. There may also be a subtle shift in objective: from using the text as a document to reconstruct or write history to understanding the text as an act of communication. The present guide to practice emphasizes this latter goal of understanding the text. History and historical reconstructions are subordinated to this end.

Many people have contributed much to this project. The Conrad Grebel lectureship committee supported the research and writing. My students' questions have been a constant source of enlightenment. Willard Swartley, executive director, gave wise counsel and helpful guidance, especially in the early stages of writing. The committee of readers, Katie Funk Wiebe, John Lederach, David Garber, and Howard Charles, have each contributed to the strength of the manuscript. In light of such generous help, what shortcomings yet remain are surely due to my own limitations. Most of the first draft was typed by Brenda Denzler who spent long hours meeting short deadlines. Rosalie Neufeld and Cynthia Goerzen prepared the final copy and Cynthia compiled the indexes. The cost for the acquisition of interlibrary loan materials and for the preparation of the first manuscript were underwritten in part by faculty development grants from Bethel College, for which I am grateful. Elsie Sheriff often went beyond the call of duty in obtaining materials for me through interlibrary loan.

Finally, I must express appreciation to my family. To my wife, Elizabeth, who encouraged, helped, and above all often did more than her share of the household duties while I was writing. Then she graciously edited the manuscript for publication, in spite of an already too heavy work load. And to my twin sons, Joel and Joshua, who chafed under a summer's vacation ruined by having to be quiet and fit their playtime to dad's writing and research schedule.

Perry Yoder
North Newton, Kansas

Abbreviations of Books and Periodicals

AHwb   Akkadisches Handwörterbuch

AOAT   Alten Orient und Alten Testament

BASOR   Bulletin of the American Schools of Oriental Research

BHTh   Beiträge zur Historischen Theologie

BK   Biblische Kommentar

BZ   Biblische Zeitschrift

BZAW   Beihefte zur Zeitschrift für Alttestamentliche Wissenschaft

CAD   Chicago Assyrian Dictionary

CBQ   Catholic Biblical Quarterly

DNTT   New International Dictionary of New Testament Theology

ET   Expository Times

EvTh   Evangelische Theologie

FRLANT   Forschung zur Religion und Literatur des Alten und Neuen Testaments

GND   Good News Bible

HeythJ   The Heythrop Journal

HTR   Harvard Theological Review

HUCA   Hebrew Union College Annual

IDB   Interpreters Dictionary of the Bible

IDB(S)   Interpreters Dictionary of the Bible, Supplement volume

IEJ   Israel Exploration Journal

JAAR   Journal of the American Academy of Religion

JAOS	Journal of the American Oriental Society
JBL	Journal of Biblical Literature
JNES	Journal of Near Eastern Studies
JSOT	Journal for the Study of the Old Testament
KD	Kerygma und Dogma
ME	Mennonite Encyclopedia
MQR	Mennonite Quarterly Review
NTS	New Testament Studies
OTS	Oudtestamentische Studiën
RLA	Reallexikon der Assyriologie
SBT	Studies in Biblical Theology
SJT	Scottish Journal of Theology
TDNT	Theological Dictionary of the New Testament
TDOT	Theological Dictionary of the Old Testament
ThR	Theologische Rundschau
TLZ	Theologische Literaturzeitung
TZ	Theologische Zeitschrift
VT	Vetus Testamentum
VTS	Vetus Testamentum, Supplement
WMANT	Wissenschaftliche Monographien zum Alten und Neuen Testament
WUNT	Wissenschaftliche Untersuchungen zum Neuen Testament
ZAW	Zeitschrift für Alttestamentliche Wissenschaft
ZNW	Zeitschrift für die Neutestamentliche Wissenschaft und die Kunde des Alten Christentums
ZThK	Zeitschrift für Theologie und Kirche

From
WORD
to LIFE

Chapter 1

Introduction: Getting
Our Bearings

1.00 *From Canon to Chameleon*

In the church, the Bible is often appealed to as an authority since it is considered by many as a norm for Christian faith and life. In fact, this is what it means for Scripture to be canonical: to have some binding authority, to be a measuring stick whereby the individual and the church can discern truth from error. As a norm, the Bible is claimed to be the foundation of the Christian faith; however it appears to be a very shaky foundation, since it is interpreted in so many different ways within the church. Indeed, it sometimes seems that the Bible is more interpreted in light of theological tradition and context, rather than theological tradition being measured by the light of the Bible. The Bible's words take on one meaning in one theological context, and other meanings in other contexts. In this state of affairs the Bible seems more of a chameleon than a canon.

The history of interpretation also illustrates this state of affairs. Interpretations which were firmly held in one period become oddities in the next period. At present the intensity of this diversity has increased. This is no doubt due in part to changing attitudes toward the Bible. Today there seems to be a general waning of reliance on authority and tradition, with more emphasis placed on individual responsibility and judgment. As a consequence, there tend to be more interpretations offered, since people less bound by tradition feel freer to offer new and novel explanations of Scripture.

Notwithstanding the Bible's canonical authority in the church, this diversity is inevitable, because *there is no uninterpreted book: every act of understanding is an act of interpretation*. It is not so much the Bible as

21

such which serves as the authority, but our interpretation of it. These interpretations vary, not because people begin with a different Bible, but because their *processes* of interpretation differ. That the interpretation of the Bible varies from theological context to theological context, as mentioned above, should not surprise us. Unless the interpretation of the Bible is guided by some common external authority or tradition, people in the church will inevitably understand the text differently.

Can we escape from this interpretational Babel? Can we arrive at a greater consensus as to the interpretation of Scripture within the church? We can do this, at least to some extent, if we can do two things. First, we need to gain a clearer understanding of what people, ourselves included, are doing when they interpret Scripture. From an analysis of the process of interpretation, we will be able to recognize why interpretations differ. Second, we need greater agreement on a common process or method of interpretation if we are to come to greater agreement about the meaning of Scripture. The major goal of this book is to present a method of study which can enable us to decide the merits of competing interpretations, and to interpret the Bible more accurately ourselves. It is also meant to provide a common basis for discussing our understanding of Scriptures. To begin with the first point mentioned above, in order to think clearly about the process of interpreting the Bible, we need first to grasp three important factors in the study of Scripture: (1) What the immediate goal is when we set out to understand a Bible passage, (2) What we must know about language in order to understand the process of interpreting the words of Scripture, (3) What our own position and relationship to the Bible is when we study it. This introductory chapter will speak to these three issues.

1.10 *The Reformation and Biblical Interpretation*

The goal of modern Bible study was shaped by the Reformation. Indeed, the agenda of biblical studies since the Reformation can be seen as a working out of the implications of the Reformers' use of Scripture.[1] Consequently, we would do well to begin our study of interpretation with a look at the revolution in the understanding of the Bible which took place during the Reformation.

1.11 *The Traditional View*

In order to understand the new developments in the study and use of the Bible during the Reformation, we need to see them against the traditional views which were held at that time.

Before Copernicus,[2] people thought there were two realms of nature—the heavenly and the earthly. Each realm contained different physical essences and operated according to different laws. Likewise, in language they believed there were two realms—the language in the Bible, thought to be different in kind from all other language, and "normal" human language. Therefore, the Bible needed to be understood by special principles which were not applicable to language in general. As Saint Thomas Aquinas stated, "So, whereas in every other science things are signified by words, this science (Bible interpretation) has the property that the things signified by the words have themselves also a signification."[3] Consequently, Bible students believed the words of Scripture had both a "literal" sense—like all language—and "spiritual" senses unique to its special type of language. This notion that above and beyond the normal historical sense of the words, the words of the Bible revealed additional truth, lead to the practice of discovering four senses in the words of Scripture. There was the literal sense, or the sense according to the letter; the moral sense which guided life; the allegorical sense; and the anagogical sense which pointed to the future. A sixteenth-century poem sums up these four meanings found in the words of Scripture:

> The letter shows us what God and our fathers did;
> The allegory shows us where our faith is hid;
> The moral meaning gives us rules of daily life;
> The anagogy shows us where we end our strife.[4]

Given such a wide scope for interpreting Scripture, scholars could get a wide variety of meanings from a single scriptural text. A pruning shears was needed to control the luxurious meanings which could grow in such a hermeneutical garden. This control was provided by tradition. For an interpretation to be "correct" meant that it needed to be consistent with traditional doctrine and interpretations. As Vincent wrote in AD 434, "The line of interpretation of the prophets and apostles must be directed according to the norm of the ecclesiastical and catholic sense."[5] Thus, while the Bible was the authoritative basis of church doctrine, how the Bible was understood was safeguarded by the church as the carrier of the tradition of interpretation. In this sense, Bible study was not an open pursuit, but the writings of the authorities were governing and one's own interpretation needed to be guided by their teachings.

1.12 *Scripture Alone*

The Reformation challenged this traditional view of interpretation. The slogan *sola scriptura* was directed against the church and tradition as the final arbiter of correctness in biblical interpretation. As Luther stated, "A deed or a word of the Holy Fathers cannot be made an article of faith.... It is the Word of God that is to determine an article of faith—nothing else, not even an angel."[6] In analogy to the Copernican revolution, it might be said that this view of the Bible was a shift from a tradition-centered universe to a Bible-centered one—the Bible alone was authoritative for the Christian and the church. The church revolved about the Bible.

But such a view is simplistic. This shift was not a simple change in emphasis or place of authority. It was far more drastic and penetrating, since this shift was not an exchange of equivalent *types* of authority, as Bainton has written:

> The reformers dethroned the pope and enthroned the Bible. This is the common assertion; but when so stated it is not valid, because a book cannot replace a man. *A book has to be interpreted.*[7]

Sola scriptura was a code word which signaled a change in the idea of what constituted a valid interpretation—from the Bible as interpreted within the framework of the church and its traditions to a reliance on an interpretational process in the present. In this sense, the shift was not from church to Bible, but rather a change in *how* and *by whom* the Bible was to be correctly interpreted.

That the heart of the revolution about Scriptures lay in the *interpretation* of Scriptures rather than in their *authority* can be seen in the challenge addressed to Luther by Erasmus in his book *Freedom of the Will*. Erasmus argued that the authority of the Bible was not the problem—all accepted that. The problem is that the plain sense of Scriptures is not self-evident since there exists such a variety of interpretations. Once tradition was rejected as the guide to Scriptures' interpretation, what was to be put in its place—ignorance?[8]

The problem with "Scripture alone" was—and is—that *there is no uninterpreted Scripture*. Every act of understanding is at the same time an act of interpretation. The crucial question of the Reformation was how is Scripture to be understood.

1.13 *The Historical, Objective Meaning*

Since there was no uninterpreted plain sense which could be agreed on, on what was a valid interpretation of the Bible to be based? If the Bible was to be at the center, unguarded by tradition, what was needed was a definite sense of Scripture upon which people could teach, preach, and build doctrine. Otherwise by removing tradition as a guide to interpretation, the Reformation opened the door to people giving the text any interpretation they chose.

First, to obtain this authoritative sense the multiplicity of possible interpretations needed to be reduced. In place of the traditional spiritual senses, Luther substituted the plain, simple, or normal *historical* sense of Scripture. For unless this usual, grammatical sense was held to, the Bible, instead of being the canon which rules the church, was a "reed that the wind tosses."[9] *The normal historical sense became the valid and authoritative meaning of Scripture for the Reformers.*[10] It was history and language which were to guide the understanding of Scripture rather than received tradition. These replaced tradition as controls to prevent individuals or the church from reading what they wanted into the text.

This raised further questions: How did one arrive at the simple grammatical sense of Scripture? What was necessary for a sound historical understanding of the Old Testament and the New Testament? At this point there seems to have been some ambivalence among the Reformers. Luther, on the one hand, held that the Bible was a simple book to understand—so simple in fact that an illiterate plowboy might understand it better than the pope. The meaning of the words of Scripture lay on the surface, so to speak, so that unaided common sense was sufficient for understanding. This answer, however, did not really satisfy Luther, since he went on to say that the interpretation of the plowboy was to be accepted before that of the pope's *if* he were lead by sounder arguments.

What were these sounder arguments? Luther put great emphasis on the historical setting of Scripture since Scriptures needed to be put in their original setting so that the meaning which the original author intended could be recovered. Consequently, Luther stressed the importance of the study and knowledge of Greek and Hebrew for ministers.[11] We might say, then, that in part sounder arguments were historical reasons gained by the use of reason in studying the Bible.

Putting Scriptures in their context was just the breakthrough in understanding which had characterized Luther's own pilgrimage. When he began his lectures on the Psalms at the beginning of his teaching career, he began with the traditional notion that the New Testament gave the true "spiritual" meaning to the Old Testament letter. Luther's great illumination came when he put the Old Testament words in their historical context, seeing the words as addressed with actual meaning to their original audience. He concluded that it was the meaning of the words in their original context which is significant.[12]

Likewise, Luther did not despise the role of reason in understanding and argument. His challenges to the Catholic Church were to be shown wrong by *Scripture* and *reason*. The plowboy's interpretation was sounder than the pope's only if supported by stronger arguments. In general, reason and revelation could be seen as necessary complements.[13]

Calvin, perhaps the most able exegete of the Reformation, came to a similar conclusion. In his commentaries, his objective was to lay bare the thought of the original author. His criterion for discovering the validity of an interpretation was: Does it agree with the author's thinking? Calvin also held that the Bible comes to mankind in normal human language. This means that the true sense of Scripture is the objective, simple sense which is arrived at by the use of the intellect. This understanding is therefore open to all who apply their minds to it.[14]

Thus, there seems to be a tension in the Reformers as to how to arrive at a valid interpretation of Scripture. On the one hand, the Bible is an open book understandable by all through the use of reason. As such, it can serve as an immediate authority for all Christians; the pope and tradition do not need to be consulted. On the other hand, reason and knowledge of the original languages, as well as their setting, are invaluable aids for proper understanding, since the normal grammatical and historical sense is the normative sense. Likewise, the Reformers in their exegesis, although stressing the plain sense, yet also derived "spiritual" sense from at least some parts of Scripture. Looking back, it might be suggested that the problem was that a common historical method of understanding was not yet available to accompany the new position of the historical meaning of Scripture.

In summary, by placing the Bible alone at the center of faith, the Reformers could no longer rely on church tradition and authority as a guide to Scripture's meaning. Since they still needed an authoritative sense of Scripture, however, they chose the normal historical sense which was more "objective." In setting up the normal historical and grammatical sense as the authoritative sense of Scripture, by implication they replaced tradition and authority with history and philology (the study of language) as the guide by which an authoritative sense could be discovered. The shift from church tradition to Scripture alone implied a shift from using church tradition to using history and philology (historical method) as the means to interpret Scripture.

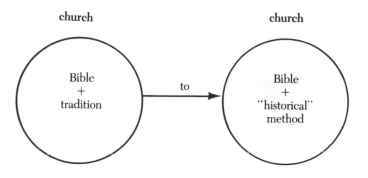

Before, it was the Bible interpreted within tradition, now the Bible interpreted by a historical method through the use of reason. Modern biblical studies can be looked upon as an attempt to develop just this method for which the Reformation called.

1.14 *The Challenge to Tradition*

Because of the Reformers' concern with the study of the Bible in its normal grammatical sense, the historical, human form of Scripture came more and more into focus.[15] The Bible's various books were seen to display the signs of different styles and diverse periods. In short, the awareness grew that there was a human historical aspect to revelation.[16]

This historical study of Scriptures lead the Reformers to question traditional interpretations. For example, John Calvin understood "seed" in Genesis 3:15 as a collective noun, rather than as a singular one, referring to Jesus. This, of course, is in accord with the demands of the context.[17]

But perhaps the most striking and foreshadowing development was the challenge to traditional beliefs about the Bible. First, the Reformers challenged the prevailing ideas about the extent of the canon. They reduced the number of books in the Bible by questioning the authority of the Apocrypha. The result was that the Protestant canon emerged.

Books which had been a part of the church's Old Testament from early times onward were now Scripture no longer. Luther, in fact, was quite radical in his views of the canon. For example, he wrote concerning Revelation, "And so I think of it almost as I do the fourth book of Esdras, and I can in nothing detect that it was provided by the Holy Spirit."[18]

Second, the Reformers felt free to challenge the traditional ascriptions of authorship to certain books in the canon. Luther held, for example, that Isaiah and Jeremiah did not write the books bearing their name, but a scribe who had great freedom did so. He also held that James, Hebrews, and Revelation were not written by apostles.[19]

Third, in their careful study of Scripture, the Reformers found what appeared to be errors. Luther realized that Matthew 27:9 does not quote Jeremiah but rather Zechariah. This mistake was not unsettling for Luther since for him inspiration did not necessarily mean absolute inerrancy. "The Holy Ghost has an eye only to the substance and is not bound by words."[20] Calvin was aware of similar discrepancies. Stephen in Acts says that 75 persons went down into Egypt, (Acts 7:14), while Genesis 46:27 gives 70 as the number. This difference is based on the Septuagint, the Greek translation of the Old Testament, which mentions 75 in Genesis rather than 70 as in the present Hebrew text. Calvin argued that Luke was aware of this discrepancy but followed the Septuagint even though it was in error because the people were familiar with this translation and would have been disturbed by any divergence from it. Thus, error was deliberately incorporated into the text for the sake of communication.[21]

A modern illustration of this principle would be the use of Reed Sea as a translation of the Hebrew text, in place of Red Sea for the body of water involved in the Exodus. This change might upset people who have "canonized" the King James translation. A person speaking to a "King James" audience might refer to the "Red Sea" for purposes of communication instead of "Reed Sea."

In any case, it can be seen that by emphasizing the centrality of Scriptures and the careful, reasoned study of them in partial freedom from traditional interpretations and beliefs, the Reformers challenged both cherished interpretations of Scripture and long-held beliefs about Scripture.

1.15 The New Perspective for Bible Study

Having now sketched briefly several important results of the

Reformers' thrusting the historical sense of Scripture into the center of the life of the church, we can now summarize some of the assumptions and implications which lie behind this new understanding and function of the Bible. Since these assumptions are basic for grasping an objective historical sense of Scripture, they continue to be important for study methods today which aim at this goal.

1.151 Language Is Language

During the Reformation, as we have seen above, the "spiritual" senses were rejected in order to have a single valid interpretation. Before the Reformation, these "spiritual" senses were attributed to the Bible because it was thought the Bible's language was of a special nature. In rejecting these "spiritual" senses and emphasizing the normal historical sense as valid, the Bible's language no longer needed to be regarded as meaning in a way different from all language. On the contrary, its language and historical setting were to be considered as carefully as that of any ancient document.

This led to perhaps the most basic assumption behind the new approaches to Bible study which grew out of the Reformation—*language is one*. The same standards and rules which apply to the valid interpretation of nonbiblical documents apply to the Bible as well. There is a general hermeneutic, a general process of understanding language, that is the same for all languages. There is no special "holy" language with its own special grammar or philology. Or again, the words in the Bible don't "mean" in a way different than words "mean" in ordinary language. The investigation of the meaning of biblical words must proceed according to the common rules developed in linguistics for the investigation of the meaning of words in any language. To state this principle negatively, there are in principle no unique methods of studying language which apply to the Bible, solely because it is the Bible. On the contrary, unless an interpretational principle has universal validity, it does not have validity in the particular. *Any rule of biblical interpretation to be valid must be valid everywhere in literature.*[22]

1.152 Reason Is Above Tradition

A second basic assumption is the *autonomy of reason*. Again in the Reformation the interpretations established by tradition were rejected on the basis of interpretations growing out of the present study of Scripture. (Luther's appeal above was to be shown wrong on the basis of *Scripture* and *reason.*) It was reason based on present experience, observation, and study that was the route to true understanding and explanation. As a result, in the Reformation, the objective study of Scripture replaced the traditions about Scripture as the path leading to a valid understanding. This meant, as seen above, that nothing was to be accepted just because it was accepted or supported in the past, no matter by how great an authority figure. Instead, through the use of reason, the most likely interpretation of the biblical words was to be sought.

One implication of this assumption is that *beliefs about the Bible must be based on study of the Bible rather than the study of the Bible being controlled by beliefs about it.* The outcome of the study of the Bible should no longer be controlled by theological dogmas about the nature of the Bible. This liberty to pursue the study of the Bible, unfettered by assumptions about where the interpreter must come out, is at the heart of the Reformers' slogan *sola scriptura.* It is a commitment to go wherever the evidence and reason lead in order to obtain a valid interpretation.[23]

1.153 *Test Everything*

A third attitude which developed from the Reformers' quest for validity was a stance or *attitude of skepticism* rather than passive acceptance. Skepticism in the sense used here is not a position of believing nothing, but rather an inquiry into the objective basis of beliefs and ideas before accepting them. This scepticism came to be manifested in several ways. One way was the rejection of tradition and traditional interpretation. Here the question was one of validity or verification—why should an ancient interpretation or doctrine be accepted as true? What evidence or rationale is there for it? Rather than accepting all as true until shown to be false, nothing is held to be true until shown to be true. This attitude obviously led to the questioning of many, if not most, of the accepted views and interpretations of Scripture in the course of history following the Reformation. Some were accepted after examination, while others were not. Such a radical questioning was of course seen as very threatening by the church. But if things are not accepted as true just because they have been believed in the past, then they must be challenged and tested to see what truth they do in fact possess. The burden of proof thus shifted—it is the church's doctrine or traditional interpretation which has to be shown as a reasonable conclusion from the evidence, rather than just assuming they are true until overwhelming evidence showed the contrary. As a result, biblical scholarship came to test traditional understandings not because it wanted to discredit the Bible, but because it was interested in holding to what was valid.[24]

1.154 Work Inductively

Finally, in order to arrive at a valid interpretation there arose an emphasis on evidence or *data used inductively and objectively*. To study inductively meant a close examination and study of the text, searching for clues to aid in the understanding of the material. Likewise, it was the use of reason using these clues which suggested and supported new interpretations and views of Scripture. Objectivity meant that arguments about the correctness of interpretations were to be based on the evidence available and how one judged that evidence rather than on tradition or dogmatic assertions.

In this context, objectivity means that views are open to scrutiny, discussion, and verification, rather than that they are free from all presuppositions. It is true, as has often been claimed, that all understanding is based on certain things being assumed or presupposed. This does not mean all understandings are equal. Some presuppositions are misleading—they lead to misunderstandings—while others lead toward a proper understanding. For instance, if you presuppose that you are now reading English, this is a necessary assumption in order for you to come to a correct understanding. If, however, you presuppose that you are reading Spanish, this presupposition will cause you not to understand. To claim validity for an interpretation is not to claim a presuppositionless understanding. Likewise, to claim that a given interpretation is based on certain presuppositions is not to deny its validity. The question is: are the specific presuppositions in question a help or a hindrance to understanding the historical sense of the text. Are they informed by the data and do they make the best sense out of the data available? Objectivity means that others can verify our conclusions. They can repeat our study, examine our data, and come out at the same place or if not, show where we went wrong. Objective interpretations are open to public testing and verification.[25]

1.20 The Linguistic Background: Says—Means—Application

As we have seen, the goal of Bible study in the Reformation was to arrive at the normal, historical meaning of Scripture. Such a definite, objective meaning was necessary if the Bible alone was to guide the church rather than the church putting Scriptures to its own uses by reading back meanings into the text. This goal seems both clear and proper. We know, of course, that this aim was not always reached. Then, as now, there were many competing interpretations, each claiming authority.

One major reason for this continuing disagreement about the meaning of biblical texts is lack of agreement on how to study and interpret Scripture. If we take the Reformation's goal of objective historical sense seriously, we must develop those methods which will help us uncover this sense.

Likewise, since the normal historical sense is open to all to find if they but search properly, the results of study must be open to others to duplicate and verify. If it is not, we cannot be sure whether an interpretation is accurate or merely a personal prejudice.

The most significant reason for failure to develop a method which leads to an objective historical sense of Scripture, verifiable by others, is lack of knowledge about the nature of language itself. This lack manifests itself most frequently in the common misconception which assumes that what the Bible says is what it means and what it means ought to be applied. On the contrary, in the Bible, as in language generally, we must distinguish between what the text says, what the text means by saying that, and how that meaning applies. Ignoring these distinctions not only leads us to misunderstandings, but prevents us from developing a method of study which will deal adequately with the problems of interpretation which we face in reaching a valid understanding.[26] In order to grasp clearly how we must study the Bible in order for it to function as the Reformation hoped it would, we must take seriously these aspects of language.

1.21 *Language Is Ambiguous: The "Says"/"Means" Distinction*

The first important feature of language which we must take into account is that language is, by its very nature, ambiguous. What the text says can mean several different things. This is because the same sounds, words, or sentences can have several different meanings. For example, the sound "s" in English may mean a variety of things. In the word "bats," it may indicate plural—more than one "bat" is meant. Or it may indicate third person singular of the verb, as in "He bats the ball." If the plural is meant, it would be a misunderstanding to construe the "s" sound as meaning the third person singular, although this is a possible meaning of the sound.

Or again at the word level, "bat" may mean, among other things, a mammal which flies or an object with which one attempts to strike a ball. Again, if one takes it as referring to a mammal when in fact it means an object for striking balls, one is mistaken—even though "a flying mammal" is a possible meaning.

Likewise at the sentence or phrase level, alternative legitimate meanings are possible. The sentence, "The eating of bats makes my flesh crawl" can have a variety of senses. Is it when someone or something eats bats that causes the effect or is it the feeding of the bats themselves that produces this? Or again, "Watch out for flying bats." Should we watch out for the mammals or pieces of wood? Again, a proper understanding requires that the correct set of alternative possible meanings is chosen.

Clearly there is a difference between what is said and what is meant. What is said is one thing; what is meant in the saying is another. We know this distinction from our own use of language. A parent may caution a child before attending church service that he is to be quiet in church. However, if in the course of the service the child does not sing or respond when directly asked a question whose answer he knows, that parent may take the child to task for not participating properly in the worship service. If the child replies that the parents asked him to be quiet and he was merely complying with their request, the parent might say, "You did not understand what I meant when I said, 'Be quiet.' "

In another situation, what is meant may not be what is literally said. A husband had given his wife a dress for Christmas. Later, in remembering past Christmases, the wife remarked that on several Christmases her husband had given her clothes but that she had never given him any clothing. To this the husband replied—"Well, that's because I'm not vain!" The wife retorted, "I suppose I am." For the husband to now say, "I didn't say that," is of course true in one sense, but obviously false in another since that is what his words reasonably mean in that situation. Again, 'says' and 'means' are two different things.

Exactly the same situation confronts us when we read the Bible. Take the familiar commandment, "You shall not kill" (Exodus 20:13). What does "kill" mean—take no life at all? No, we usually do not think of this as applying to animals—but the text does not say it doesn't include animals. Does it mean take no human life at all? No, again, since in the next chapters the law provides that in certain cases the taking of life was permissible (Exodus 21:12-17, 29; 22:2). Thus although the text says "kill" we should understand it to mean "murder." *Thus to know what a text says is not to understand what it means.* This is not because the text does not say what it means, but because what it says, like "kill" above, may have more than one meaning.

A second reason why language (the says) is ambiguous is that it is an open, creative system. New expressions or word combinations can be formed, new sentences constructed, even new words can enter the language. Likewise, old words and phrases can be used for new experiences and situations. This flexible and creative nature of language makes misunderstanding possible. An old meaning of a word may be understood when in fact we are to grasp a new meaning. Or the reverse is possible; we may attribute a new meaning to a word when a word is actually being employed in an older sense. When we read in Paul, for example, words like "faith," "law," "sin," it is almost impossible not to understand them in terms of modern English and our current theological context. Yet, because of the constant change in language, it would be surprising if our meanings and the ones in Scripture were the same. We must be constantly alert for words to be used in different ways with different meanings.

This feature of the openness in language—the new and creative usage of language—also means that within the Bible the same term may come to mean different things. For example, in Old Testament times, the "Day of Yahweh" was a day the people looked forward to, since it was a day of judgment in which God would vindicate them and punish their enemies. For the prophet Amos, however, the "Day of Yahweh" was a term which he applied to God's judgment on Israel itself (Amos 5:18-20).

1.22 Understanding Language: Bridging the Says/Means Distinction

Given the ambiguity of language, it is easy to understand why a variety of interpretations exist. Yet not all interpretations have an equal validity; some indeed can be judged to be misinterpretations. That ambiguity does not lead to chaos, to pure subjectivity in interpretation, to words meaning anything we want them to mean is due to two other major features of language—it is a *conventional* means of communication between people and it has reference to a *certain situation.*

Language is not a private matter, nor is it a random series of words or sentences, but it is structured according to shared customs. It is this conventional or patterned nature of language which allows its intelligi-

bility between people. This means that users of a language have in common certain unconscious agreements (conventions) about how words are
used, how sentences are built up, about how to construct and use different types of language, as well as a host of other things. Knowing these
conventions we have competence in a language—adequate knowledge
of how to "send" and "receive" the language. Obviously, the more of
these rules, or patterns, people have in common, the easier the communication between them; the fewer in common, the more difficult.

The fact that our use of language is governed by conventions
should not surprise us. Much of what we do in life is governed by "rules"
or conventions. We eat with utensils rather than with our hands because
in our culture this is how people eat. We don't stuff our mouths or talk
with our mouths full of food. Knowing these customs we act in socially
accepted ways. To break them would be rude. Or again, we shake hands
when we meet because this is how we show friendliness. To refuse to do
this is to communicate unfriendliness. Women wear their dresses a
certain length, men wear coats and ties in certain situations because it is
expected, it is what we do to be normal.

Language, too, is customary. We need to follow its conventions if
we are to make sense. If we do not follow them, we may well produce
nonsense. An example of a language custom or convention in English
would be the word order, subject-verb-object in a normal declarative
sentence. "Mary hit John." We know who hit whom, because according
to convention the subject precedes the verb while the object follows. If it
were not for this convention, we would not know who hit whom. Note
that the information as to which noun is the subject is not stated; it is not
in the "says," but is a presupposition we bring to the sentence based on
the conventions of English. We see from this example how conventions
reduce the ambiguity in language.

Besides the fact that language is conventional behavior, structured
according to shared customs, it also takes place in a context and depends
on this context for understanding. The other side of this fact is that a
change in context may change meaning. To take up our example of
"bats" once more, if you are spelunking in a cave and someone says to
you, "Watch out for the bats," you take one kind of precaution. If,
however, you are walking across a baseball diamond where players are
taking practice swings, you take another. The context has changed, and
the meaning has changed. Examples of this abound in the Bible. In 1
Corinthians 10:33 Paul talks positively of pleasing men, but in 1 Thessa-

lonians 2:4 he warns not to please men, while in Galatians 1:10 he says he himself is not pleasing men. What Paul "says" means different things in different contexts. By taking the historical context seriously, we safeguard the words of Scripture from being empty molds for modern content.

As part of context, who the author is, is an important clue for understanding. The same word may mean different things in the writings of different authors. For example, the word "faith" in Paul may have a different meaning than it has in James.

By way of illustration, we may compare language to a triangle, each corner of which stands for an important factor in determining the meaning of a text. These factors together lead to meaning.[27]

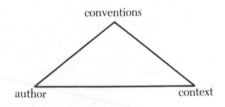

1.23 *The First Task of Bible Study*
     The first task of Bible study is to move from the ambiguity and openness inherent in language to the definiteness needed for understanding; it is to move from what is said to what is meant in the saying. Understanding can be seen as a continuum:

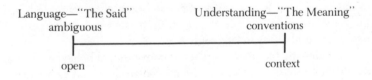

In keeping with the nature of language, then, a Bible study method needs to be able to uncover the structures and context of a passage so as to move us from the left side of the continuum "says" to the right side "means." The further right we can move on the continuum through the use of conventions and context, the more definite and valid will be our understanding. *A method, through allowing the discovery of the conventions and context of a passage, will bring about understanding by*

moving the interpreter from what the text SAYS to what the text MEANS.

If "says" and "means" are different, as argued above, how can people apparently go from "says," what is in the text, to meaning without any consideration of context or conventions? Doesn't actual practice deny the theory? That understanding is taking place apart from conventions and context is an illusion. Actually, everyone understands what is said on the basis of some context and conventions, since all understanding is founded on this. If the context and conventions are not those of the author, they are those of the reader. For example, "The women should keep silence in the churches" (1 Cor. 14:34). What does this mean? Can women sing? Lead songs? Pray? Can they teach Sunday school classes? Speak in Sunday school? Give testimonies? Make announcements? Often this passage is understood to mean women may not preach. Why? Because this is what we do not let women do at present in many churches! This understanding is based on a definite context and conventions, but they are *our* context, not the author's. If the church is to hear the voice of Scripture in what is said, rather than its own voice, it must seek the original historical meaning of the words. This historical, determinate sense of Paul's words can only be found by placing them in the context and conventions of *his* time and language.

Thus, all understanding is based on placing the words in some context and understanding some conventional meanings of the words. The question is, on *whose* conventions and contexts are we going to base our understandings, on those of biblical times, or our modern ones? Taking the Bible seriously, we would seek to understand it based on the conventions and context of the biblical texts, not ours. There is no escaping the process outlined above.

1.24 Applying the Text: The Means/Applies Distinction

Just as we cannot immediately read off the meaning of a passage of Scripture without first exploring its contexts and conventions, so we cannot go immediately from what the text meant then, to what the text means for us now. To a lesser or greater extent, three major factors prevent us from going immediately from what the text meant to how the text applies now.[28]

1.241 Descriptive/Prescriptive

First of all, as is generally recognized, not all material in the Bible has the same force for immediate practice or theological thought. This difference is sometimes captured by the terms "descriptive" and "prescriptive." By descriptive is meant those features or actions which represent the cultural or individual element in the Bible. They reflect the historical situation in which the Bible was written. The prescriptive materials are those which communicate a norm or prescription which was considered or intended to be binding in a given situation. For example, in the biblical narratives we have many examples of what belonged to the cultural customs of the times. Abraham held slaves, practiced polygamy, and lived in a tent. The fact that Abraham did these things does not show that such things are to be copied. The author in writing these things is merely describing. They are not a binding statute. This seems simple enough, but it is easy to overlook this distinction and to use such cultural or historical practices as a biblical authorization for our own practices. For example, I once saw a poster which said, "Plans are biblical—Moses had plans, Nehemiah had plans." But in the stories about these men, plans were not put forth as a norm or principle. Rather, they had plans because plans were and are a part of normal human experience and existence. We could likewise say that hair is biblical—Moses had hair, Nehemiah had hair.[29]

1.242 *Historical Conditioning*

Once we have sorted out what is prescriptive, however, we cannot go at once to the application. This is because the prescriptive material itself was shaped by the historical situation in which it was given. The classic illustration in the Bible is Jesus' teaching on divorce (Matthew 19:3-9). Deuteronomy 24 contained the law regarding divorce. Jesus, however, says that this law was given because of their hardness of heart. It was conditioned by the recipients of the law. This, Jesus infers, means that the law was a concession to them and their situation—it does not represent God's ultimate will, although commanded by God. Rather, Genesis 1 and 2 contain God's will for marriage. On this basis Jesus then gives his teaching on divorce.

From this historical shaping of Scripture we can learn at least two principles which we must consider in application. First, we need to see what the total range of the biblical witness is.[30] We dare not take a single text and build an application on it without regarding what else is in the Bible. In the example above, Deuteronomy 24 alone did not provide an adequate base for a teaching on divorce. Genesis 1 and 2 needed to be considered. The Bible often says a variety of things on a subject because it is addressed to a variety of situations.

Second, all words are given in a specific context and are shaped to that context. We must take this context seriously. If we do not, our application may be more a repeating of an earlier culture and its own limitations than a realization of God's will for us today in a different setting. That is, since revelation was shaped, so to speak, to the audience, we must discover this historical shaping so as to discern what might represent a command or concession which was called for in that particular historical or social situation. Or we may see why in different situations, different answers are given or needed—as on the issues of divorce. The divorce law did not state that it was a concession. This is an aspect of the text which our process of understanding must uncover. We can see these principles in action when we apply Paul's instructions regarding slaves to our times. Seen from our perspective today, these seem to be shaped by Paul's situation, the culture and political-social system in which he lived. A proper application of these instructions needs to take Paul's context seriously. Given a different social setting, we in the United States have decided that the church should not support slavery, but rather work to abolish it.

1.243 Cultural Relativity

Our knowledge of the historical conditionedness of the Bible's message opens up the wider factor of historical or cultural relativity, in general. Cultural relativity exists because words and practices have meaning as parts of a larger cultural whole. When the culture changes, so does the meaning of elements within it. Thus practices or ideas which mean one thing in the biblical context may mean quite another thing in ours. In addition, because of the changes in culture, some practices regulated in biblical times are irrelevant to our own times. On the other hand, we face issues not known in biblical times.

To take this last point first, Paul writes twice about the eating of meat offered to idols (1 Corinthians 8; Romans 14). This was evidently a significant problem in the early church (of Acts 15). For people in North America today, this teaching does not seem to have any direct immediate application for us. On the other hand, we face problems not discussed in the Bible—genetic engineering, artificial prolongation of life, and abortion—to name just a few.

Not only does the Bible reflect a different set of practices and teachings from what we find in our culture, but to take practices over directly from biblical times to our times is inevitably to change the meaning of the practices. For example, Paul commands his readers in several letters to greet each other with a kiss. This command is not normally carried out in our churches because we feel strange about men kissing. Indeed, it may mean something different in our culture than it did in Paul's.[31]

1.25 Making Application: Bridging the Means/Applies Distinction

In order to avoid these pitfalls we should attempt to apply principles, the spirit of the Bible, more than the letter of the Bible. We can do this in several ways.

First, principles stated in the Bible should take precedence over historical description and historically conditioned commands. On the one hand, these principles may keep us from applying individual, specific commands which may not represent God's best intentions for us. On the other hand, since principles are more general, less tied to specifics, they usually have a wider range or scope of application. This means that the same principles can take on a variety of forms in different cultures and thereby help us transcend cultural relativity.

Again, Jesus' teaching on divorce illustrates this principle. He looked for general statements of principle regarding male-female relationships rather than basing himself on a practice commanded by law. Laws and other prescriptions are normally given to correct faults, not to spell out the ideal. Thus a law on divorce does not spell out the ideal for marriage, but what to do when something goes wrong. Too often by taking such corrective statements as ideals—as for example in Paul's teachings on social roles and relationships—we turn remedial instructions into normative models. General principles can do much to put such teachings into a proper perspective. We must recognize oftentimes the built-in limitations of specific instructions and laws. Rather than extending them beyond their limits, we should look to principles for guidelines. By using principles for application, we will avoid the pitfall of using specific teachings in inappropriate ways.

Second, in application we should attempt to apply the "why" rather than the "what" of the Bible. This means we should look for the principle behind the specific command or application. Jesus asked about the "why" of the divorce law. This influenced his evaluation of its significance for application. Likewise we need to ask why Paul teaches as he does about meat offered to idols or slaves' obedience to masters. In this way we look behind the letter to the principle on which the letter is based. It is this implicit principle which we seek to apply.

In a like manner, from a study of descriptive material, we may see theological principles at work, principles being taught by example. This material too can then have a theological and ethical relevance for us, even though the details of the story do not. For example, although we don't live as Abraham did, his obedience to God's call can serve us as a model. Likewise, God's providence as illustrated in these stories can sensitize us to God's providence for us today.

The principles we discover are applied to our situation by way of *analogy*. We seek to express these principles in relevant contexts and ways that make sense in our own day. This use of analogy has two immediate benefits. First, it allows us to transcend something of the cultural gap between ourselves and the Bible. For example, instead of "greet one another with a holy kiss," Phillips paraphrases, "greet one another with a hearty handshake." Here the principle of greeting fellow Christians in a warm way is given a new form of expression. This is more in keeping with our cultural mode of greeting, since handshaking communicates in our situation what Paul was interested in expressing, while kissing does not.

Second, it allows those passages which treat irrelevant practices to speak to our times. By looking at Paul's principles—his motives and reasons—when he wrote concerning meat offered to idols, we can gain some valuable principles for Christian ethics today. These in turn can be applied to quite different practices in our modern situation. Likewise, we can find principles in the Bible which we can apply to situations which are not regulated in Scripture, such as abortion. Thus by searching for principles, we allow the biblical message to become alive in our own situation and life. We allow it to become incarnated, so to speak, in a new historical and cultural situation.

1.26 *The Second Task of Method*

Again, we may use an illustration to help summarize these points.

The task of method is to help us to move from meaning to application by the use of principles and analogy. This is application at its best, using a stable canon to speak anew to changing social situations. In this way the Bible becomes a dynamic factor fixed in one sense, yet flexible and alive in another. Thus, as Sanders has written, it becomes "adaptable for life."[32] Such a method will also help us in the following ways.

First, there is a possible gain in objectivity. When the apparent meaning of a text does not seem to be in accord with our theology or what we feel is proper practice, we too often study the text anew to find the "real" meaning. The assumption is that our understanding is faulty. If we study hard enough, however, we will find the "real" meaning which will coincide with our theology or practice. In this the Bible is adapted to our situation by finding new meanings in it. Some of the study done on Paul's teachings regarding women, it seems, was motivated in this way. This does not necessarily mean such study is compromised from the beginning, but real dangers lie here. Meaning has been confused with application; to know the meaning is not necessarily to know the application.

Once we realize that we cannot go immediately from meaning to application, we can be more open to finding meanings which diverge from our present thinking. We may, for example, admit that Paul condoned slavery, without thereby binding ourselves to the support of slavery in our own time. Meaning is one thing—to be found as sketched above. Application is something quite different—discerning the significance for us today of what was meant then.

Second, there is the aspect of consistency. For a study method to be valid, it should operate consistently. Using the principles of application listed above should lead to greater consistency. On the other hand, disregarding them leads to inconsistency. In fact, the more closely the application is a literal practice of the historical meaning of Scripture, the greater the inconsistency. As a first step to decrease this inconsistency, a division between description and prescription needs to be made. Since this will still not solve the problem (e.g., sowing two kinds of seed in a field or wearing clothes made of two types of fiber, although prescriptive, are not practiced, Leviticus 19:19), the historical conditionedness of Scripture will need to be recognized. Once this is done, cultural relativity will soon enter in in order to increase the consistency of application. Why do we use grape juice rather than wine in communion or why don't we take wine for our stomach's sake? (1 Timothy 5:23). Having realized the necessity of these steps, it will then be seen that principles from the Bible applied by analogy are our best guide to Christian conduct today.

1.30 *The Eight Steps to Understanding*

From our survey of the Reformation's use of the Bible and our study of language, we can state three points:

1. The process of understanding of the Bible is to be based on a reasonable judgment of the evidence regardless of tradition and doctrine (*sola scriptura*).
2. Our goal in Bible study is to find the normal, "objective," historical sense of Scripture as a basis for our understanding.
3. Our understanding moves from what the Bible says to what it means and then to how it applies.

To illustrate this process of understanding we can combine the two diagrams used above:

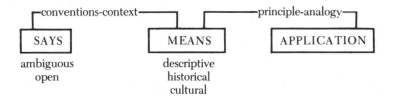

The goal of study is to discover those bridges which help us move from stage to stage of understanding. The method which will be presented below enables us to move from says to means to application because through it we discover the links which connect them.

Each of the eight steps outlined in the following chapters is necessary, because each makes its own contribution to our understanding of a passage. Furthermore, none of these steps arrives at the meaning of a passage by itself. Instead, the steps reinforce each other since it is the combination of evidence from all of these steps which points us to a valid interpretation.

The story is told of a group of blind men who went to the zoo. While there they entered into the elephant's cage to see what manner of beast this was. One grabbed the tail, another the trunk, another the leg, and another the ear. The man who seized the tail declared the elephant to be like a rope. The man with the trunk thought him to be more like a hose; the man with the leg, like a tree; and the one with the ear, more like a leaf. Having only a part of the picture each drew the wrong conclusion. Likewise, each of the study steps arrives at a part of the whole, so all steps must be used together for a correct understanding.

The steps in a method not only need to be comprehensive, but they also need to be arranged in the proper order so that each succeeding step can build on the results of the preceding one. Thus, while some of the steps may not always appear to be very exciting or productive, they do their part in leading toward understanding by providing the necessary information and understanding for later steps. To leave one or more stages out weakens the validity of the results obtained—indeed, it may lead to a misinterpretation.

Below is a brief survey of the eight steps grouped under the headings "says," "means," and "application." This will give a broader perspective of the whole method before we begin our step-by-step study. Since it is intended as a survey, the descriptions below are not complete for each step. In the following seven chapters, steps two to eight will be explained in detail. [33]

1.31 Discovering What a Passage Says
1. Textual analysis/using a translation

In the first step of study we seek to discover as best we can what the biblical writer actually wrote. Since none of the original manuscripts remain, we only have copies of copies. These copies may differ from one another in what they say. Where they do differ, we must first decide which of the alternatives in these copies best reflects what the author wrote. Since this step presupposes, at a minimum, a knowledge of the original languages, it will be omitted below when we actually perform the study steps. [34]

For the person who does not read Hebrew and Greek, the "says" of the text is found in a translation. It is important to use an accurate, literal translation for Bible study since this will most nearly represent in translation the "says" of the original. Paraphrases like *The Living Bible* or dynamic equivalence translations like *The Good News Bible* which attempt to translate meanings are to be avoided. Examples of more literal translations would be *Revised Standard Version, The New American Standard Bible, New English Bible,* and the *New International Version*.

1.32 Discovering What a Passage Means
I. The Conventions

2. *Structure analysis*

This step has several phases. First, we must determine what is an appropriate passage for study. To do this, we must find the smallest compositional unit on which a study should focus. Second, we need to analyze the structure and style of a passage. This is necessary in order to be clear about the conventions which lie behind the form or shape of a passage. Since the meaning of a passage is expressed in and through its structure, we need to discover this in order to lay a firm foundation for the further steps in understanding. As will be seen, misconceptions as to the meaning of a passage can arise when the way in which an author expresses himself is overlooked.

3. *Form analysis*

The Bible contains a variety of forms or literary types such as parable, story, laws of various kinds, and letters, to name a few. It is important for us to identify what type of material we are studying, since the different types convey their meanings in different ways. For example, Jotham's fable teaches a lesson about kingship (Judges 9:7-15). It is not meant to communicate information about trees. It is important for us to know whether we are studying a fable or a historical narrative, so as to understand what the author meant to communicate. Different types of language also have differing implications which we must recognize lest we misapply Scripture. An example used above was the difference between remedial instruction and principle. Since the structure of a passage may be crucial for discovering its literary type, this step builds on structure analysis and must come after its completion.

4. *Word analysis*

In studying a passage we must understand the meaning of individual words and phrases. To understand a word's meaning in a passage, we must analyze both its general meanings and its particular, specific meaning in the passage we are studying. To do this, we must see how it is used in general and its place in the structure of a passage. Likewise, the meaning of a word is affected by the type of literature in which it is found. For example, words in legal material may have meanings or nuances not found in general speech. Thus, we must be careful to match the meaning of a word to the passage as a whole.

II. The Context

5. *Tradition analysis*

Words or ideas expressed may have a specific intellectual back-

ground. We need to know what traditions or ideas are being drawn upon
or lie behind a passage. The background information obtained by putting words in a wider intellectual, social, or theological context can be
very illuminating. It can also help us to see what an author did *not* say,
but assumes is known by the readers. Missing this assumed knowledge
may lead us to an incorrect interpretation. For example, knowing the
anti-kingship tradition in Israel would help us to a deeper understanding
of Jotham's fable.

Some biblical writers, as we shall see, not only drew on certain
cultural and theological traditions, but used literary sources in composing their units. These sources were sometimes in an oral form, sometimes
in a written form. In this study step we will study both the literary
sources which an author used and how he modified or selected from
them. By discovering the principles of selection and modification, we
can gain valuable insights into the meaning of our present text.

6. *Transmission and redaction analysis*

Often there was a gap between the time when a passage was composed and the time of its being placed in a biblical book. The words
spoken by the prophets are an example. Few if any of the prophets
collected their works together as we now find them in the Bible. The
teachings of Jesus would be another example—the original words are by
Jesus, the Gospels by others.

We need to discover how a unit survived from the time it was first
composed until it was included in the work where we find it today in the
Bible. Knowing who preserved the material, where and why, provides us
with valuable clues as to how the material was understood and used in
Bible times. For example, knowing what group preserved a psalm and
how they used it would shed a great deal of light on the meaning of the
psalm.

Not only was the biblical material preserved, but also it was in the
end arranged in a work or book as we find it in the Bible today. The
person who put together a work is called a "redactor"—like the redactor
of the Psalms. Redactors arranged the material according to a certain
plan and relationships. They had purposes which guided them. We discover a redactor's purpose by studying the arrangement of material. The
other side of this is that by seeing the relationships which exist between a
passage in a book and its function in the plan of the book as a whole we
gain important insights as to the meaning of a passage. In this study
phase we will focus on the passage after its composition, while in pre-

vious ones we looked at what came before, what was drawn upon in the composing.

7. Historical analysis

Finally, to see a passage in its context, we need to see it in its historical setting. The conditions within which an author was writing as well as those of his audience help us recover the original sense of a passage. They also help us discern how to apply the passage appropriately today. This step of analysis follows after the study of the plan of the book, since we look at the book as a whole in its historical setting, asking questions such as the purpose of the book and the time of writing.

1.33 Discovering the Application of a Passage
III. The Application

By following the seven steps outlined above we should be in a position to state the meaning of the passage in its original context. In this sense, we have become communication partners with the author. Now we need to make application to our lives in the present. This step comes last, because until we reach a valid historical understanding of what was meant, we cannot apply this meaning to our own context. In making application we will state what principles are at work in the passage and how they apply by analogy to our situation today.

1.34 The Presentation of the Steps

The chapters following provide a step-by-step guide to inductive Bible study. In order to make the various steps as clear as possible, a uniform presentation will be given in each chapter for each step.

First, an introduction will place the study step in a general perspective. This should make it easier to grasp its rationale, why it is used, and what results are to be obtained.

Second, a principle or axiom of Bible study will be stated. Each of these principles forms a step in an inductive study of the Bible by pointing to some aspect of language which must be examined in order to understand what was being communicated. Third, a series of keys or operations will be presented. These are the questions that need to be answered in that step of study. These questions will point to the clues which will enable one to carry out the task of this stage of study.

Finally, four illustrations will demonstrate the application of the keys to different biblical passages. From these examples, it should become clearer how to proceed.

1.35 The Examples

The four passages I have chosen to illustrate the method are Genesis 12:10-20 (Abram and Sarai in Egypt), Amos 2:6-16 (oracle), Matthew 5:38-42 (not returning evil), and Romans 13:1-7 (the Christian and the state). I have used the same passages to illustrate each stage in the method because a method is a series of interlocking stages. If different examples are chosen for each step, this interlocking is inadequately illustrated. As will become apparent, in the actual study of the Bible some steps are much more productive than others in a given passage. By choosing only fruitful examples, this aspect of method is lost.

These four passages, which are quite different types of literature, were chosen in order to illustrate how to study a variety of materials. They are samples of four of the most important types of material we have in the Bible—narrative, prophetic speech, Gospel, and letter. The representative character of the examples should make for maximal transference to your own study of other passages.

The examples are studied in detail for the sake of illustration. Each stage of study was attempted on each passage, as a study which could stand on its own merits. Only such an approach can really model adequately the various steps. Obviously, the passages could be studied at greater depth. I have sought a balance between short illustration and a full-blown scholarly monograph. As long as the techniques being illustrated are clear, the illustrations will have served their major purpose.

1.40 The Studying Subject

So far we have discussed the objective of study—the normal historical sense—and the object of study—language. We need now to turn our attention to the one who studies. In thinking about the involvement of the individual in the study process, our comments will focus on two topics: the role of the Holy Spirit in the study process and the immediate social context within which a person studies Scriptures.

In the Christian tradition, the Holy Spirit is considered a help and guide to a correct understanding of Scripture.[35] However, with the Reformation's emphasis on the historical sense of Scriptures known through the use of reason, it was granted by some that one not possessing the Holy Spirit could also understand, at least partially. With the continuing emphasis on the historical and descriptive dimension of Bible study, it became apparent that religious beliefs were not essential to the study of the Bible. Today, Bible scholars of widely differing beliefs can gather and discuss together the meaning of Scripture. They can cooperate even in the production of a commentary series, such as the *Anchor Bible*. What then is the Spirit's role in interpretation?

Several solutions are possible. One could hold the Spirit to be essential to some steps of study or understanding and not to others. For example, the Spirit might be considered crucial to correct application of the text. Through the Spirit the Christian church discerns the times correctly, applies Scripture aptly by this analysis, and is enabled to live out this application. But the historical sense of Scripture can be gotten without the Spirit.

This type of thinking reminds one of the "God of the gaps" type of argument. That is, God is involved when we do not know how to explain something. As we become more knowledgeable, the gap keeps getting smaller and God's role becomes less and less. In Bible study method, we are pretty sure how we do textual criticism or find the meaning of words. However, when it comes to application, we are much less certain. There seems to be more room for intuition, for unspecified factors to affect the outcome. Here, then, we invoke the Holy Spirit. This we might term "the God of the methodological gaps."

How can we avoid this? One possibility would be to affirm that the Spirit is a guide to understanding in all phases of study. This might be argued from two considerations. First, we might state by way of hypothesis that a religious life and outlook form a necessary presupposition for correctly understanding documents which themselves arise from a religious experience. The reader today is linked to the past author and audience by sharing the same religious realities about which they wrote. This common experience of God, then, forms a vital link in the bridge of understanding. It provides the bonds necessary for an empathetic relationship with the text and a will to understand the reality from which it flows. This experience becomes a part of the experiential background which we use to decide the probability of conflicting interpretations.

Someone may write a poem, a sonnet for instance, out of the passion of being in love. As one who has experienced such love reads this, there is a potential for understanding the poet based on sharing a similar type of experience.

But the Bible is not only a testimony to people's experience of God; it also has a normative aspect. How do people respond appropriately to this God? Biblical religion was neither only a mystical experience nor an

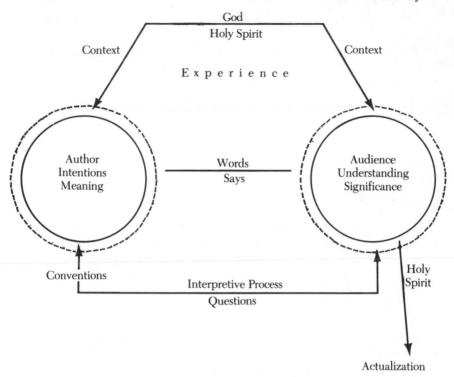

intellectual exercise. There is a practical side to religious experience in the Bible—obedience. As we live in accord with the truth of our understanding, our capacity for correctly understanding that truth widens and deepens. There develops a reciprocity between understanding and obedience. Faithful obedience is the counterpart to faithful understanding. This means that the study of the Bible for understanding is not a spectator sport. The subject is involved.

This participation, again, has a potential for understanding which is missed by studying the Bible from outside as an uninvolved observer. Although we may read a book of bicycle repair and study the diagrams carefully, some things may not seem to us to make sense. But once we actually start working on a bicycle, the rationale of the procedure becomes evident.[36]

The social context within which the Bible is studied is also an important factor. I would propose the thesis that study should be done within a community. This is so for at least three reasons. First, people have various gifts or talents. By cooperating together, these various strengths can be used. Individuals often bring different perspectives and questions which can contribute to a fuller understanding. In this way, results can also be tested and further refined.

Second, studying together makes experience and obedience more likely. It allows alternative visions to arise, visions grounded in the biblical vision.[37] There is also accountability to live in the light of what is held to be true.

Third, groups tend to be conservative. There is therefore a testing and verification which makes for more objective interpretation. It is less likely that interpretation will reflect personal prejudices or untested presuppositions.

Perhaps the diagram on page 50 can indicate something of the complementary function of method and the Holy Spirit. Neither method alone nor Spirit alone is adequate. Both are components of a correct understanding.

Part I
THE CONVENTIONS

Chapter 2

From Surface to Skeleton: Structure Analysis

2.00 *Structure*

At a church meeting on the issue of leadership styles, someone quoted 1 Corinthians 6:5, "Can it be that there is no man among you wise enough to decide between members of the brotherhood?" to support the idea that a strong individual should lead the church. If we look at this verse in its context, however, we see that it has quite a different meaning. Paul has just told the Corinthians that they will judge the world and angels. How much more then they ought to be able to decide disputes among themselves rather than going to secular courts of law. This central point is the immediate setting of verse 6:5. Surely, Paul means here, cannot the Corinthians, who pride themselves on their wisdom, who as Christians will judge both the world and angels, find even one wise person to decide a case between Christians! In context Paul is not advocating one-person rule in the church.

In the above illustration an interpretation of the text missed the point because it did not take the verse quoted in the context of its passage. But how do we determine what is the relevant context? How do we decide what is the appropriate amount of text to study? This brings us to the first step in Bible study, isolating a passage for study.

2.10 *Basic Units*

Customarily people have chosen as units for study the ready-made divisions as we find them in our English translations—the chapters and verses. Most often, then, Bible study means reading and discussing the Bible either verse by verse or chapter by chapter. This way of proceeding, however, is not really very satisfactory.

To understand why, we need to back up a bit in order to put our discussion in a broader perspective. When people communicate through language, whether written or spoken, they need to organize their language in a way that makes sense. Usually they speak about this or that topic which forms the focus or organizing point for what they are saying. When finished with that focus they go on to another "paragraph" which is focused differently. Organizing language by units in this way is a general convention or principle of language: *language is not haphazard, but is arranged in units of communication.*

This linking together of words and sentences into units is called *coherence*. In reading or listening to someone we expect what is being written or said to be coherent, that is, to be tied together in such a way that it makes sense. To make sense out of language we need to catch these inner connections in what is being said or written.

In the study of the Bible we need to begin with the assumption that the Bible writers were attempting to communicate to their audience by writing in organized units. These compositional units or paragraphs are the smallest unit of communication in the text. It is on these units that inductive study needs to focus. To take less than this is to chop up the ideas of the author and perhaps misunderstand them as a result of studying them out of context as in the example above. To take a larger bite is to include too much for a properly focused study.

Unfortunately, chapters and verses usually do not represent these basic units of communication. Verses are too small a unit, dividing a text into fragments; chapters are usually too large, often including several units which ought to be studied separately. Thus most editions of the Bible today indicate paragraph divisions in order to point to units of communication in the text.

For a practical illustration of these basic units look at Matthew 5. Here you can see that some verses are much more closely linked together than others. Verses 3-12 are connected more tightly than verse 12 is to 13. In the same way verses 17-20 seem to go together, while verse 21 marks a break. Verses 21-48 in turn seem related having six units with a similar beginning. Thus you can see from just reading the text that certain verses clump together to form a unit.

Even within a basic unit, smaller segments can be seen. For example, verses 13-16 seem to go together, since verse 13 is more closely related to verses 14-16 than it is to verse 12. But 14-16 are closer to each other than to verse 13, which seems to stand by itself.

2.11 **Axiom: Biblical writers wrote not by chapters or verses but by integrated units of communication. One of these basic units forms the foundation for the further steps of study.**

2.12 *Procedures*

Select a book of the Bible for study and identify a chapter or chapters as having material you are interested in studying. Now read this material carefully and closely, looking for clues like those listed below which can aid you in locating the basic unit(s) within a chapter.

A. *Analysis*
1. First, look for clues which indicate the boundaries of a unit, signs that a unit is beginning or ending.

    a. Are these phrases which mark the beginning or ending of a story or a topic? They frequently speak of time or place. An obvious beginning phrase is, "One day, as he was teaching ..." (Luke 20:1).

    b. Is the goal of the unit reached? Is the story finished, the tension resolved, or the topic completed?

    c. Is the unit bounded on either side by the ending of one unit and the beginning of another?

    d. "Editorial comments" may also mark the division between units. "Now the men of Sodom were wicked, great sinners against the Lord" (Genesis 13:13) is an example.

2. Second, look for signs which indicate a transition from one communication focus to another.

    a. Is there a change of actors, scene, theme, or topic? "After he had ended all his sayings in the hearing of the people he entered Capernaum" (Luke 7:1) is such a phrase.

    b. Is there an abrupt transition in which the material seems unconnected? Perhaps there is a certain grammatical roughness—a change in tense, verb number, person being addressed, or in antecedents of pronouns. The break between Genesis 13:18 and 14:1 is an example of a drastic break. "So Abram moved his tent, and came and dwelt by the oaks of Mamre, which are at Hebron; and there he built an altar to the Lord.

    "In the days of Amraphel king of Shinar, Arioch king of Ellasar, Ched-or-laomer king of Elam, and Tidal king of Goiim...."

      c. Is there a change in type of material, for example, from narrative to speech?

      d. Read several chapters to get a feel for the author's style, the type of unit he uses, and how he joins them together. This broader view may help you decide how to divide up the material you are studying into basic units.

   3. Third, observe whether the formal structure of a unit is complete. If we are reading a joke we expect a punch line at the end. Consequently, we would not end the basic unit of a joke until we reach the punch line. With this completion of the formal structure of the joke, we feel that the unit is completed and another basic unit can begin.[1]

B. *Synthesis*
   1. Choose one of the basic units you have isolated for further study.

   2. Explain why it is a basic unit.

      a. What sets it apart from the passages on either side of it?

      b. What serves to unify the material?

      c. What can you say from your analysis thus far about the meaning of the passage—its focus, topic, or emphasis, for example?

Often several of these clues operate together. When several lines of evidence converge, you can have confidence that you are on the right track.

A problem may arise, however, because within a basic unit you may also find segments or subparagraphs. It may be easy to confuse these segments for basic units. In looking for breaks in the text you must weigh both the quantity and quality of the evidence found. If this is done you can usually see that the breaks between the basic units are greater and of a different kind than the subdivisions within a unit: the smaller segments contribute to the point and structure of the unit. You have already seen an illustration of this difference in the example used above, Matthew 5:13-16. The break between verses 12 and 13, and 16 and 17—the division between units—is more pronounced than between the segments 13 and 14-16, which represents a division within a unit.

2.13 *Illustrations*
Genesis 12:10-20
   In Genesis 12 we find a narrative about Abram. Although the units

may not seem to be clear at first, after reading the chapter carefully you can see a break at verse 10, which begins the story of Abram's descent into Egypt (clue 2). Here we find the phrase, "Now there was a famine in the land. . . ." This phrase, "now there was" sounds like the beginning of a story, which further reinforces our decision to divide the text here (clue 1a).[2] This story begun in verse 10 continues to the end of the chapter and perhaps has its ending in verse 13:1 where Abram finds himself back again where he was before he went down to Egypt (see 12:9). However, since Lot is mentioned in this verse, but nowhere in 12:10-20, perhaps this verse is beginning the next unit. Because of this mention of Lot and the function of this verse as a transition to the next story, we will not consider it a part of the basic unit (clue 2a). The story itself seems self-contained. The plot begins in verse 10. It reaches its resolution in verse 20 (clue 1b). The basic unit consists of Genesis 12:10-20.[3]

Amos 2:6-16

In Amos 2 we find another type of material, prophetic speeches. By reading through the chapter you can observe that the phrase, "Thus says the Lord" followed by the phrase, "For three transgressions of . . . for four, I will not revoke it" occurs three times—in verses 1, 4, and 6. Each of these phrases begins a new, self-contained prophecy dealing with a specific country which is the focus. Also, verses 3 and 16 end their unit with a closing phrase.

Using clues 1a and 1c, we can divide this chapter into three basic units, verses 1-3, 4-5, and 6-16. We will choose verses 6-16 for study.

Matthew 5:38-42

Sometimes finding the basic units appears easy, as for example in Matthew 5, which we have looked at above. In verses 21-48 we have a series of teachings, each beginning with a traditional idea, such as "You have heard that it was said, 'Do not commit adultery' " (v. 27, GNB). This idea is then contrasted with a teaching which Jesus gives, "But I say to you. . . ." The boundaries between the units in this series are clear, since each begins with essentially the same phrase and contains a contrast between old and new teaching. One unit ends where the next begins (clue 1c). In this case each of these individual teachings, or antitheses as they are called, is a basic communication unit and can serve as the focus for an inductive study. Matthew 5:38-42 is one of the six antitheses found in this chapter, being the fifth in the series.

Romans 13:1-7

Romans 13:1-7 forms a distinct unit. 13:1 begins with a new topic, while verse 7 completes the discussion of this topic, the state (clue 1b). By reason of its topic, this unit seems set off from its context.

2.20 *Literary Structure*

Once a basic unit has been selected for study, the next step is to discover how the unit is organized, the structure of the unit. As seen above people speak or write in organized units of communication. This organization structure is necessary in order for them to communicate effectively. This means that within the unit they have arranged their language in a certain particular way. Through uncovering this structure of a unit, we can gain valuable insights into what is being communicated by the unit. We can see how it is focused and how its various parts contribute to this focus. Thus, the question to ask after you have isolated a unit for study is "What is the structure of this unit; how is the language patterned or arranged?"

Some people find this step of analysis difficult because they are not used to analyzing what they read from a literary angle. Rather they read for "content." In this phase of study, however, we are searching for the literary scaffold, the way the unit is built up from its various parts.

2.21 Axiom: Finding the parts of a unit and how they fit together is the essential first step toward discovering the context within which the words and sentences of a passage are to be understood.

2.22 *Procedures*

Read the unit to see how many major parts or segments there are in it; where are the "breaks" or "joints" in the unit? These segments of the unit will serve as the building blocks for your outline of the unit's structure. Then see if there are further divisions within each major segment. In this analysis you are searching especially for ways in which the language of the text itself may point to the unit's parts and their relationship within the unit. The following are clues which may help to divide the unit into the parts which make it up.

   A. *Analysis*
      1. Search to see if there are phrases or words which may indicate subsections.

   a. Words like "behold," "now," or "therefore" may indicate turning points in a unit.

   b. Are there repeated phrases or words? Are there oppositions?

   c. Are there words or phrases which serve as headings? Rhetorical questions which begin subsections?

2. Analyze the style, the way in which words are used, very carefully. Look for breaks or changes in style.

   a. Are there changes in the tense or subject of the verbs?

   b. Is the passage primarily in first, second, or third person? Does the audience or the person of the pronouns change (from first person to third person, for example)?

   c. Do certain syntactic patterns dominate: simple sentences, complex sentences? Are a few modifying words used, or many? Are there descriptive phrases or lack of description? Does the sentence structure change, from simple to complex, or from active to passive?

   d. Do certain types of words—common nouns, proper names, active verbs, stative verbs, classes of nouns, or verbs—dominate? Are there changes in vocabulary, in the types of words used? Perhaps there is a shift from concrete words to abstract ones, from animate to inanimate, or from proper nouns to common ones. There may be variations in word frequencies; certain words may cluster in a particular part of a passage.

   e. Are there changes in the tone of the passage? Are there "editorial comments" giving of information or are value judgments made?

   f. Is the passage poetry? You might prepare a scansion of the poetry. (This topic is beyond the scope of this outline; see the description in *IDB* s.v. "Poetry.")

3. Look for changes in the type or function of the material. For example, a shift from speech to narrative often indicates subsections within a unit. Likewise by looking at how the material functions within the unit, what its contribution is to the whole, you can see subdivisions in a unit. These may be changes in the amount of information or detail given.

4. Finally, observe the content of the unit. Find the different story units or scenes in a narrative, or topical points in an argument which represent subdivisions. These may be marked by a pause or a break. Also, look for the main focus or thread running through a unit

which gives it coherence. Where is the stress, emphasis, or center? What is essential to the story line or line of argument and what might be background information or a parenthetical comment?

B. *Synthesis*

1. After the analysis of the unit into segments, prepare an outline of the structure of the passage. Such an outline can take the form of a chart (page 64).[4]

2. Since this outline is to show the structure of the unit, try to use formal or functional labels for the segments if you can. Examples of such terms would be: introduction, speech, resolution, example or illustration, reasons, and conclusion. Also, group the subpoints in the outline under the main point with which they go. Make sure your label for a segment fits all the material in it. If it does not, break the segment down into subsegments or change the label.

3. Indicate what clues or markers have led you to outline the structure of the passage as you have.

4. How does this outline shed light on the meaning of the passage?

2.23 *Illustrations*
Genesis 12:10-20

As seen above, Genesis 12:10-20 forms a basic unit (13:1 may be seen either as a transitional verse, or as the ending of the present unit).

The first verse gives the circumstances of the story, "There was a famine in the land, so Abram descended to Egypt to sojourn there because the famine was severe in the land." The next verse, however, backtracks, since it pictures Abram not in Egypt, but on his way there, "And it happened as he drew near to enter Egypt." This phrase sets the stage for Abram's speech to Sarai, "Behold now I know that you are a beautiful woman. When the Egyptians see you they will say, 'she is his wife' and they will kill me but keep you alive. Say now, please, 'you are my sister' in order that it will be good for me on your account and I will live because of you." The narrative then continues, reporting that things happened exactly as Abram foresaw. When they entered Egypt, the Egyptians saw that she was a beautiful woman, and they praised her to Pharaoh. Because of her, things went well for Abram and he was enriched. So far, so good, according to Abram's plan, except for one unforeseen problem. Sarai was taken into Pharaoh's harem. His enrichment was at the expense of his wife.

But then something unexpected happens—Yahweh intervenes. He

afflicts Pharaoh and his household because of Sarai. Pharaoh consequently summons Abram, asks why he deceived him by saying Sarai was his sister, and commands him to leave. Verse 20 records the execution of Pharaoh's command—Abram, his wife, and all that was his is expelled from Egypt.

The structure of the story seems to be:

1. A general setting for the story is given at the beginning (v. 10). While this functions as an introduction to the story, the motif of famine is not mentioned again in the story. This first segment of the unit is loosely related to what follows (clue 4).

2. Verses 11-13, a speech, constitutes the second section of the unit (clue 3). This speech has its own narrative introduction, which separates it from verse 10. It is in this speech that the story really begins, since it is here that the plot is hatched and the seeds for the future tensions are planted. This speech itself has a definite structure;

    a. A statement of the problem—Sarai's beauty and the possible execution of Abram because of the Egyptians' desire for her.

    b. A command on how to cope with the situation—to deceive the Egyptians regarding Sarai's status.

    c. An expectation of what the outcome will be—prosperity and life for Abram.

3. The narrative which follows has two sections. The first (vv. 14-16) reports how the outcome predicted by Abram was realized. Things went exactly according to Abram's plan—but Sarai was now lost to Abram. This part of the narrative serves both to fulfill the expectations raised in Abram's speech, and to raise a new tension, the loss of Sarai. In the second section (vv. 17-20) God, who has not been mentioned up to this point, now intervenes in Abram's plan. Abram's ruse is discovered, and the story quickly ends with his expulsion. This scene functions as the resolution of the plot and its tensions. It ends with the wrap-up of the story: Abram and Sarai leaving Egypt.

There are elements of style which parallel and reinforce this analysis of the structure of the story (clue 3). In the initial speech of Abram, Sarai is termed "his wife," but she really is used as a pawn in his scheme, both to save his own skin, and to prosper. In the next section where his plan is carried out, Sarai is called only "the woman," an impersonal label appropriate to her role of pawn. Tension now exists between appearances, her pawn status as "the woman" and her real status as the wife of Abram. This corresponds to the function of this segment of the unit, which raises a problem and thereby creates a tension. God's action resolves this tension and restores Sarai's previous status to her. Thus in the last segment of the unit, she once more changes from "the woman" to Abram's wife.[5]

Another reinforcing feature of the language is that the story line is narrated by the use of a third person impersonal phrase, "and it was/happened." This phrase occurs in verses 10, 11, 14, and 16. In the first three instances, it introduces the next section or scene of the story as analyzed above. In verse 16 it finishes the scene where Abram's success is noted, "and he had sheep, oxen, he-asses, menservants, maidservants, she-asses, and camels." The fourth segment begins with (v. 17) "But Yahweh struck. . . ." This introductory phrase is in stark contrast to the ending just noted in verse 16. Furthermore it is the only scene of the story which begins with a personal actor. This break in the narrative pattern lends emphasis and a feeling of abrupt unexpectedness to God's intervention. These two stylistic features reinforce the formal structure we have found and add insight and emphasis to the dynamics of the story.

We can summarize the results of our careful reading in chart form:[6]

Scene	Structure Markers	Stylistic Features
I. Introduction, verse 10	"and it was . . ."	

II. Speech, verses 11-13
    a. Statement of the
       situation/problem
    b. Command-solution
    c. Prediction-resolution
	"and it was . . ."	Sarai = wife

III. Narrative, verses 14-20
    a. Fulfillment and problem
       verses 14-16
    b. Resolution, verses 17-20
	"and it was . . ."
	"and it was . . ."
	"Then God . . ."
		Sarai = woman
		
		Sarai = wife

Amos 2:6-16

In Amos 2:2-16, we have a prophecy of Amos directed to Israel, the Northern Kingdom. The passage is poetry, mainly synonymous poetry.[7] The speech is the last of a series addressed to various nations. The previous ones were directed against, first, the foreign nations round about Israel, and second against Judah, the Southern Kingdom. The speech addressed to Israel begins, as all the previous speeches do, with the set phrase, "Thus says the Lord, Because of three transgressions of Israel, because of four I will not turn it back" (v. 6a). After this introduction, a series of Israel's transgressions are mentioned in verses 6b-8. With verse 9, however, there is a change in content; God now begins to rehearse some of his past gracious dealings with Israel. This historical flashback extends through verse 11. To the historical survey is added yet another transgression in verse 12. Then in verse 13 we see another change in the type of material, a description of the coming judgment. This description continues to the end of the unit in verse 16. The unit closes with the ending, "Oracle of Yahweh." We could outline the structure of the unit as follows:

1. Introduction—"Thus says the Lord," followed by a stereotyped general statement of judgment (v. 6a).
2. A list of particular sins occurring within Israel (vv. 6a-8).
3. Historical flashback to the beginning of the nation, plus a transgression (vv. 9-12).
4. Description of the coming judgment (vv. 13-16).
5. Closing phrase (16).

These divisions are further confirmed by the differences in the language between the parts of the unit (clue 2). For example, in verses 6-8, the verbs are in third person, past-present tense, and the people are spoken of in the third person ("they"). With verse 9, however, the verbs are in the first person, "I," and the people in verses 10-12 are addressed directly in the second person ("you"). With verses 13-16, the verb tenses change again, from past to present and then present to future. The person of the verb likewise changes to third person. The people once again are talked about rather than being addressed directly. The following chart may help us to visualize these shifts in language more clearly and to see how these shifts correlate with the segments found above.

	verb subjects	verb tense	person of the people addressed
1. Introduction (6a)	3rd person	past/present	3rd person
2. Israel's sins (6b-8)	3rd person	past/present	3rd person
3. Historical flashback			
(9-11)	1st person	past	2nd person
Verse 12	2nd person	past	2nd person
4. Judgment (13-16)	1st/3rd person	present/ future	2nd/3rd person
5. Closing phrase			

This close coincidence between subject matter and style is strong evidence that our analysis of the structure is correct. Here, again, by a close reading we can see the subdivisions and the structure of the unit clearly.[8]

Koch has indicated several relationships between segments of the unit which bind it together and increase its coherency. For example, the earth or ground is mentioned in verse 7a in the list of sins, in verse 10 in the historical flashback, and in the judgment. The sins are oppression of the needy and weak. In the judgment, it will be the powerful and mighty who are brought low.[9]

Matthew 5:38-42

Matthew 5:38-42 is one of a series of antitheses in which Jesus contrasts his teaching with what people have been taught or might ordinarily think. From reading the passage we observe that it begins with a contrast, the first part being a quotation from the Old Testament, "You have heard that it was said, 'An eye for an eye and a tooth for a tooth' " while the second part presents the contrasting teaching of Jesus, "But I say to you, Do not resist one who is evil." Following this general teaching, Jesus gives a series of five cases or specific examples. These cases (in verses 39-42) continue to the end of the unit. The structure of this unit seems to be a very simple one consisting of two parts (clue 3):

> 1. General teaching—the antithesis, "You have heard . . . but I say. . . ."
> 2. Specific examples illustrating the teaching.

If we look more closely at the five examples we can see that they also have a certain common structure (clue 2c). They all begin with a hypothetical general case. For instance, the first example begins, "But if any one strikes you on the right cheek." This supposition is then followed by a command, an imperative, "turn to him the other also." This command tells us how to respond in the hypothetical situation. Thus we might outline the structure of this unit as follows:

> 1. General teaching—antithesis
> 2. Five specific examples
>   a. Situation—command   d. Situation—command
>   b. Situation—command   e. Situation—command
>   c. Situation—command

If we read this passage in the Greek, we would also note a shift in word usage which reinforces this outline. In the antithesis Jesus used the second person plural "you" (ye) while in the examples he uses the second person singular "you" (thou). This change in number reinforces the break we have traced above between the antithesis and the examples (clue 2a).

The change in person relates to the difference in function between the two parts. The antithesis is a general teaching aimed at all in general, thus the "you" plural. In the examples, however, Jesus seems to be thinking more concretely of actual possible instances in which an individual might find himself—thus the "you" singular (clue 2). The style is brief and direct. The use of imperatives and the second person singular indicates that this is a call to action.

Romans 13:1-7

Finally, to take an example from yet another type of literature, we will analyze the structure of Romans 13:1-7. This very famous passage begins with a quite general exhortation, "Let every person be subject to the governing authorities." Paul follows this exhortation with a series of supporting arguments, which continue through verse 5, then repeats the general exhortation once again. In verse 6 Paul turns to a specific matter, the payment of taxes. In verse 7 he returns once more to general language, commanding each person to pay the other his or her due. This he more closely defines by a series of further examples. The unit seems to be divided into two parts, verses 1-5 which are general in nature, and verses 6-7 which deal with specific obligations, primarily the payment of taxes (clue 3).

If we look at this unit yet more closely, we see that there are further structural contours. In the first section, verses 1-5, the arguments which Paul raises in support of his general statement seem to fall into two parts. Verses 1b-2 contain theological arguments, ending with the statement that those who resist will incur God's judgment. The second set of arguments in verses 3-5 contain practical considerations—we ought to obey because we will be rewarded if we do good, but punished if we do wrong. This whole section then seems to be recapitulated in verse 5b— we ought to be subject to avoid God's wrath (a theological reason) and for the sake of conscience (a practical reason).

From the standpoint of style, each of these subsections begins with "for" (*gar* in Greek), which seems to indicate the beginning of a new argument in support of the general thesis at the beginning (clue 1).

The second major section, verses 6-7, also seems to be subdivided into two parts. The first part, verse 6, deals with the specific matter of tax payment. Verse 7, however, reverts to a more general tone, like that of verse 1a, with its command to pay everyone what is due. This is followed by a series of specific instances of what this might mean—taxes, revenue, respect, and honor. This command at the close seems to round off the unit, returning to the general exhortation at the beginning in verse 1a.

We can diagram the structure of Romans 13:1-7 as follows:[10]

Outline	Verse	Structure Markers
1. General thesis, "let every one . . ."	1a	
a. Theological reason	1b-2	"for"
b. Practical reason	3-4	"for" . . . for . . . for"
c. Restatement of thesis	5	"therefore"
2. Application		
a. Specific—payment of taxes	6	"for"
b. General—give to all their due	7	

Paul's use of the second person and the rhetorical questions which he uses ("would you have no fear. . .?) indicate that this is no abstract argument, but a dialogue addressed to people whom he is trying to persuade to a certain point of view or action.

2.30 *Logical Structure*

As we have seen above, when people speak or write they organize their language in ways that make sense. To make sense each sentence, phrase, or segment within a unit needs to have some sensible relationship to what came before and what will follow. If it does not, language becomes disjointed and perhaps incoherent. In this step of study we will seek the logic which lies behind the structure of a passage. By understanding this underlying logic, we will see more clearly how the parts are connected to the whole.

This stage of study, then, focuses upon *explaining* the structure of the passage. By what logic or train of thought are the segments bound together into a whole? Through this step of analysis, you will provide the reason or rationale behind the literary structure which you have just found. In addition, you may also need to examine the arrangement of sentences or phrases within a part or segment of a passage in order to see what rationale lies behind their particular order or arrangement.

An analogy may help illustrate the difference between literary and logical analysis. In dissecting an animal, we may lay bare the circulatory system—the veins and arteries and the heart. This is the formal structure, the anatomy. However, we have not really understood these parts as a system until we understand how each part functions as part of the total system, the physiology.

2.31 **Axiom: It is only when we understand the functional aspect, the rationale or reason behind the structure, that we have really begun to understand the language of a unit.**[11]

2.32 *Procedures*

The clues for this section will be given in a general fashion. Begin by studying the literary structure you have found. Determine what logic links the segments of the passage together. The major type of links which you can expect to find are the following:

A. *Analysis*
  1. Developmental links: Sometimes a section simply adds on to or runs parallel to what has gone before. This is most often the case in narrative.
    a. Material which adds on is material which continues to develop the story or line of argument. "... he came and took ... and lifted up...." (Mark 1:31).
    b. Material which is parallel serves the same function as previous material in the unit. In either case, the material stands on its own.

  2. Supporting links: Sometimes a segment or phrase supports another. Such material is not independent but dependent—its function is to support another part. A supporting element may help in the following ways.
    a. Clarification: It may either say the same thing in different words or it may add new information by way of clarification. This helps the audience to grasp more readily what is being said. "I am not come to destroy, but fulfill" (Matthew 5:17).
    b. Cause-effect: Some of these relationships are reason-result, grounds-conclusion, or means-purpose. "... being now justified ... we shall be saved" (Romans 5:10).
    c. Orientation: This type of material is related to the unit by giving information about the situation—the time, place, people addressed, and circumstances of the action.[12]

B. *Synthesis*
  1. Your explanation of the structure can take the form of an outline. You

may repeat the outline which you developed in the preceding step, adding to this the logical relations which link the segments together.

2. You should explain how this understanding of the unit's structure affects the understanding of the unit.

2.33 *Illustrations*
Genesis 12:10-20

In Genesis 12:10-20, we saw above that the story was divided into three major segments. The first part, verse 10, gives the motivational background for Abram being in Egypt. It seems to have no further function within the story. Its relationship to the unit is one of orientation (clue 2c). The plot of the story begins in the second part (v. 11) which contains the speech of Abram. This speech is preceded by its own phrase of orientation, "And it was as they drew near to enter Egypt...."

The speech as seen above is segmented into three parts: (1) A statement of the situation which is causing or will cause a problem—Sarai's beauty. (2) A command is given to resolve the problem—Sarai is to say she is Abram's sister. (3) The expected outcome of this action is stated—Abram will live and prosper. This speech is tightly knit logically. The present situation serves as the grounds or cause which justifies the deception. Likewise, the expectation is the purpose of the proposed deception, the deception forming the means to the desired ends (clue 2b). We can outline the logic of the speech as follows:

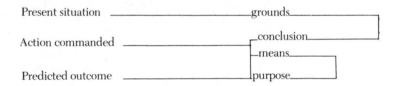

From this diagram we can see that the action—the command to deceive—is presented as doubly valid, once by the nature of the present situation and once by the expected outcome.

The narrative section of the unit is straightforward, telling how Abram's analysis of the situation was justified and how his expectations were exactly realized. Note in reading this section, how closely the language of the narrative repeats that of the speech. In verse 14 it is reported that the Egyptians saw that Sarai was a beautiful woman, while

16a repeats almost word for word the fulfillment which Abram predicted in his speech (v. 13). This narrative is in a sense the mirror of the speech—it reports how Abram's speech came to realization in the course of events.

These verses, however, contain a strand of material which is not linked to the speech—verse 15, which is sandwiched between the phrases reporting the fulfillment of the speech. This verse tells that Pharaoh's officers not only saw Sarai and praised her to Pharaoh, but also that the woman was taken into Pharaoh's harem. This strand then sets the stage for the next scene of the story, which is linked developmentally (clue 1) to the present one by giving the resolution of this unforeseen development.

The second scene of the narrative begins abruptly with a new actor, Yahweh, who intervenes in this matter. This intervention provides the backdrop for Pharaoh's summons of Abram and his terse speech to him. The speech ends with the command—"take and go!" Verse 20 reports the execution of these commands. The unexpected turn of events narrated in this scene is brought about by the two narrative elements unforeseen or unmentioned in Abram's speech: that Sarai would end up in Pharaoh's harem, and that God would intervene and act on Sarai's behalf. The element unforeseen in scene two, the speech, calls forth the unforeseen actor in the last scene. Again, this section is linked developmentally to the preceding ones.

We can now see something of the intricacy and delicacy of this short and seemingly simply constructed story. The speech in scene 2 is linked to the narrative in scene 3a by the link of prediction—fulfillment. Scene 3b, however, is linked to the narrative in scene 3a by the unpredicted. This interplay in the development of the unit between the foreseen and unforeseen highlights the tension which exists in the story between the plans of man and the providence of God. In outline, the story would look like this:

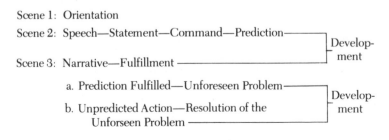

Scene 1: Orientation

Scene 2: Speech—Statement—Command—Prediction ── ⌉ Develop-

Scene 3: Narrative—Fulfillment ──────────── ⌋ ment

    a. Prediction Fulfilled—Unforeseen Problem ── ⌉ Develop-

    b. Unpredicted Action—Resolution of the ── ⌋ ment
       Unforseen Problem ────────────

Amos 2:6-16

In Amos 2:6-16 we saw quite a different type of material and structure. We observed that the passage, following the stereotyped introduction to the unit, was divided into three main sections—a listing of Israel's sins (vv. 6-8 [12]), a historical flashback (9-11), and a description of the coming judgment (13-16). The first and last section seem to have a cause and effect connection, since the listing of Israel's sins forms the reason or grounds for the coming judgment (clue 2b). The judgment thus forms the logical outcome or conclusion to Israel's present sins. The middle section, the historical flashback, however, seems to break the logical coherence of the passage. Its present function seems to be to sharpen or heighten the magnitude of Israel's sins. Israel, because of her history, could have been expected to act quite differently than she is now doing. The present sins are the opposite of what would be expected. Thus the historical flashback functions to raise this counter-expectation to mind and thereby underlines the gravity of Israel's sins. This in turn increases their weight as the grounds for the coming judgment. The passage seems to have the following logical structure:

Introduction

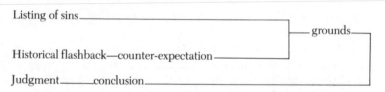

Listing of sins

Historical flashback—counter-expectation

grounds

Judgment_____conclusion

Within each of these units there are further logical linkages which connect the phrases and sentences to each other. The listing of the sins and judgments in the first and last sections are constructed developmentally (clue 1). Likewise, the historical flashback is constructed on the principle of narrative development.

Matthew 5:38-42

Matthew 5:38-42 is divided into just two parts. The first part is the antithesis, where Jesus presents his general teaching "do not resist the evil person" as a contrast to the usual practice, "an eye for an eye and a tooth for a tooth." The second part is a series of five specific examples illustrating this general teaching. These examples seem to be related by clarification to the initial statement, which is the general element in a generic-specific relationship (clue 2a).

We saw above that each of these specific examples had the same structure—the presentation of a hypothetical situation with a command about how to respond to that situation. From this consistent structure and the logic of the passage, we may conclude that when Jesus says, "Do not resist the evil person," he did not mean to do nothing in return, that is, to remain passive or nonresistant, since each illustration of the meaning has a command to act. Rather, what he meant was not to respond in the normal human way, since each action commanded is rather unusual. The understanding of the general statement in light of the specific content given by Jesus also points to the logical relationship of "do not resist the evil person" to an "eye for an eye." The contrast is not between responding to evil (eye for eye) and not responding to evil at all (do not resist), but rather, between *ways* of responding. An old way of responding to evil is contrasted with the new way being taught and illustrated. Here, by grasping the logic of the structure, we begin to approach the contextual meaning of the text.

The five examples which are given do not seem to have a logical relationship to each other, but rather represent a list of circumstances in which people may find themselves in the course of their daily lives. They include personal insult, being sued, being imposed upon by government officials, and being asked to loan things or money. These examples would seem to be linked developmentally (clue 1).

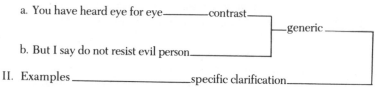

I. Antithesis
    a. You have heard eye for eye———contrast———
                            ———generic———
    b. But I say do not resist evil person———

II. Examples————————specific clarification————

Romans 13:1-7

    The structure of Romans 13:1-7, as we have seen, is the most complex of any of the units being studied. We will begin by diagraming its structure and then comment on it.

    I. Theology (vv. 1-5)
        A. Thesis (la)
            "Let every person be subject to the governing authorities."

1. Theological argument (1b-2)
   "For there is no authority except from God, and those that exist have been instituted by God. Therefore he who resists the authorities resists what God has appointed, and those who resist will incur judgment."

2. Practical argument (3-4)
   "For rulers are not a terror to good conduct, but to bad. Would you have no fear of him who is in authority? Then do what is good, and you will receive his approval, for he is God's servant for your good. But if you do wrong, be afraid, for he does not bear the sword in vain; he is the servant of God to execute his wrath on the wrongdoer."

B. Restatement (5)
   "Therefore one must be subject, not only to avoid God's wrath, but also for the sake of conscience."

II. Application (vv. 6-7)
   A. Specific (6)
      "For the same reason you also pay taxes, for the authorities are ministers of God, attending to this very thing."

   B. General (7)
      "Pay all of them their dues, taxes to whom taxes are due, revenue to whom revenue is due, respect to whom respect is due, honor to whom honor is due."

As you can see, the thesis is a conclusion based on two grounds, one theological and the other practical. After these parallel arguments, Paul restates his conclusion in summary fashion. The whole of this section in turn forms the reason behind a specific result—the present payment of taxes. This result is stated twice, in slightly different ways. The first is just the statement—that this is why you are now paying or should pay taxes. The second statement begins with a general proposition, but makes immediate application to the paying of taxes among other things.

Usually it is verse 1 which receives the major attention and emphasis in this passage, but from the logical structure as outlined above, we can see that this statement, like the whole of the first section, really forms the foundation—the reason—for the second part, the logical result. Thus it would seem that Paul's emphasis here is on the matter of taxes rather than on general submission to government, since he uses that general principle to indicate the appropriateness of tax payment, the actual focus of the passage.

I. Theology

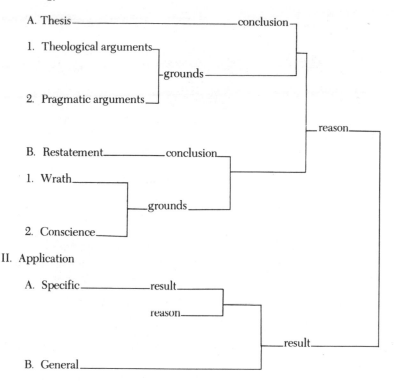

    A. Thesis——————————————conclusion

      1. Theological arguments

          grounds

      2. Pragmatic arguments

               reason

    B. Restatement——————conclusion

      1. Wrath

         grounds

      2. Conscience

II. Application

    A. Specific——————result

         reason

              result

    B. General

Alternately, you might consider the present payment of taxes a further argument for the general thesis of verse 1a. It seems to be more likely, however, that paying taxes is a result of submission to government rather than a reason for it.

2.40 *The Compositional Structure*

After you have analyzed the structure of a passage as best you can from a literary point of view and have attempted to discern the inner logic of the unit, you must consider whether or not the unit is a compositional unity. From your study so far, you may have noted parts of a passage which seem not to fit with the rest. The answer to this problem may be that the passage is a compositional mixture. That is, the passage as we now have it may not be the work of a single author at one time. There are several options here. It may be the result of the work of several authors being joined into one unit; or perhaps several units composed by the same author, but at different times, have been fused together. Or again additions may have been introduced into the unit in the course of its transmission and collection into a book.

These processes are especially true of the units which were originally composed orally and transmitted orally. They may have been written down at a time which was quite distant from the time of their "original" composition. Many of the biblical "authors" in fact did not collect their compositions into books nor arrange them in the form we now find in the Bible. The material about Jesus and his teachings, for example, were not collected by Jesus, but by later writers. The people who did the collecting and arranging, often called "redactors," may have fused together what were originally independent units. Likewise, they may have added additional comments. This was necessary when the separate units were gathered together into a book as we now find in the Bible.

Note, however, that when the author of a unit quotes a source like the Old Testament, this does not make the unit a composite. The question here is whether more than one author has worked or reworked the unit.

2.41 Axiom: A unit may be the result of the fusion of two or more compositional pieces or it may contain additions.

2.42 *Procedures*

In looking for signs of composite authorship, look for the following clues:

A. *Analysis*
   1. Are there duplications, redundancies, or unnecessarily repeated information?
   2. Are there inner inconsistencies?
   3. Are there tensions in the word flow and rough joints in the structure; are there digressions for no apparent reason?
   4. Are there changes in style or vocabulary in the unit; are some parts marked by different language?
   5. Are there changes or differences in perspective, theology, or interest in the unit?
   6. Is there material which obviously assumes a different authorship?

Are there secondary comments, explanatory notes, or supplemental material?
7. Does the material found together in the passage occur separately elsewhere? Have two separate "blocks" of material been fused together?
8. Are there anachronisms, that is, can part of the text be shown to come from a later time?[13]

B. *Synthesis*
If you find what seems to be clear evidence of composite authorship, you need to determine the type of the multiple authorship.
1. If the unit has had several additions made to it, you can classify it as an *expanded unit*—a basic compositional unit with expansions. These expansions are often explanations or comments on the unit. Sometimes they are expansions for emphasis.
2. If the unit has been formed by an "editor" joining what may have been two or more units, it is a *composite unit*.
3. If it shows no sign of multiple authorship, it is a *simple unit*.[14]

2.43 *Illustrations*
Genesis 12:10-20

Genesis 12:10-20 seems to flow smoothly. The narrative is very spare—on the surface each phrase seems to be important to the story. However, certain problems in the narrative have been seen. There is, first of all, the break between verses 10 and 11. But any shift here is probably due to a shift from a general introductory setting to the specific beginning of the plot. A redundancy has been seen in verse 10; famine is mentioned twice—once at the beginning and once at the end verse (clue 1).[15] Since verse 10 is a transitional verse, some have seen verse 10 placed here by a later editor in order to fit this story into Abram's travels in Canaan which are resumed again in chapter 13.[16] The double mention of the famine may have arisen from this, but it may also be repeated for emphasis or style.[17] The list of animals in verse 16b also appears awkward, since male/female donkeys are separated by the mention of servants.[18] Would a later editor destroy a nice orderly list to make it rough? More likely not, unless pressing motivation can be shown. Thus, all in all, this unit appears to be a simple unit.[19]

Amos 2:6-16

Amos 2:6-16 is not compositionally clear-cut. There appears to be a major break between verses 8 and 9 and 10, as we have seen above in our examination of both the formal and logical structure. In verse 9, God shifts to first person from third person, while in verse 10 the people are no longer "they" but addressed as "you" (clue 3). As seen, we have here a very rough transition in the language. Likewise, between verses 9 and 10, not only is there the difficulty in the flow of language, but the sequence of events is backward—verse 9 seems to be describing the conquest, while verse 10 relates to the Exodus from Egypt (clue 2). The vocabulary used here is similar to that found in Deuteronomy and related writings (clue 4). (See transmission analysis, chapter 5.) Finally, as we shall see in the next chapter, where Amos uses this type of speech elsewhere in the book, he does not have a historical flashback. For all of these reasons this unit appears to be an expanded unit with verses 10-12 being an addition.[20] Either a historical flashback was extracted from an originally separate speech by Amos and joined to this unit, or one of the gatherers and transmitters of Amos' words added it here to heighten the effect of this prophecy.

It should not surprise us to find material added to Amos, since we find material elsewhere in the book which is clearly not written by Amos—for example the first verse of the book, or chapter 7:10-17, which were written about Amos by later editors or redactors (see transmission and redaction analysis in chapter 6). Thus, we must keep in mind that the present collection of Amos' sayings and their arrangement was not due to Amos. Others not only collected and arranged them, but joined units together and added material to them.

Matthew 5:38-42

Initially Matthew 5:38-42 seems structurally to be very straightforward—a simple unit as we have in Genesis 12:10-20. But if we look at the parallel account of this teaching in Luke 6:29-30, we find a great difference (clue 7). In Luke, to begin with, we have a list of only four cases instead of five, as in Matthew. These four are being struck on the cheek, being sued, being asked to lend something, and having something being taken from you. The case of being asked to go one mile is not mentioned by Luke. But even though Luke has four cases, only the first three are the same as those in Matthew, since Luke's last example is not found in Matthew. Even more striking is the fact that there are no antitheses here in Luke—or anywhere in Luke for that matter. Thus, in Luke, these cases are not given as examples of what it means to not resist the evil person. Instead, they are listed as illustrations of what it means to love your enemies, which is found in the next antithesis in Matthew. It seems probable, then, that Matthew has joined two teachings into one unit (clue 7). He has taken a general teaching, "do not resist the evil person," and joined to it the five examples which presently follow it in order to make it concrete. This unit would thus be a composite unit; it is made up by Matthew's fusion of two originally separate traditions.

Romans 13:1-7

Romans 13:1-7, on the other hand, appears to be a simple unit coming from Paul. There does not appear to be any strong evidence that it has undergone major change since Paul wrote it. This is disputed by some, not on the basis of evidence found in the unit itself, but on the basis of the apparent abruptness of the unit in its present context in Romans 12 and 13. That is, the end of chapter 12 seems to find its natural continuation in chapter 13:8-10. Even if this observation were true, and this will be discussed in another step, this would not be evidence that the unit itself is not, in its present shape, a simple unit.

Chapter 3

From Structure to Type:
Form Analysis

3.00 *Form*

During a time spent in voluntary service as an itinerant Bible teacher, our family traveled a great deal in the United States and Canada, sometimes pulling a small travel trailer from place to place. Because of the extra load, we tried to find easy, level roads on which to drive. Once in the Western United States we decided to take a shortcut across part of Nevada and Oregon. According to the map the road looked straight and level with no mountains or other obstacles to pull our trailer over or around. But after we were on the "shortcut" for a while, it became clear that what looked flat on the map was really very hilly. In fact, we just barely seemed to make it over some of the hills we encountered. We were misled by our map, not because it was incorrect or inaccurate, but because it was a "flat" map; it showed the routes and the distances between places, but it did not show the third dimension, the rise and fall of the terrain. Without considering this third vital dimension we interpreted the terrain incorrectly.

Many people read the Bible as a flat book. They fail to read and understand the Bible against the historical environment in which it was written and originally understood. When this background is removed the words lose their original context within which they made sense and were understood. This makes the Bible flat, because its words are all understood in a single context, as if they were all written at one time and place. Lacking the dimension of historical depth, people are misled as to what is in fact the meaning of the text.

But there is yet another way in which the Bible is treated as a flat book. It is often read as if it were all the same type of literature. People

80

usually assume that the Bible, for example, is all written in descriptive narrative or in some propositional form. Actually, the Bible contains many different types of literature. In it we find parables, different types of poetry, biography, and narrative to name only a few types. These different types of literature need to be taken into consideration if we want to understand the Bible accurately.

Language can be likened to a game. As there are a variety of games—football, baseball, soccer—so there are a variety of literary types, each having its own rules (conventions). For example, in America we enjoy the game of baseball. If we traveled to England we might encounter another game called cricket which would seem similar. There would be a batter, a pitcher, and fielders. Yet the rules of the game would be quite different. As long as we tried to understand cricket by the rules of baseball, we would be hopelessly confused. But once we realized that this is a different game with different rules, we would begin to understand what was happening on the field of play.

Just as there may be external similarity between games and yet their rules may be quite different, so there may be external similarity between different types of language and yet their conventions (rules) may mean various things and be quite different. It is not until we understand the type of literature we are reading that we can truly understand it. Thus, in this step of study we will try to discover what literary conventions or norms have influenced the way an author has composed a unit. Once we discover the "rules" which guided the composition of the unit, we will then be able to understand the type or form of literature being written.

Returning to the analogy of a game, we can see why we need to discover the conventions or rules in order to learn what type of unit is being written. In a game, when we find the rules of baseball being followed, we have a baseball game. When the rules of baseball are not being followed, we do not have a baseball game, since not just any game using a bat, a ball, fielders, and bases is baseball. Likewise, in language, when we find the rules of parable composition being followed, we have a unit belonging to the form "parable." Where these rules are not being followed, we do not have a parable, since not every figurative story is a parable. Therefore, in determining the form of a unit, we look to see what conventions of composition were being followed.

Why do these different forms of language exist? Why do we need different rules of composition? They exist in a language because language is used: (1) to do different things, (2) to communicate different types of content, and (3) to do this in different social settings. These three factors are the unwritten presuppositions behind the conventions of a form and govern its use.[1] We must become aware of these presuppositions in order to "take" a passage as it ought to be taken. Each of these three aspects of a literary form will be discussed in turn.

First of all, language has many different functions; it is used to do a wide variety of things. For example, language may be used to report an event. For this function descriptive narrative is used. Or language may be used to illustrate a truth, lesson, or point, in which case a parable would be appropriate. Language may be used to regulate behavior by writing laws or issuing commands, or to entertain as in a story or a joke. These different functions are reflected in the way language is used.

In each of these cases we can see that there is an appropriate fit between the type of language used and its function. We take this for granted, since this is how language works in everyday life. For example, a parable would be an appropriate form to use to relate a religious concept. Because of this presupposition an author would use a parable to teach about God. On the other hand to regard a parable as descriptive narrative and to seek in it a historical event would be to violate the conventions of a parable. This understanding of a parable would be incorrect since it runs counter to the presuppositions which govern the use of parables.

Second, language is used to speak about a great variety of topics. To do this different forms are used. For example, some types of language are felt to be more appropriate to use in talking about God. We would not ordinarily use a joke to speak of God, but we would use a sermon. Even in writing or speaking about the same general topic different types need to be used depending on the aspect of the topic focused on. A treatise about celestial mechanics uses a different type of language than does a poem about the beauty of the night sky. These two types of language not only have different functions, but they also communicate a different type of information. The treatise depends on accurate description; the poem, on aesthetic beauty. Thus we can see that different subjects and themes demand that different types of language be used in order to talk of them. Again, to use the wrong type would be to communicate poorly. Likewise, to mistake the type used would be to misunderstand. To take a poem about the night sky as a scientific description would be to miss the point and misuse the poem.

Third, language is used in a vast range of social situations. The social situation includes, for example, the audience which is being addressed. We tend to speak differently to children than to adults. We speak differently with our friends than with strangers, and we speak still differently with a newspaper reporter (or we should). Variations in the situation also influence the way language is used. A teacher speaks one way in the classroom to a student, but in a different way privately in the office. If both are serving on the same committee, the teacher speaks with the student in yet another way. Likewise, husbands and wives use language differently, depending on whether they are in private or in public. Such examples could be multiplied almost endlessly. The point is that the context in which language is used influences or even determines the form of language used. When an unsuitable type of language is used we are put off. For example, if an after-dinner speaker at an informal gathering enters into an elaborate technical lecture instead of telling jokes and giving a short, witty speech, we may be upset by being a captive audience for something which we would just as soon be spared. Likewise, to criticize a witty speech in such a circumstance for not being profound or intellectual enough is surely to miss the point.

Having seen that these three factors influence the way we use language, the question arises, *how* do they do this? How do we know which language game to use? We have already noted that language is conventional, shared behavior. One set of these conventions or rules tells us how to speak about different topics in different contexts to accomplish different things. That is, customs have evolved about how to use language depending on circumstances. An example would be using full names rather than nicknames when announcing names at graduation ceremonies. Why do we do this? Custom tells us this is the proper way to do in that social context. Custom tells us what type of language to use in a given situation.

These traditional rules which guide us in forming our language are of two major types. They influence us in: (1) the way we organize or structure our language and (2) the words we use and how we use them. *We can define a form*, then, as a classification of units which share the same conventions of structure, style, and subject matter.[2] It is easy to see that structure of a limerick (5 lines) is different from that of a sonnet (14 lines). Likewise, the vocabulary in a lecture on astronomy is different from that of a poem about the starry heavens. They differ because they follow different rules; they are different games.

Just as we cannot see customs or the rules of a game, but only how it is played, so we cannot see the conventions which distinguish one form of literature from another directly, but must discover them from the way language is used. Since the structure, style, and subject matter determine the form of a unit, the steps outlined below help us discover the conventions relating to these. These conventions are found by comparing passages in order to find similarities. If we find a feature shared by several passages which are independent of one another, we can assume we have found a literary convention which has shaped the composition of the units. Why is this so? If two or more literary units share the same feature, it would be for one of three reasons: (1) One unit is the model and the others are copies or imitations of it—that is, they are dependent on it. (2) Pure coincidence. (3) All are playing the same language game—they are written following the same rules of composition.

3.01 **Axiom: Each passage of Scripture belongs to a certain type or form of literature which has its own conventions; a valid interpretation or understanding must be in accord with these literary presuppositions.**

3.02 *Procedures*

You should note that the same type of conventions do not mark each form. Some forms will be distinguished by their structure, e.g., limericks and sonnets; others by their style, e.g., legal material; still others by their content,[3] e.g., a doxology which is a hymn of praise addressed to God. In reading for common features between units you must be attentive to the various kinds of conventions illustrated below. As a search strategy, you should begin with an outline of the structure and a list of characteristics which describe your passage. You can use these as a beginning point for comparison with other passages.

    A. *Analysis*
      1. Conventional structure
        The first step in determining the form of a unit is to determine if the structure of the unit is unique or whether it is shared by several units. Sonnets, for example, share the same structure; they have 14 lines with certain rhyme schemes. Any poem which you find today having this structure you would classify as belonging to the type "sonnet" because it follows the conventions of sonnet writing.

        Likewise, in the Bible when several passages have the same structure and appear to be literarily independent, their similarity is explained by assuming they are composed according to the same rules. Since they are written according to the same rules they belong to the same literary form, just as in the case of English sonnets.

To do this comparative work, it is helpful to proceed as follows:

a. Read the remainder of the book or work in which the passage being studied is found in order to determine if there are other units with a similar structure. Keep in mind the importance of key words in indicating the structure of a passage.

b. Read other books with similar material to see if passages with a similar structure can be found. A commentary may suggest similar passages.

c. Outline the structure of all the similar passages which are found. This will make it easy to compare their structural similarities and dissimilarities.

d. Determine whether the passages are literarily independent. Is it probable that these passages are similar because they are following the same compositional conventions, or are they all the work of a single author or copies of one another? If they are all literarily dependent, then there is no clear evidence that you have a form rather than the unique style of an individual or copies of it.

2. Conventional subject and style

a. Besides a common structure, the members of a form may have distinctive subjects, themes, or motifs in common. These you see in the way words are chosen and used. Indeed, common elements of expression may be the form's identifying element. For example, when you read a story as in Judges 9:8-15 in which trees talk, you know that you are reading a fable because talking trees and animals are a convention of fable telling. Fables have certain other common patterns, for example, the actors are trees or animals. Thus, not every story in which animals and trees talk may be a fable. For example, in Numbers 22:28-30 an animal talks, but since the major actor is a human—Balaam—this story is not a fable.

In comparing passages with one another you need to be attentive not only to individual elements of content, but to the function of these elements within the unit as a whole. This is why it is so important to be clear about the structure and the function of elements within a passage before comparisons are made between different passages. Content which is parallel must not only be the same in substance, but must also have the same function within the passage.

b. A certain style or features of style may be conventional in a form. For example, "then" sentences are characteristic of legal material; rhetorical questions, of arguments; and metaphors, of various poetic types. A certain type of vocabulary or certain specific words or expressions may also be characteristic of a form. For example, woe oracles in the prophets begin with the key word "woe."

3. *Social presuppositions.*
Certain social roles and effects are often assumed in a passage. These too may be conventions of a form.
   a. Who is speaking and who is listening? What social roles are being presupposed? For example, when you find words in a passage addressed to God, the first thing you will think of is that you have a prayer. You would not consider this type unless the words were addressed to God.
   b. What effect is sought? Is the passage to inform, to entertain, to stir to action? What function, intention, or purpose did this type of unit serve? Jokes have one type of intention and function, sonnets another, and law yet another. These differences can be helpful in guiding you to a correct understanding of a form.
      Using these clues—the structure, the subject and style, and the social presuppositions—you are now in a position to determine what type of language a passage contains.

B. *Synthesis*
   1. Arrange the units by degree of similarity. Which passages seem to be the most similar, which the most dissimilar? This may be done by using a continuum: a line on which the units may be placed as below.

most similar _____ most dissimilar

Looking now at the similaraties and dissimilarities, are the features of the unit being studied close enough to those of the other passages to say that it shares with them a common form or pattern of language? If they do appear to share a common pattern of composition, list the elements they share or at least those which most of them share. Not all elements of each individual passage will necessarily be found in every other passage which belongs to the same type, nor necessarily in quite the same way or order. The common characteristics listed can serve as the keys to identify other passages which may belong to the same type. These keys define the form.

   2. What should you do if you find no passages similar to your unit? No matter how you try, you may not find other units with significant similarities to your own. In this case, characterize the distinctive features of the unit. This will stand instead of an assignment of the unit to a particular form.

   3. Indicate the significance of your findings for the meaning of your unit.
      a. What does the form of your unit imply about the meaning?
      b. How does the recognition of conventional language in your unit shed light on its understanding?

3.03 *Illustrations*
Genesis 12:10-20
In Genesis 12:10-20 we found the following structure (see page 64).

I. Introduction
II. Speech
   A. Statement of the situation—problem
   B. A command—solution
   C. Prediction—resolution
III. Narrative
   A. Fulfillment and problem
   B. Resolution to the problem

Our first step, in line with clue 1 above, is to see whether in Genesis 12—36, where we find the rest of the patriarchal stories, we can observe stories with a similar structure.

We do not need to read more than four chapters before we find a story with a very similar pattern. Genesis 16:1-16, which tells of the conception and birth of Ishmael, begins with a brief general setting or introduction (I in the above outline). This is immediately followed by a speech of Sarai, "Behold now, the Lord has prevented me from bearing children; go in to my maid; it may be that I shall obtain children by her" (v. 2). In this speech we can see the same three-part structure outlined above: there is a statement of the situation, "The Lord has prevented me from bearing children" (problem). This is followed by the command to action—"go in to my maid" (solution). Following the command Sarai states the expected outcome—"it may be that I shall obtain children by her" (resolution). Thus in this passage we find part II of the outline above with all of its three parts in exactly the same order.

A narrative follows in which the command is carried out. It seems that the expectation of Sarai will be realized, since Hagar becomes pregnant. This corresponds to IIIA in the above outline—a narrative in which the speech is fulfilled. But an unforeseen consequence arises: Hagar adopts a haughty attitude toward Sarai and ill feeling develops between them (problem). Sarai mistreats Hagar and as a result Hagar flees. It looks as if Sarai's expectation will not be realized. In this circumstance God intervenes to bring about a resolution by appearing to Hagar. This corresponds to point IIIB in the outline, the solution to unforeseen problems. The pattern in this passage seems identical to that found in Genesis 12:10-20. It has the same major parts, which function in the same way: a speech which tightens the narrative spring followed by a narrative which describes the fulfillment of the speech's command and the rise of an unexpected problem which comes from the fulfillment. In the end the climax of the narrative fulfills the expectation of the speech.[4]

This same pattern can be seen again in the story of Jacob's theft of Esau's blessing (Genesis 27:1-40). Here the pattern is a bit more complicated, because after the brief general introduction (v. 1) we find two speeches instead of one. In the first, Isaac speaks to Esau, while in the second Rebekah addresses Jacob. However, both of these speeches follow the same three-point structure. Both state the situation, give a command—Isaac to Esau, Rebekah to Jacob—and state what they see as the outcome. In addition to this structure there is a dialogue at the end of Rebekah's speech since Jacob is not so sure that the plan will work as his mother suggests. He fears that the plan will bring him evil rather than good.

In these last two speeches, a new feature is present in the third element. Here we not only find a general expectation, as in the past two stories, but also a promise—a direct first-person involvement and obligation on the part of the speaker to see that the future expectation is in fact realized. The element of promise is weaker in Isaac's speech than in Rebekah's. In Isaac's speech he obligates himself to simply eat what is brought so that the desired outcome, a soulful blessing for Esau, will come about. In Rebekah's case, she obligated herself to prepare a tasty dish. Thus the formulation of the future expectation can be either general, using the third-person impersonal or passive, as in the previous stories, or, as here, in the first person where an obligation is contracted with the person addressed. We might classify these two different formulations of the future expectation as prediction and promise, respectively.

Since, according to traditional source divisions, the stories we have been examining all come from the J source or strata of material,[5] they may all be dependent literarily on one another. That is, this striking similarity in structure may be the result of J's unique style of telling stories. In order to find if this structure is more widely used, we will go to the book of Judges, which like Genesis has many stories about the heroes of Israel's early history. If we can find the same pattern there, we will conclude that this pattern in Genesis 12:10-20 is due to a general storytelling convention rather than to J's creativity in narrative art.

In Judges 16:4-21 we find the story of the seduction of Samson by Delilah. The story has a structure very similar to the stories we have just seen in Genesis. It begins with a speech by the Philistine rulers, who begin summarily with the command, "Seduce him, and see in what is his great strength and how we can overcome him." Then follows a twofold expression of the future consequences, "that we may bind him in order to torture him and we will give, each of us, a hundred in silver."[6] The speech has only two of the three parts of the outline given above; it lacks the statement of the problem. But this is clearly presupposed in the speech. In any case the speech is followed by a narrative which details how the command was carried out and the expectation fulfilled. Delilah is paid for her treachery, and Samson ends up in a Philistine city, bound in fetters, grinding at the mill in prison.

In Judges 4:4-24, which is the prose account of the defeat of Sisera, we find the same structure. The story begins with Deborah's speech to Barak. She gives the situation, God has commanded an action, then comes the command, "Go, gather your men at Mount Tabor, taking ten thousand from the tribe of Naphtali and the tribe of Zebulun" (v. 6). This command is followed by an expectation of what the future will bring, here in the form of a promise. "And I will draw out Sisera, the general of Jabin's army, to meet you by the river Kishon with his chariots and his troops; and I will give him into your hand" (v. 7). But Barak is not satisfied with Deborah's suggestion that he go and muster the army. Instead, he asks that Deborah accompany him. Deborah agrees to this condition but then says that the future will turn out differently; the glory of the battle will not be Barak's but a woman's. A change in the means commanded by Deborah means a change in the future expectation. This indicates the strength of the logical connection in this story-type between the means commanded and the results expected. The narrative then continues by relating how they followed the command, what happened as a result, and how Deborah's prediction that a woman would gain the glory of the battle came true. It was Jael who succeeded in killing Sisera, not Barak or one of his men.

Finally, we find the same structure again in Judges 13:2-25, which announces the birth of Samson. In this story it is an angel who is the spokesperson. The speech begins with the familiar, "behold now," followed by a sentence stating the problem: the woman is barren and without child. But now the barren will bear, contrary to all normal expectations. Then comes the imperative, what she is to do in this situation. The woman should eat a special diet while pregnant, and the child is to be reared in a special way. From this flows the future expectation (the result): he will be a Nazarite and will begin to liberate Israel from the Philistines. In the narrative that follows, however, we do not find the fulfillment of the speech. The bulk of the following story instead tells of Manoah's desire to see the heavenly visitor and when he finally does, the offering up to him of a sacrifice. This story appears to break the pattern we have been seeing; the speech is not fulfilled in the story.[7]

We have just seen that the structure which we saw in Genesis 12:10-20 is found in narratives in the book of Judges which are literarily independent of J. Consequently we presumably have here a convention of Hebrew narrative art which has influenced the structure of these stories. This convention explains why they follow the same pattern. Since in this convention the speech is linked to the narrative by expectation-fulfillment, these stories may be called speech-fulfilling stories. The narrative tells how the expectation raised in the speech comes to fulfillment.[8] There is something of an inevitable causal link between the action commanded and the result expected. The story narrates how this came about. These stories are in a sense "closed" stories. From the opening speech you know how the story is going to end; you just do not know the way to the end. A modern analogy might be the Columbo detective stories on television. Since the first scene shows who committed the crime, the tension revolves around how Lt. Columbo is going to unravel the mystery, not who did it.

It might be thought that this three-part pattern in the speech and the linking of the speech to its narrative by expectation-fulfillment is too general or vague to represent a specific convention. After all, how else could one begin a narrative through the use of speech? Implicit in this objection is the idea that the similarity which we have seen is not due to the conventions of a form, but rather a combination of coincidence and natural necessity. That these narratives are indeed formed according to a specific convention of storytelling rather than by general necessity can be seen from the fact that not all speeches set at the beginning of narratives have either the structure we have seen or the same function within the unit. They are not linked to their narrative by means of expectation-fulfillment.

For example, another major type of beginning speech containing imperatives is found in Genesis 22:1ff., which recounts God's test of Abraham. The initial speech is a simple one, consisting of a series of commands, "Take, go, and offer." The only digressions are the closer specification of who is to be offered—"your son, your only son whom you love, Isaac"—which makes what is commanded unmistakable and heightens both the tension of the story and the severity of the test. The second digression relates to the place where the sacrifice is to be offered, where God defines the place by saying, "Upon one of the mountains which I will show you." This latter, a modifying clause, is no future expectation of what will result from the carrying out of the imperatives, as in the previous group of stories; rather, it is an indication of the goal of the action. Its concern is to specify more exactly the obedient action which is commanded by the imperatives—the sacrifice is not to be carried out at just any place, but at a specific place to be designated by God later. The story then flows from these imperatives. It is an account of what happened when Abraham acted upon them.

A similar story is found in Genesis 35:1ff., where again the initial speech is by God addressed this time to Jacob. Again it consists of a series of imperatives, "rise, go up, dwell, and make an altar." The narrative following tells of Jacob's obedience to these imperatives.

While in these last two stories God addresses a man, the same type of speech is also found between people. In Genesis 24:1ff., Abraham addresses his servant regarding the selection of a wife for his son Isaac. The speech is longer than the previous ones since Abraham binds the servant by oath to carry out his wishes. Also, the servant inquires what to do in the case of certain contingencies, for example, if the girl will not return to Canaan with him. But in general, we find here a commanding speech of Abraham solemnized by an oath which sets the story moving. The remainder of this lengthy account (at least by Genesis' standards) concerns how the servant was able to carry out the commands of his master.

This type of initiating speech is not confined to Genesis. In Judges 6:25ff., there is a brief story which begins with God addressing Gideon. "Take and tear down," he commands. The story then recounts what happened when Gideon carried out these instructions. Likewise, in Judges 14:1ff., the story of Samson's first marriage or attempted marriage is begun by Samson's speech to his parents, "I saw a woman. Take her for me." They demur, but again Samson commands, "You take her for me because she pleases me." The story then flows from the attempt by his parents to carry out this command and what happens as a result.

These speeches and their relationship to the story as a whole are clearly different in structure and thought from the first group. First, they consist almost exclusively of imperatives. There is no three-part structure: no statement of the situation or the problem, nor is any expectation expressed, nor is it suggested why such a thing should be done. The actions are just commanded. These speeches may be called command speeches, since their main function in the narrative is to inform the main actors what they should do. The narration which follows recounts their obedience, or attempted obedience, and what results, if any, came from following the commands.

As a whole these narratives seem to have a two- or three-part structure. There may be an initial statement, giving the circumstances of the command; for example, Genesis 24:1 states, "Abraham was old . . . and the Lord had blessed Abraham in all things." This part, however, seems to be optional, since it is missing in three of the five stories mentioned above. Next comes the speech with its commands, which in turn is followed by the narration of obedience to these commands. These narratives may be labeled "obedience stories," since obedience is the thread which runs through the story and unites the parts, giving it coherence.

Having looked at obedience stories which follow a different structure, it seems clear that Genesis 12:10-20 and other speech-fulfilling stories have their specific pattern because they are based on different conventions and belong to a different type of story.

So far we have characterized the speech-fulfilling stories by their formal conventions, their rules of structure. Looking at the content, there do not appear to be any obvious, common themes or motifs which link these stories. They all have to do with common people, that is, there are no kings or princes as the major figures. But this does not provide us with a clear clue from content to help characterize these stories.

With regard to the social setting, we do not seem to have any definite information. We might infer that such stories were told where Israelites gathered together and talked of their past. In the recounting of the significant events and people of the past, the speech-fulfilling narrative form would have been used, among others like the obedience story, to relate these great events in a gripping and attention-holding way. We will also see, below, how this form could be used to make a dramatic lesson.[9]

Amos 2:6-16

Amos 2:6-16 has been outlined as follows (see page 65).

1. Introduction, "Thus says the Lord" (v. 6a)

2. Israel's sins (vv. 6b-8)
3. Historical flashback (vv. 9-12)
4. Statement of judgment (vv. 13-16)
5. Closing phrase

Again, the first step in analyzing the form is to determine whether this structure is unique to this passage or whether Amos follows this pattern elsewhere. If we read the remainder of Amos we will see that the speech of Amos to Amaziah in chapter 7 has essentially the same outline. Verse 16 begins with a general command to listen: "Hear now the word of Yahweh." This is followed by the mention of Amaziah's sins, "You are saying, 'Do not prophesy against Israel, and do not mutter against the house of Isaac.'" This accusation of wrongdoing is followed by the familiar prophetic phrase, "Therefore, thus says Yahweh." The final part of the speech describes the judgment that will befall Amaziah and his immediate family. We can outline the passage 7:16-17:

1. Summons to hear, "hear now"
2. Listing of sins, "you are saying . . ."
3. Introduction to the judgment, "Therefore, thus says Yahweh"
4. Statement of judgment

There are several differences between 2:6-16 and 7:16-17. First of all, 2:6-16 does not begin with a summons to hear; rather, it begins with "Thus says Yahweh" a phrase which occurs in the middle of 7:16-17. Second, there is no historical flashback in 7:16-17. Third, there is no closing phrase. The correspondences however, seem more significant. Both have a list of transgressions and a description of judgment. These two elements are clearly linked by a structural marker. In 2:6-16, "behold" in verse 13 serves this function, while in 7:16-17 "therefore" has the same function. Both have the phrase "thus says Yahweh," although the phrase occurs in different places within them.

In Amos 4:1-3 we find a passage which displays the same basic structure as 7:16-17.

1. Summons to hear, "Hear this word, cows of Bashan . . ."
2. Listing of sins, "Who oppresses the weak . . ."
3. Introduction to the judgment, "The Lord Yahweh swears by his holiness. That, behold . . ."
4. Statement of judgment, "They shall lift you up by hooks . . ."
5. Closing phrase

The agreement in structure is striking, and much too close to be mere coincidence.

If we would study other units in Amos, we would find a number of passages which follow this same pattern. Other passages, although a bit different, seem to have a similar structure. Amos 3:9-11 begins differently, but has the same basic outline. Likewise, the woe oracle in Amos 6:1-7 follows this pattern, but the judgment and its introduction in verse 7 are quite brief when compared to the fairly long list of sins preceding it.

We can conclude therefore that in basic outline, Amos 2:6-16 is not unique in Amos, although its historical flashback does set it apart from the other similarly structured units.[10]

The next step is to discover if other prophets—that is other independent authors—followed the same pattern in their speeches. The answer in short is yes. If we look, for example, at Micah chapter 3, we can recognize three basic units there—verses 1-4, 5-8, and 9-12. The first and last units are very similar in structure to what we have just observed in Amos. This is especially clear in the passage 9-12.

1. Summons to hear, "Hear this now, heads of the house of Jacob . . ."
2. Listing of sins, "who abhor justice . . ."
3. Introduction to the judgment, "Therefore"
4. Statement of judgment, "on your account Zion will be a plowed field . . ."

The passage in 5-8 begins like Amos 2:6-16 with the phrase, "Thus says Yahweh." This is followed by a statement of wrongdoing. Then as we expect, "Therefore" introduces the statement of judgment in verses 6-7. Verse 8, however, is different; it is a counter expectation, a contrast between the fate of the false prophets, who have just been described in the judgment, and that of the true prophet Micah. Here we can see a deviation from the basic pattern we have been tracing.[11]

This basic pattern occurs not only in the books of collected prophecies, like that of Amos and Micah, but it is also found in the oracles of various prophets which are now scattered through the history book of 1 and 2 Kings. For example, in 1 Kings 14:7-11 we have the words of Ahijah concerning king Jeroboam which are spoken to Jeroboam's wife when she came to consult him about her ailing son. Ahijah begins, "Thus says Yahweh, the God of Israel." A short historical review follows: "Because I exalted you from among the people, and made you leader over my people Israel, and tore the kingdom away from the house of David and gave it to you." This sets the stage for the listing of Jeroboam's sins: "yet you have not been like my servant David, who kept my commandments and who followed me with all his heart, to do only that which was right in my sight; you also have done more evil than all who were before you, and have gone and made for yourself other gods and molten images to provoke me to anger, and have cast me behind your back." Next comes the introduction to judgment, "therefore, behold," which is followed by the statement of judgment, "I am bringing calamity on the house of Jeroboam, and will cut off from Jeroboam every male person, both bound and free in Israel, and I will make a clean sweep of the house of Jeroboam, as one sweeps away dung until it is all gone." The form of this passage is quite similar to what we have seen, with the exception of the short historical review which serves as a prelude to the description of Jeroboam's sins. Similar passages are also found in 1 Kings 16:1-4; 21:19-24; and 2 Kings 1:3-4. In 1 Kings 11:31-32 and 2 Kings 22:16-17 there are speeches with the same structure, but the accusation and the judgment are reversed. That is, in all the examples we have examined up till now, the listing of sins comes first, followed by the description of judgment. In these last two speeches, however, the judgments are depicted first, then the transgressions are given.[12]

From this brief survey, it is clear that this structure of Amos 2:6-16 is unique neither to the passage nor to Amos, but represents a widespread convention of prophetic speech. While Amos 2:6-16 with its historical flashback varies from most of the units we have examined, in 1 Kings 14:7-11 and 1 Kings 16:1-4 we also found short historical reviews attached to the statement of sins. While in these two passages in Kings the historical summary comes before the accusations rather than after, as in Amos, the function of this historical material seems to be the same in all three instances: it is to present God's gracious deeds toward the accused and thereby underline the perversity of the transgressions. All in all, we have in 2:6-16 a specific form of prophetic speech: it is structured according to a widespread convention.

The common outline or identifying key for this form of material is given by Westermann as follows:[13]

  1. Accusation
     a. General accusations (Amos 2:6a)
     b. Specific accusation (Amos 26b-8)
  2. Messenger formula—"Thus says the Lord"
  3. Announcement of judgment

a. Intervention of God (Amos 2:13)
b. Result of intervention (Amos 2:14-16)

In the parenthesis we have indicated how the material in Amos 2:6-16 would follow this outline. Below is another outline which has been suggested for this form.[14]

1. Introduction (2:6a, "Thus says the Lord")
2. Reference to present (2:6b-8)
3. Transition (2:13 "behold")
4. Disaster (2:13-16)
5. Concluding formula (2:16)

The second outline has the advantage of being more general and descriptive; it omits reference to the "messenger formula" which as we saw is not always present and when present, not necessarily in this position.

In order to further verify our findings, we should look to see if these passages are also characterized by a common content (clue 2). We can see that the content is uniform. In all of these passages, there is the listing of sins and the description of judgment. In all cases, it is God bringing the judgment. This type of speech characterized by this structure (clue 1) and the phrase "thus says the Lord" (clue 2b) we will tentatively call the speech of judgment.

The social roles presupposed do not seem to be quite so clear. In fact, we do not have any evidence in most cases as to what the actual context was for these speeches. We do not know, for example, where Amos was when he spoke 2:6-16.[14a]

The passages we have been looking at in Amos and elsewhere may seem so typical of the prophets that it might be thought that this is the only suitable way for a prophet to talk to the people when delivering God's words. We might think that the similarity between the speeches we have seen is not so much that these passages are conforming to a convention of the language, but that this similarity reflects necessity—how else could a prophet deliver the words of God? This is not the case, however, as the prophets used a great variety of forms to communicate. A single example will make this evident.

If we begin to examine the style and structure of Amos 5:21-24 it is immediately apparent that the language and structure are different from Amos 2:6-16. First, it does not have the formula, "Thus says Yahweh," but instead God begins speaking in the first person "I" without any introduction. There is no listing of sins nor a description of judgment. Instead, we have God expressing his attitude toward Israel's religious practices. The content of this unit is quite different. Verse 24 contains an exhortation, not for better worship patterns or rituals but for better social patterns and structures. It seems clear that this is a different form of speech than the speech of judgment and has its own conventions which are appropriate for its own special content and social context.[15]

If we grant that the prophetic speeches fall into different forms or types of language, each of which has its own special function, how does this help us understand the prophets or prevent us from misunderstanding?

Two examples will help to make clear the usefulness of knowing the form and its conventions for understanding the material. The unit we just looked at, Amos 5:21-24, is many times misunderstood, because it is assumed that the prophet is giving a list of Israel's wrongdoings. People understand this unit as if it followed the pattern of the speech of judgment, where we do find a list of wrongdoings. However, the statements at the beginning of 5:21-24 are not directly linked to words of judgment. Furthermore, regarding content, Amos is not listing in 5:21-23 the same type of actions he is listing in 2:6-8. In Amos 5:21ff., Amos is reporting God's attitude toward what are essentially good actions—indeed, what has been commanded by God. The problem is not with the deeds mentioned, as was the case in the speech of judgment, but with either the attitude behind the deeds, or the social context in which the deeds were being done. What God is calling for in Amos 5:21-24 is not an abandoning of the things mentioned, but in addition to these to do acts of social justice, to establish social justice as a prerequisite for proper worship. When we read this passage as a call for abandoning sacrifice, songs, and assemblies, we misunderstand the passage because we are reading it as a judgment speech with its list of acts which are evil in themselves. Applying the wrong conventions to a unit leads to misunderstanding.

A second illustration is Amos 3:13-15, where we find a speech by Amos which apparently consists of only the summons to hear, verse 13a, the identification of the speaker, verse 13b, and the words of judgment, verses 14-15. The listing of sins is missing in this passage. I have heard verse 15, "I will smite the winter house with the summer house; and the houses of ivory shall perish, and the great houses shall come to an end," used as an indication of Israel's sins. It was because of having these

houses that God's judgment was to come upon them. Now in a general
way this may be true; in fact, support for it may be found elsewhere in
Amos. But it is wrong to argue so from this passage, because, as we can
see from the structure, it is exactly the *reason* for judgment that is missing in this unit. What the prophet is proclaiming, is the shape the judgment will take, not the reason for the judgment. From the way judgment
will take place one cannot necessarily infer the reason for the judgment.

If we look again at the speech in Amos 7:16-17, we see that the
reason for judgment is given in verse 16, and the form of judgment in
verse 17. Here, the form of judgment has no relationship to the reason
for it. (Having a wife, children, and some property are hardly deeds de-
serving of punishment!) On the contrary, although these things are quite
right in themselves, they will bear the consequences of the coming judgment. Thus, by being aware of the different forms of prophetic speech
and the functions of the different structural elements within each of the
forms we are both aided in our understanding of the prophets and
prevented from using their words in inappropriate ways.

Matthew 5:38-42

In Matthew 5:38-42 the task of defining the type of literature is a
bit more difficult than in the previous two passages because only here, in
Matthew 5, do we find antitheses. In this sense these passages are
unique, belonging to no traditional form of language. To examine this
passage more closely we may divide the passage into its two main parts,
antithesis and illustration, and study each separately. Perhaps the parts
which Matthew combined, by themselves do belong to a genre of
speech.

Although the antitheses are unique to Matthew 5 in the teachings
of Jesus and indeed in the entire New Testament, it has been argued
that Jesus, by putting his words into the form "you have heard . . . but I
say . . ." is reflecting a teaching formula or convention used by the rabbis in their exposition of Scripture. When a rabbi was teaching Scripture
he might say concerning a verse, "I might understand by this," and then
go on to give a possible literal interpretation of the passage. He would
then follow this literal interpretation with the words "but you must
understand . . ." which would introduce what he considered to be the
real meaning of the passage. Thus the phrases "I might understand by
this . . . but you must . . ." were used to contrast a possible literal meaning with what the passage actually meant (clue 1). Following this line of

argument, we could say that, while the use of antithesis is unique in the New Testament, Jesus is actually following a convention or practice used in the exposition of Scripture.[16]

Further evidence to support this understanding of the antithesis would be Jesus' statement in Matthew 5:17-20 where he declares he has not come to destroy the law and the prophets, but to fulfill them. By his reinterpretation of Scriptures through these antitheses, Jesus is showing how his teachings do, in fact, fulfill the law.

But there are some ways in which this hypothesis does not quite fit. First, the beginning phrase, "It was said to them of old," is the type of phrase used to introduce a quotation from Scripture in Matthew.[17] The passive, "it was said," was used in order to avoid the direct mention of God. Thus this phrase really means in Matthew, "God said to them of old." This is quite different from the rabbis' hypothetical introduction to a possible interpretation, "I might think." Second, in the second part of the contrast Jesus says, "but I say . . ." not as in the rabbinic formula, "but you must (interpret it another way)." Third, the rabbinic formula is not attested before the second century AD, although it may well have been used before that time.[18] All in all, then, while Jesus' use of a contrast may be traditional, we cannot say that he is using a specific conventional structure or form to make the contrast. Indeed, it may have been his variation from the conventional that gave his words the powerful impact they had (Matthew 7:28-29).

The illustrations which Jesus used to indicate what he meant by the general statement, "resist not the evil person," seem, however, to be similar in form to material we find elsewhere in the Bible. Their form, as we have seen above, is "whoever may do this to you, you must do so and so to them," as in "Whoever may strike you on the right cheek, turn to him the other also." This form seems to be the equivalent of "if anyone . . . then . . ." which is exactly how in fact the RSV translates these illustrations (clue 2b). This pattern is familiar to us from the laws in the Old Testament. In Exodus 22 we have a series of laws with this form, for example:

> If a man delivers to his neighbor money or goods to keep, and it is stolen . . .
> then, if the thief is found, he shall pay double. If the thief is not found,
> [then] the owner of the house shall come near to God, to show whether or
> not he has put his hand to his neighbor's goods. (vv. 7-8)

This type of law has been called casuistic or "case" law since it presents a case and then covers several eventualities which might be expected to occur. In the example above the case is stated, and two possible alternatives follow.[19]

The similarity between this legal form of case law and the form of the illustrations given by Jesus makes it appear that Jesus was following the convention of law and that his illustrations are consequently a type of law. This would seem to fit well with other considerations concerning the Sermon on the Mount. The idea of a teaching on a mountain, of course, makes one think of Mount Sinai and the giving of the law. This is further reinforced by 5:17-20, which, as mentioned above, immediately precedes the antithesis. Here Jesus stresses the value of the law and the necessary fulfillment of it. Taken in this way, the literary type of this material would be "law," law in which Jesus intensifies the requirement of the Mosaic law.

There are, however, several reasons why this material is probably not to be seen as law. First, we do not really have a complete parallel with the legal material. In law we expect a given case to have a series of provisions in order to cover all or the most probable eventual circumstances. In Jesus' illustrations we do not find this. He does not say what to do, for example, if struck on the left cheek or in the stomach. Thus the illustrations do not really seem to be laws, although their form certainly seems lawlike.

Second, as has often been noted, Jesus himself does not practice this teaching. According to John 18:19-24, when Jesus answers the high priest, he is struck by one of the officers standing by him. Jesus, rather than turning the other cheek, says, "If I have spoken wrongly, bear witness to the wrong; but if I have spoken rightly, why do you strike me?" (v. 23). And finally, although the illustrations seem to be formed like laws, they appear to lack the binding quality of law.

In light of these objections to taking the material as law, it has been suggested that Jesus is here actually making a parody of case law—he is following the form of law, but the contents are so different that he is actually making fun of law (clue 2). There is seen here a clash between structure and content. If we examine the second half of each illustration, the part that follows "then," we can see that what Jesus asks is not only quite unexpected, but silly. In each case the victim is asked to aid the initiator. Even granted that these statements are directed to victims rather than to the oppressor and thus do not deal with restraining the wrongdoer, we do not expect victims to add to the aggression of the aggressor. By contrast, what we might expect by way of Christian counsel is that Jesus would command us to love or forgive the one who wrongs us or merely not to hit back. Because of this jarring effect of the commanded action which seemingly demands the completely illogical, we have here an imitation of the case law form in order to poke fun at law which is supposed to say what is the logical thing to do in each situation. Perhaps Jesus is saying that the Christian life is not that simple; it cannot be governed by law or the letter of the law. To try to live by law would miss the point of what Jesus is teaching.[20]

Another suggestion about the genre of these illustrations is that they comprise a series of "focal instances."[21] A focal instance is a type of teaching which is marked by three characteristics. First, it gives a specific instance which is addressed to individuals, as these illustrations are doing. Second, it is extreme; it points out what might be considered the ultimate case in which a principle might apply. Third, such a case reorients our thinking.[22] If such an extreme case is included in what we might be called upon to do, or if that is really how we might act in such a situation, certainly then in *less* provocative circumstances we should respond in like fashion. Such focal instances show us not only specific cases, but in effect say, "Not only in this specific case, but in everything up to and including this case, this is how you are to respond" (clue 2b). Here the series of focal instances changes our thinking about how we are to respond to others. In the remaining antitheses in Matthew, we can find other examples of such focal instances—5:22, 23-24, 28. Outside of the antitheses we find this type of teaching in Matthew 23:8-10 and 8:21-22[23] (clue 1).

From the standpoint of content and context this last suggestion seems to fit well. Jesus is giving extreme examples of what it means "not to resist the evil person." In the context, they are illustrative of how Jesus' new understanding is to be worked out in life. As such, the focal instance is a wonderful teaching device for riveting a principle of action to the minds of the listeners. We conclude, then, that the form of this material is that of a "focal instance." Taking the passage as a whole we seem to have here the exposition of Scripture by means of focal instances.[24]

Romans 13:1-7

We will begin our analysis of Romans 13:1-7 with a look at its literary context. In the book of Romans, beginning with chapter 12, we

find a type of material which is called "parenesis."[25] This word comes
from the Greek word *parainesis* which means "advice." This material is
ethical and practical in content and in style marked by exhortations and
commands (clue 2). Notice how chapter 12 begins: "I appeal to . . . do
not be conformed to this world but be transformed . . . [command]."
Following these introductory words in verses 1 and 2, we have a series of
admonitions regarding the daily living of the Christian faith. That
Romans 13:1-7 forms part of this parenetic material is clear from the beginning, where we find a command in the third person, "Let every
person be subject to the governing authorities" (clue 2b). The whole
paragraph revolves around the single practical issue of relations to
government, in particular the very specific issue of the payment of taxes.

Labeling our passage "parenetic," however, does not exhaust our
form analysis, since Paul's ethical admonitions can take a great many
forms. If we look, for example, at the exhortations in Romans 12, it becomes immediately apparent that there are a variety of styles and structures used. Some of the admonitions are quite short and snappy, like
"Contribute to the needs of the saints, practice hospitality" (v. 13) or
"Live in harmony with one another" (v. 16). Other admonitions,
however, receive a much more extended treatment. In 12:18-21, for
example, Paul develops the theme of not taking vengeance. In this
passage, as in 13:1-7, we find an extended argument revolving around a
single topic. That is, there is a general teaching or exhortation given, and
then arguments follow to support it. It appears from this structure that
these arguments are designed to persuade the reader of the importance
and necessity of obedience to the command. Thus we find, in parallel to
Romans 13:1-7, that there are parenetic units which are "mixed"; they
not only have exhortations but also a developed rationale to support
them (clue 1).

This type of passage, where a point is argued, has been called a
"diatribe," an argument which attempts to persuade someone to a point
of view or to an action[26] (clue 2). Another way in which we might
describe this form is to say that it is an exhortation which is argued.
Other examples of the diatribe, or exhortation with argument, can be
seen in James, chapters 2 and 3.[27] James 2:1-12, for example, begins with
a command to "show no partiality." This is followed by an extended
argument to persuade the readers of the rightness of this counsel. Note
the frequent use of rhetorical questions to drive home the point—as
paralleled in Romans 13:3 (clue 2b).

Thus we can conclude that the structure of Romans 13:1-7 is not unique, but is a conventional pattern called a diatribe. In this pattern here is a statement and an argument. The argument has a dialogical quality, since it presupposes a discussion going on between the writer and reader. Rhetorical questions are one way of showing this dialogue and confronting directly the audience to whom the letter is written.

3.10 *Changes in Form*

Having established the type of material which is found in a passage, we can now work from the other end; we can observe how a passage differs from the norms or conventions of its type. Just as we saw similarities between passages above, we also noted dissimilarities. It is important to note these deviations since they offer valuable clues for our understanding of a passage. These deviations often point to a major element of significance in a passage, because an author through the manipulation or bending of the standard rules is able to grasp the attention of his audience and draw them to the point which he is making.

In Amos 5:1-2, for example, we find a lament. The lament was a type of poem customarily used following the death of an individual (see, for example, David's laments after Saul's and Jonathan's deaths, 2 Samuel 1:17-27). The lament was also used for a nation following a disaster, as we find it used in the book of Lamentations. In Amos, we find it used of a nation which, far from suffering calamity, was in fact experiencing success and prosperity. Amos was speaking to the nation as if it were already dead. Thus there is a head-on clash between Amos' use of the lament and the normal situation in which this literary type was customarily used. This clash undoubtedly called attention to Amos' message.[28]

All deviations from the norm, however, do not have this significance. They may only reflect normal historical change. Since the various examples of a literary type are written over a long period of time, they are bound to reflect changes which occurred naturally through time, changes which reflect the development of the type itself. For example, we pronounce and spell English words quite differently today than they did in Chaucer's time. About 600 years separate us from Chaucer, about the same amount of time that separated David from Ezra and Nehemiah. We can thus expect Hebrew to have undergone great changes through a period of 600 years, as English has.

These changes take place in a language not only in such matters as spelling and pronunciation (phonology) but also in the literary forms. Chaucer wrote poetry, but most, perhaps even almost all, poems today are written differently; that is, they conform to a different set of conventions than did Chaucer's poetry. These changes are natural and inevitable because as language is passed on from generation to generation there is slippage in the transmission. The next generation does not learn the language perfectly; they do not speak it exactly as their parents did. Linguists call this "language drift," and it remains fairly constant over time for all languages. In addition to this "natural" change, there are also historical and social causes for language change—invasions, new social institutions, revolutions, or changed cultural patterns. These changes are often reflected in the changes which language types undergo through time. Or to put it the other way around, changes which we note in a type may well reflect social and intellectual changes in the society.

The discovery of a unit's deviation from the conventions of its type can be quite significant for the understanding of a passage. Deviations which reflect historical changes in a genre may reflect changes in the social setting or in the function and intention of the form. Since these factors are important in the interpretation, any evidence for them is very valuable. Likewise, alterations for the sake of communication are bold indicators as to where the focal point of a passage lies. These breakings of the conventions of a form are often like underlining or italics today; they focus the attention of the audience on what is really important.

3.11 **Axiom: All examples of a form differ to a lesser or greater degree from the model or pattern, since literary types, like all language, are not static but are constantly changing through time as they are used by individuals in specific situations.**

3.12 *Procedures*

In order to determine what historical and individual changes or developments took place in a form it is helpful to be able to arrange the different examples of the type in chronological order. Sometimes this can be done; at other times it may not be possible. If it can be done, then the examples can be examined to see what changes occurred over time. From these changes and what is known about biblical history, it may be possible to indicate the social forces which influenced or coincided with the changes.

In comparing your unit with other members of its type, look for changes in the three areas you used above as keys to identify the form: (1) changes in structure; (2) changes in words and style, motifs, and theme; and (3) changes in the social presuppositions. The following clues can help you to understand a particular passage against the background of its type.

A. *Analysis*
   1. What are the significant, or even unique, features of the passage in terms of its deviation from the norm in:
      a. Structure—how is this passage's structure different from the expected pattern? What differences in style are there?
      b. Words—what new subjects, themes, and motifs are found or old elements omitted?
      c. Style—is the style different from that normally found?
      d. Social situation—are new roles or social contexts presupposed? Here you may only raise the question. The specific details of the social context will be studied in historical analysis, chapter 7.

   2. What changes have taken place in the history of the form, changes in its structure and content? Where does the present passage stand in this development, and how does it reflect it?

   3. What historical or cultural factors do these changes reflect and how are they related to the unit under study? (This investigation may well be deferred until the investigation of the historical context of the basic unit is undertaken.)

B. *Synthesis*
   From these clues you should decide whether differences are due to historical changes, to accident, or to the author's intentional deviations from the norm. What is significant about the unique features of the passage? These clues should provide you with insights into the inner compositional dynamics of a passage. Indicate how these insights aid in discovering the meaning of the passage. The following section will illustrate these principles.

3.13 *Illustrations*
Genesis 12:10-20

We have already assigned Genesis 12:10-20 to a class of narratives we labeled "speech-fulfilling" stories. These stories had two basic parts: a speech in which a course of action was commanded and certain outcomes were predicted, and a narrative reporting how the anticipated outcome came to fulfillment. As seen above, Genesis 12:10-20 follows this basic pattern except that the anticipated outcome raised an additional problem, the loss of Sarai. This surprising twist led to another—Yahweh's unexpected intervention to restore Sarai and preserve Abram's anticipated outcome. Such a deviation from the expected pattern would have underlined for the Israelite audience the actions of God in the story. It draws the audience's attention to the contrast between the prudent plans of man and the providence of God. Through this highlighted counterpoint the author makes vivid an important point about faith and human ability to control the future. Even by the best-laid plot Abram was not able to bring about a prosperous future. It was God, by his gracious providence, who did it. The next story about Abram (chapter 13) shows Abram more reliant upon the promises of God and less on his own rights and cunning.

In Genesis 16 the author follows the same outline as in Genesis 12:10-20, but here it is Sarai who takes matters into her own hands. She is going to have a child one way or the other, Yahweh notwithstanding. But instead she loses not only the child, but her maidservant, Hagar, as well. Once again God intervenes to unscramble the tangled outcome.[29]

These deviations from the form would seem to be due to the author of these two passages, rather than to historical development. First, historical development among these stories is not immediately evident, with one exception, which we will discuss below. Second, the communication value of this deviation seems clear as just outlined, while any social causes for it are unknown (clue 3).

The one case where it does seem that historical development has taken place is Judges 13, the announcement of the birth of Samson. As noted above, the narrative that follows does not fulfill the speech. Indeed, one needs to read on through the next several stories to reach any kind of fulfillment for the speech in 13:3-5. Here it seems likely we have the adaptation of a narrative technique, originally used to tell an individual story, now used to build suspense for a whole cycle of stories.[30] If this analysis is correct, this adapted use would be later, logically, than its original use in the individual narrative. Thus Judges 13 would represent a later historical development of the speech-fulfilling narrative.

Amos 2:6-16

Development or changes in the prophetic speech of doom are readily apparent. There are two striking differences which set off speeches of Amos and the prophets who came after him from the speeches of the prophets who came before. The prophets who came before Amos, whose speeches we can read in the books of Kings, addressed themselves to an individual, namely, the king. It was a one-on-one confrontation, the prophet versus the king.[31] However, from Amos on (from the eighth-century prophets down to the destruction of Jerusalem), the majority of speeches in this form are addressed to groups of people while the king is seldom addressed directly. In Amos, there is only one speech to an individual, that to Amaziah the priest, in chapter 7. There are no speeches to the king as an individual. We can see two clear and connected shifts in audience: (1) from individuals to groups or even to the nation as a whole, and (2) from the king to citizens. We will need to examine the causes for this change when we investigate the historical background (see chapter 7). Since they exercised such a dramatic effect on the message, these causes were crucial to the message of Amos and the following prophets (clue 3).

A second difference is the type of sins listed. In the prophets' speeches in Kings, the sins are mainly moral or cultic in nature. Following after other gods and retaining the golden calves at Bethel and Dan, or sins like adultery or murder are the accusations made against the kings. However, in Amos these sins are barely mentioned; although Amos was active in Bethel, the golden calf there was never singled out for censure. Instead, a major thrust of Amos and the following prophets, in their speeches of doom, was social justice: the sins singled out were social sins, oppression of the poor, weak, and needy. Perverted justice, crooked business dealing, and callous unconcern for others were the usual matters against which the prophets spoke.[32]

This shift in audience and message was not unique to Amos or due to a particular desire on his part to communicate more effectively. It can be seen in other preexilic prophets as well. Since these changes cannot be explained on the basis of Amos' own individual style, they must be the result of some more far-reaching shift in the social or cultural context within which the prophet was active (clues 2 and 3). In order to understand the dynamics back of these changes we will need to understand the social and intellectual developments which took place between the time of Elijah, for example, in the ninth century and Amos in the eighth. Since this is the task of a later step in analysis, we will need to wait until then for a solution to this development. But discovering these social and intellectual changes are vital for a well-founded understanding of the message of Amos.

Regarding the particular unit we are studying, Amos 2:6-16, we saw that it deviated from the normal pattern of the messenger speeches of doom by containing a historical flashback in verses 9-11 (12). Although this was not the norm, several speeches in Kings were found which also had a historical review of God's grace attached to the list of transgressions. Since we raised the question under structure as to whether this was an original combination by Amos or by a later editor we need to wait until we discuss these verses in a later step before we can say whether Amos' own uniqueness shows through here.

In any case, in Amos the historical development which has taken place in his speeches of doom points to the importance of another area of study, the historical context, for understanding his message. That phase in our study will need to build on the insights discovered here.

Matthew 5:38-42

We do not seem to have enough information to do this step in analysis for Matthew 5:38-42. Since, as we have seen, antitheses are unique to this passage in Matthew, it would be impossible to demonstrate historical development among the examples of the type. What we have in the antithesis instead of a type, is a form class, a group of units which have the same form or structure, but which are literarily dependent.

Within the form class, however, there may have been a historical development. The series of antitheses begins in 5:21 by strengthening the law; the first two antitheses reinforce two of the Ten Commandments. But the series ends by either repealing the law, as in antithesis 4 which commands not to swear at all, or by going far beyond the law as in 38-42 and the antithesis that follows. It may be that this development in the scope of the antithesis reflects a historical development.[33]

This change in scope from the first to last antithesis offers us a valuable clue for understanding our passage. Jesus is radically reinterpreting the law, not just tidying it up. But this reinterpretation is still seen as the fulfillment of the law's binding quality, as Matthew 5:17-20 shows. This raises a central issue for the understanding of Jesus' teaching here: how is such a drastic reinterpretation to be seen as a fulfillment, rather than as a repudiation of the law? This will be the concern of a further stage of study. It needs to be seen, however, that by noting the unique or developmental features within a group of related passages we discover a basic dynamic operating within a passage.

Romans 13:1-7

Here again, there is little that can be done to show historical development. In this case it is because teaching material is general advice which is addressed to specific situations. Therefore, additional insights into a passage like Romans 13:1-7 will come at a later stage when we begin to discover its specific context.

3.20 *Summary*

To summarize your efforts up to this point, you have found a basic unit for study. You have analyzed its structure and style so that you can see its construction clearly and understand how the individual elements function as part of a larger whole. You have studied the logic and the compositional unity of this structure.

Building on this detailed study of structure, in the present chapter you have sought to understand the conventions of language which this unit expresses. These conventions belong to the level of language we call form—the type of language used. Without the initial, careful study of structure, you could not carry out an accurate assessment of a passage's form. Once you have assigned a passage to a given class of literature based on similarities among the passages in the type, you turn to a study of the dissimilarities between the passages. From these differences you draw out clues as to the significant elements of meaning in a passage. Many of these significant elements point you to yet further stages of investigation. But this data is invaluable for helping you to ask the right questions in order to understand the passage.

Chapter 4

From Form to Content:
Lexical Analysis

4.00 Lexical Analysis

Thus far in our study we have focused on passages as wholes. We have analyzed them into their compositional elements and studied these parts as logical parts of the larger whole. From this viewpoint, we have observed the various conventions which operate in the formation of a unit, conventions which have shaped the structure and determined the literary type of a unit. However, we also need to analyze passages at a finer level, the level of words.

It may seem strange to begin now to talk about words and their meaning, since usually when we think of Bible study, we think of studying the meaning of the individual words in a passage. But the unit of meaning is not typically the individual, isolated word, but the phrase, sentence, or basic unit. Thus it is necessary to place the words in the wider context of the unit's structure and its type in order to understand them fully and correctly. Meaning, then, is not expressed so much by separate words, but by larger units through the use of words.[1] This is why we have first examined structure—how the building blocks are arranged—and type—how the language is being used—before we now begin the study of the words—the individual building blocks used to construct these units of meaning.

An illustration may help make this important point more emphatic. A single word by itself can be very ambiguous—for example, the word "sail" can be either a verb or a noun. The word "red" can refer to either a color or to someone's politics. What is actually to be communicated must be seen from the larger context of the phrase, sentence, or basic unit. From this unit of meaning we understand which "sense" the word

110

has in its present context and how it helps communicate the meaning of the larger whole. In the sentence, "Give me the red sweater," it is clear that "red" is a color and is being used to distinguish one sweater from another in a series of sweaters. The crucial issue is what a word means in a particular context.[2]

Having said this, it is still true, of course, that if we do not understand the meaning of words, we will not understand the passage. The study of words can be decisive for the meaning of a unit. To do this properly, as we have just seen, words need to be looked at in context. The principle to keep in mind is that *the passage is the context for understanding words, rather than the words studied in isolation determining the meaning of the passage.*

This point is important because often when it is disregarded the study of words takes the place of the study of passages. When this happens, the words are usually equated with the "concept" or "thought" which is being communicated. This often leads to words being studied in relative isolation from the contexts in which they occur. Words, however, are not used as isolated units of meaning. Rather, they are used in phrases, sentences, and passages to communicate meaning. Therefore, word studies can never be a substitute for the study of passages, but rather must be seen as an aid to the latter.[3]

4.01 *Etymologies*

A popular way in which words are studied that pays little attention to context is defining words by their etymology. The etymology of a word is its so-called "original meaning," or the "original meaning" in the language from which the word comes. Unfortunately, etymology often has nothing to do with the actual usage of words, but is rather the imposition of an abstract notion like "original meaning" onto actual usage. How many times, for example, have you heard that since we know that "radical" comes from the Latin word for "root" we know that a "radical" solution is one that goes to the root of things. What the word "radical" meant in Latin is irrelevant; the question is what does it mean in English? A radical solution is usually a solution which would make things quite different from the way they are now and from what we naturally expect to happen. For example, a radical solution to poverty in America might be to guarantee every family an income of 20,000 dollars a year and limit income to no more than 30,000 dollars. While this would be a radical solution, quite out of keeping with the way we now do things, challenging some of our basic assumptions, it surely does not go to the roots of poverty—discrimination, unequal abilities and opportunities, chance of birth. This radical solution treats the symptom rather than these root causes. Or, again, it is a cliché that "church" means "called out." Why? Because the Greek word for church, *ekklesia*, is made up of two words, *ek* which means "from" (but also "by"!) and *klesia* which comes from the root meaning "call." What is needed is rather evidence to show that this word was ever *used* in the New Testament with this sense.

4.02 *Translation*

Finally, it is necessary to keep in mind when we are searching out the meaning of words in the Bible, that we are studying words in Greek, Hebrew, and Aramaic, the languages in which the Bible was written. Therefore, we need to be careful that we are getting at the meaning of *these* words and not the meaning of the words used in a translation. To look up a word in an English dictionary is of quite limited help in word study. It can give us the meaning of the English translation, but not the biblical word itself. To do a satisfactory word study will mean tracing the meaning of the word as it is used in the original language.

4.03 *Meaning*

Most frequently, when we think of "meaning" we think of something to which words refer like a concept or an object. While it is true that words are used to refer to objects or ideas, it is not very helpful to proceed to define words this way, since we usually find words used in contexts in which nothing could be pointed to as an illustration of that to which the word refers. For example, in the sentence "lasers are a hot new product" we understand the word laser although we may never have seen a laser and have none handy to point to. Or again, we use words to talk about "objects" we've never experienced like "unicorn"! Therefore, from a reader's or listener's standpoint we must normally figure out the meaning of words from language itself, from context.

How do we learn the meaning of words from language? A general principle which has been given for learning the meaning of a word is, *to find the meaning of a word we need to study its usage*.[4] That is, rather than trying to define the meaning of a word in an abstract or theoretical way, we look instead at how the word is used in the language. From this usage we deduce its meaning. This way of proceeding is quite helpful and productive, since the way words are used is something we can observe and others can verify. By working this way, the meaning of a word is defined in an inductive and concrete manner rather than abstractly and in ways not open to verification.[5]

But how does the way a word is used indicate its meaning? From a word's usage we can see with what other words it occurs. It is from these contexts with other words that we infer its meaning. For instance, we talk about many things real and unreal which we will never see: protons, antimatter, and unicorns. We know the meaning of these words, apart from any direct experience of them, from reading or hearing about them in context. *It is from our experience of the contexts within which these words are used that we come to know what they mean.*[6]

But how does knowing the context in which a word is used help us to understand its meaning? As we have seen above (1.30), language has no direct relationship to meaning. In terms of words, this means that there is no necessary link between a word and its meaning. What then is the tie that binds a word to a given meaning? The link is one of convention: this is the way we use a word in this language to talk about things. It is from learning these conventions or customs which govern how words are used that we learn the meaning of words. For example, from our knowledge of how "unicorn" is used, we know that it is a word used to talk of an imaginary, one-horned beast in fairy tales. Knowing these conventions we can talk about unicorns, although we will never see one. In fact, if we were to use "unicorn" for an animal which we actually saw, people would think we did not understand the word "unicorn," since it conventionally refers to an *imaginary* animal. We know this convention from the contexts in which the word occurs.

These conventions which regulate the contexts in which a word may occur we may call semantic conventions. Just as there are grammatical conventions which control word order (subject to precede verb, object to follow verb in declarative sentence), so there are semantic conventions which govern what words can occur together. For example, "green grass" fits together but not "green dreams." Although both follow the rules of grammar, "green dreams" does not follow the rules of meaning or semantics of English. That is, we do not use "green" to talk about dreams. If someone persisted in talking about "green dreams" we would either conclude that the person did not know the meaning of "green" or a new convention would be established—green would come to refer to a certain type of dream.[7] To know the meaning of "green" is to know that it goes with "grass" but not with "dreams."

To summarize: the way we use words to communicate is conventional (governed by "rules"). Knowing the contexts of a word we can figure out the conventions of a word's usage. That is to say, we know the meaning of the word because by following these conventions we can communicate in a way that makes sense to the speakers of a language.

These semantic conventions which are learned from the way a word is used govern two types of relationships which exist between words. First, there are the horizontal relationships. These are the relationships which exist between words in a phrase or sentence as in the above example "green grass." Part of a word's meaning is found by seeing with what other words it can be combined. Second, there are the relationships which exist between words of the same kind, such as "green," "blue," "yellow," etc. Part of a word's meaning is defined by the way it relates to these other members of its group. Green is partly defined by the words on either side of it, yellow and blue: it refers to the color between these two. We can also see this clearly in the words "high" and "low" or "big" and "little." What is meant by "low" is partly defined by what is conventionally considered to be "high." We will discuss these horizontal and vertical relationships in turn.[8]

A word's horizontal relationship can be determined by discovering the distribution pattern of the word's usage, with what other words or types of words it occurs or does not occur. As we have just seen, a word cannot occur with just any other word, but only with words which are compatible with it. For example, the word "easy" is grammatically an adjective and can modify any noun and be grammatically correct. However, it is not compatible in meaning with just any noun; that is, it does not make sense when used with them. An "easy plan, course, or recipe" makes sense, but an "easy bird, pencil, or table" does not. In English "easy" normally can occur with nouns which indicate a course of action, but not with wild animals (birds) or manufactured products (pencils, tables). The words with which a term can occur set the boundaries or the limits of the meaning of a term. These restrictions on occurrence as indicated by a word's distribution pattern (in what contexts it can occur) define the word by setting it apart from other words which have different distribution patterns and consequently different limits of meaning.

For example, "strong" and "powerful" are words with similar meanings—they occur in many of the same contexts, such as a "strong man" or a "powerful man." But there are also contexts which they do not share. It is normal to say a "strong rope" but not a "powerful rope"; "strong tea" but not "powerful tea"; a "powerful motor" but not a "strong motor." These two words have different distribution patterns (they occur with different words). This shows us that they have different meanings because different rules govern their usage. From the above, we can say "powerful" is applied to objects that do something, while "strong" is applied to objects which are static. They overlap when applied to animate objects, such as strong or powerful men, animals, etc. This difference in meaning of "strong" and "powerful" is learned by seeing the horizontal context in which they are used.

Words also have vertical relationships with other related words. These related words are words with a similar distribution pattern (and meaning). Such a word group of associated words would be "warm," "cold," or "hot." The meaning of each of these words is based to some extent on its relationship to the other words in the group. We call this a vertical relationship because any one of these three words can apply to the same context. For example, all three of these words can modify coffee:

hot
warm   coffee
cold

The speaker or writer picks one of these words from the vertical column and places it in a horizontal relationship with coffee.

It is important to see a word in the context of its word group since the meaning of a word is partly determined by the type of relationship it has to the other words in its group. Words in such a vertical list or group may be related to each other in different ways.[9] Some relationships like "hot," "warm," and "cold" are graded ones; some are partially synonymous, such as "strong" and "powerful"; while others are opposites like "weak" and "strong." Some words in a group are more general, while others are more specific. An example of this would be "ram" and "ewe," which are included in "goat." The type of relationship which exists between members of a word group helps to define a word by showing how an area of meaning is divided up by the various words in such a group. Such is the case with the example just given of "ewe," "ram," and "goat." "Ewe" is specifically used to refer to only the female goats. Another type of relationship—"hot" and "cold"—are relative measures.

To say that something is "hot" is not to give it any specific temperature, but to indicate that it is not cold or warm. This can be seen in phrases like a "hot" stove, "hot coffee," and a "hot day." The temperature of a hot day is cool by comparison with the temperature of a hot stove. Likewise, a hot cup of coffee is hotter than a hot day, but cooler than a hot stove. All these statements are relative, gaining their meaning from the other temperature choices available by convention.

Seeing a word in the context of its word group is important in order to know what choices were available when a certain word was selected. This perspective enables us to see the sense of the word which is chosen in a particular case.

To illustrate how the meaning of a word is dependent on what other possible choices are available in a given context, we will take an example from Deuteronomy 3:11. This verse tells us that the couch of Og, king of Bashan, was 9 cubits long and 4 cubits wide, measured by the "cubit of a man." To know what is meant by the "cubit of a man" we need to know what other kinds of cubits there were. Is it in contrast to the cubit of a woman, or of a horse? In Ezekiel 40:5 and 43:13, we find a clue for our answer. These verses speak of a different kind of cubit—a cubit which was the length of a cubit and a hand (span). Thus there seems to have been two cubits in Israel—an "ordinary" cubit, the cubit of a man being the name for this, and a longer cubit which was a span longer than the regular cubit. This would be like the difference between the U.S. gallon and the imperial gallon, which is a U.S. gallon plus a quart. The meaning of "man" in the phrase "cubit of a man," then, is "ordinary" or "regular" as opposed to "longer" or "larger." This meaning of the word "man" can only be found when it is placed in the context of its appropriate word group—what other terms can occur in this context with "cubit."

Vertical groups are made up of words with the same general meaning. They share many contexts because they share the same general meaning. But they will usually not have identical distribution patterns (unless they are complete synonyms or antonyms). This was seen above in the example of "strong" and "powerful." They differ in distribution pattern because in addition to the general meaning which they share, they also each have their own special or particular meaning which is reflected in their particular distribution pattern. It is this difference in distribution pattern between words of the same group that is the basis for deciding on the specific sense of a word. This specific sense is what distinguishes one member of a word group from the other words in the group.

As another illustration of how to define a word in terms of its relationships to the other members of its word group, let us compare the verbs "eat," "feed," and "dine." We can say, "We ate out last night" or "We dined out last night." Similarly, we can say either, "The cattle fed on grass," or "the cattle ate grass." We would not, however, normally say that "We fed out last night." We might say "The cattle dined on grass," but because of the unusual combination of "cattle" and "dined," such a sentence would be striking and thus used for effect. Usually in English, "feed" is restricted in its distribution to nonhuman subjects, while "dine" normally takes human subjects. "Eat" may occur with either, being the more general term; that is, it has a wider distribution, occurring in more varied environments, in the language. Among these three words, we infer that the common aspect has to do with the eating of food. The specific conventions are that "eat" may occur with both humans and animals, "dine" usually with humans, and "feed" only with animals. This is part of the meaning of these words—part of the meaning of feed is that it means "eating done by animals," while "dine" means special eating done by humans, or it can be used of animals for a heightened effect. These conventions then explain the general distribution of a word, why it is chosen in a particular case.

From the above examples we can see two aspects of the usage of a word: the vertical and the horizontal. The vertical aspect gives the relationship of a word to other words which have a similar meaning. This shows us what choices were available. The horizontal aspect shows the difference in occurrence between members of the same word group. This shows us the specific aspect of the meaning of a word—what distinguishes a word from other members of the word group. Through discovering the differences in distribution between a word and other members of its group, we are able to give the meaning of a word in context by showing why this word was chosen rather than others in its word group in this particular instance.

In fitting the meaning of a word to its context in a passage we must be constantly aware of the delicate shades of meaning a word can have. The trick is to match the general and specific aspect of a word's meanings to the particular context under study.

One final aspect of distribution should yet be noted. So far we have looked at a word's environments strictly in terms of the other words with which it can occur. However, the type of language used and the audience also affect the choice of words. In everyday speaking we may say "chew," but in a formal lecture we might use "masticate" instead. In talking to children, we may say "daddy sheep," but to adults we say "ram." This is an additional factor to keep in mind when we look at distribution. We should not be surprised to find that words have different distribution patterns which depend on the type of literature and situation in which they are used.

4.04 **Axiom: The meaning of a word is discovered by seeing the contexts in which the word is used and how these contexts differ from those of other related words.**

4.05 *Procedures*

  A. *Analysis*
     1. *First*, not all words or expressions in a passage need to be singled out for special study. In fact, in some passages no words need to be selected for study. In addition, the depth of study will depend on the type of word, its importance, and what you need to know to understand a specific passage.
        a. List the words which need further clarification or are pivotal to understanding a passage.
        b. Divide this list into two groups. One group will be formed by words which refer to people, places, events, customs, or objects which are unfamiliar. The second group of words would be those which need further in-depth study.
        c. To find the meaning of the first type of word consult a Bible dictionary. For example, "Egypt" is mentioned in Genesis 12:10. If you wanted to know more about Egypt, for example, how far it was from Palestine, the easiest thing to do would be to look it up in a reference book such as a Bible dictionary or atlas.
        d. The second group of words can in turn be divided into two groups. (1) There are words which you will want to analyze fairly exhaustively because of their importance to your understanding of the passage. (2) There will be other words which will not need such thorough treatment since questions about their meaning revolve around only a single issue or question which you may solve without the more extended treatment.
              For example, in Matthew 5:39, Jesus says, "If any one strikes you on the 'right' cheek." Here the question is what difference, if any, is there between being struck on the cheek and on the "right" cheek. To answer this question we do not need to examine all the

uses of "right" and other members of its word group. We simply need to see what the significance of being struck on the right cheek had for that culture. For these words, you should frame a limited question, such as "What is the difference between saying right cheek, like Matthew does, and just plain cheek, like Luke does?" Such a limited question only requires that we undertake as much of an investigation as is necessary to answer the question. Often you can answer these questions from the commentaries. By directing your focus to a specific interpretational issue, time and effort can be saved.

On the other hand, in Amos 2:6, we have the word "needy." The issue here is what type of people Amos is talking about; who were the needy in Amos's time? Such a question invites a thorough examination of the word "needy."

In addition, words may be used metaphorically, like "he eats like a pig." Here you would study the metaphorical usage of a word.

2. For words and expressions which you plan to investigate thoroughly, make a list of all the places in the Bible in which the word occurs. This can be done by using a concordance.[10] Once this has been done, further steps can be taken to analyze and classify the environments—the horizontal relationships—in which a word occurs. Try to infer the meaning of the word from these contexts. The following are some clues to help you look.
   a. With what range of terms is the word used? For nouns, look for adjectives and verbs. For adjectives, look for nouns. For verbs, with what subjects and objects are they found? From this usage, try to construct a pattern—with what types of classes of words does the word under study occur—animate, inanimate, human, non-human, abstract, or concrete, etc.?
   b. Look for a skewing of the distribution pattern, a clustering of occurrences in particular passages, books, or types of literature or social contexts. In what type of literature, style, or social situation is the word or expression at home?
   c. Look for use in narrative or law, since these tend to be concrete, to give historical and cultural settings and thus have great potential for providing clues to the specific aspect of a word.
   d. Look for parallel expressions in poetry. In poetry parallel words are often synonymous. Sometimes they are opposites, but in either case they can be an important guide to the meaning of the word.

3. Once the word's distribution pattern has been analyzed and its usage understood, it may be necessary to see how the word is different from other words in its group (vertical relationships).
   a. First list the other members of the word group. (See a concordance.)

  b. Examine the distribution of these other members of the word
     group to see how the word being studied is different from the
     other words. Do this by noting differences in distribution patterns
     and drawing out from this what are the crucial, specific differences
     in meaning. This explains why the author chose the word in the
     passage under study and what is being communicated in the
     context of the passage.
  c. For expressions, what variations occur and what is their signifi-
     cance for meaning?

B. *Synthesis*
  1. Define the words or expressions studied in terms of their distinctive
     features as seen in their distribution just analyzed. One way of tabu-
     lating the results is to set up a chart with relevant categories of mean-
     ing in columns. The word or words can be marked either plus or
     minus with regard to these categories. This provides a profile of the
     meaning of the word. The example of eat, dine, feed used above can
     serve as an example.

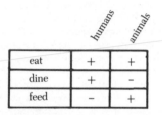

	humans	animals
eat	+	+
dine	+	−
feed	−	+

     The chart could be extended to other terms and other columns could
     be added to distinguish the new terms from these three. As an illus-
     tration, if we added "graze," we would mark minus for humans, plus
     for animals, plus for grass, and minus for grain. This would distin-
     guish it from "feed," which occurs with both grass and grain. Eat, of
     course, would also be plus for both.[11]

  2. In cases where it does not seem necessary to investigate the words in
     the word group, you may state the meaning of the word in terms of
     its horizontal relationships. Do this by characterizing the environ-
     ment within which the word occurs, the types of words with which it
     occurs. From this, state the important rules of distribution which you
     can infer. What "meanings" does the word have? See the examples
     given above of "powerful" and "cold."

  3. Fit the meaning of the word to its context in the passage. Words have
     a variety of senses or the author may be using it a novel way. Make
     sure the meaning decided on is governed by the context you are
     studying.

4. Classify expressions or stereotyped word groups according to the following three categories:
   a. Standard expressions—used throughout the language. (The English expression "over my dead body" or "he eats like a pig" would be an example.)
   b. Typical expressions—characteristic of a certain literary or theological tradition (e.g., "verbal plenary inspiration").
   c. Formulas—expressions rooted in a special situation in life. ("I now pronounce you man and wife," etc.)

One final factor must be mentioned: words do change their meaning through time. This means that the best evidence for the meaning of a word is those occurrences which come from the same time or shortly before the passage under study. However, in the Bible, since we do not have much material written at the same time, especially for the Old Testament, often it is necessary to disregard these time differences. But since this increases the chances that a mistake may be made in analysis, it is always best to weigh the evidence. The best evidence is other uses by the same author; next best are other uses from the same period; finally, evidence from remote periods. Thus, in collecting the evidence, as much as possible keep in mind the date of the passage being studied and the date of key references being used to establish the meaning of the word.

Because of this lack of material, scholars often need to resort to other types of evidence. One is the evidence of the etymology. As indicated above, this is only justified as a counsel of despair. Another is to compare the same word as it is used in a neighboring language of the same language family; that is, to look at the meaning of a cognate word. (Cognates are words in two languages which share a common origin.) This, too, is risky and must be used cautiously. One only needs to be reminded of the difference in meaning between English "deer" and German "Tier" (animal) to see the dangers involved in using such comparative evidence across language boundaries.

4.06 *Illustrations*
Genesis 12:10-20

In Genesis 12:10-20 there do not appear to be any words or expressions which merit special individual study.

Amos 2:6-16

From Amos 2:6-16 we will select just one word, "needy," for study

(v. 6b) and one expression "Thus says the Lord" (6a). Other words in this passage could be profitably studied but lack of space prohibits this.

First the phrase, "Thus says Yahweh." If you look in a concordance, you will see that the phrase, "Thus says. . ." (usually "the Lord") is a frequent phrase in the prophets. It also occurs in the narrative books and it is some of these latter instances that provide us with valuable information about how this phrase was used (clue 2c).

In Genesis 32 we have the story of Jacob sending messengers on ahead to meet his brother Easu. When they deliver Jacob's message to Esau, Jacob tells them to say, "Thus says your servant Jacob . . ." (32:4). From this we can see that in ancient Israel a message delivered by a messenger in the name of another, began "Thus says . . ." which was followed by the name of the sender, in this case Jacob. Further confirmation of this can be found in Judges 11:15. In this passage we have the story of Jephthah's negotiations with the Ammonites, in an attempt to prevent war between them and the Israelites whom he was representing. Jephthah's message, as spoken by his messengers begins, "Thus says Jephthah. . . ."

We may conclude from this very brief survey that the phrase, "Thus says so-and-so," was the conventional formula used at the beginning of a letter or message which was delivered by a messenger for another. The person who began speaking in this fashion immediately identified the fact that he was giving the words of another. In light of this, we can understand something of the social roles presumed in the passages we have looked at above. The prophet is God's messenger, who now pronounces God's message to the people Israel. The rejection of the message is thus not merely a rejection of the prophet and his words, but of God and his words. Given this context, the form of speech with which we are dealing has been called "the messenger speech of doom."[12]

"Needy" was chosen as a word for study because it is the most frequently used term in Amos for the oppressed. The question which we will seek to answer by a study of this word is who are these people whose oppression brings down God's judgment on Israel. To answer this question, we will give a fairly exhaustive analysis of the word "needy." This should demonstrate the techniques involved in the study of a word as outlined above.[13]

The Hebrew word translated "needy" in Amos 2:6 is *'ebyon*. This can be found by using either Strong's or Young's concordance. Once the word in the original language is known by using the concordance, all of its occurrences in the Bible can be found, regardless of their translation into English. Thus we find that *'ebyon* is used 61 times in the Hebrew Bible (clue 2). Looking at these 61 occurrences, we can see that they are not spread evenly throughout the Bible. The following chart will show this distribution of *'ebyon* by type of literature, at least roughly (clue 2b).

Law	9 times	Exodus 2 times; Deuteronomy 7 times
Narrative	1 time	Esther 9:22
Prophets	17 times	Amos 5 times; Isaiah 5 times;
		Jeremiah 4 times; Ezekiel 3 times
Psalms	24 times	(including 1 Samuel 2:8)
Wisdom	10 times	Job 6 times; Proverbs 4 times

It is clear from the above chart that *'ebyon* (needy) occurs most frequently in the Psalms. It is found infrequently in legal texts and wisdom literature, and not at all in the major narrative books, Genesis through 2 Kings.

If we next look at the environments in which *'ebyon* occurs, we find that they are quite different in the two major sources, the prophets and the Psalms. The term, for example, occurs five times in Amos, and in each of these instances the context is that of social oppression.

2:6	Sold into slavery for a pittance
4:1	Oppressed by the wealthy
5:12	Legal oppression by being denied justice
8:4, 6	Objects of economic of economic exploitation

Other similar references in other prophets are: Isaiah 32:7; Jeremiah 2:34; 5:28; 22:16; Ezekiel 16:49; 18:12; and 22:29.

In the Psalms, however, the context is quite different. Here *'ebyon* is used by the petitioner of the prayer to describe himself to God. See, for example, Psalms 40:17 and 86:1: "As for me, I am poor and needy; but the Lord takes thought for me"; "Incline, O Lord, your ear and answer me, for poor and needy am I." The petitioner in describing himself as *'ebyon* is giving a reason why God should answer him. *'Ebyon* then in these psalms is used as a title of religious piety and devotion; it is the label of the godly worshiper praying to God for deliverance. As such, it interchanges or is used in parallelism with "godly," "servant of God," "one who trusts in God" (Psalm 86:2 and elsewhere), and other similar terms denoting the sincere worshiper (clue 2d).

Thus in looking at the two commonest places where the term *'ebyon* occurs, we find that it is used in quite different contexts (clue 2a). This means that *'ebyon* has at least two different meanings—a "religious" meaning and a "secular" meaning. The religious meaning has to do with the need of the petitioner for God's help. This need forms the basis of his plea to God, the reason why God should answer the prayer and deliver him.[14] The secular usage, as in Amos, has to do with those who are oppressed materially, those who are taken advantage of by the rich and powerful. Here it is a socioeconomic term. Since it is the latter meaning which is important for Amos, we will only investigate this sense of the term further, in order to determine who these oppressed are and to obtain a more precise picture of what was being done to them.

In addition it should be noted that in both of these meanings, the term *'ebyon* occurs with poor (*'ani*) as in Amos 8:4 and Psalm 40:17 quoted above. This word *'ani* is thus a word which must be closely related to *'ebyon* and forms parts of its word group.

Looking again at the concordance we see that there is one passage in which the word *'ebyon* is quite concentrated (Deuteronomy 15:1-11) where it occurs six times (clue 2b). This legal passage can help us further define the word *'ebyon* by supplying another context for the occurrence of the word. The law in Deuteronomy 15:1-11 is a sabbatical year law which requires the cancellation of loans by creditors every seven years. The ones who are here receiving the loans are called *'ebyon*. In verse 11 they are called both *'ebyon* and *'ani*. From this context we can infer that the *'ebyon* are those who need to borrow money because of their precarious economic situation and who may not be able to pay it back.

Another sabbatical year law also concerns the *'ebyon*. This one in Exodus 23:11 regulates the use of the land. Here the *'ebyon* is to get the produce of the field on the seventh year, as the owner of the land is to let it rest, abandoning it for a year. From this context we can infer that the *'ebyon* was landless, and this provision was addressed to the landowners in order that the landless *'ebyon* could have access to the land and its products in the sabbatical year when the landowners left the land fallow.

The final economic provision for the *'ebyon*, Deuteronomy 24:14-15, rules that an *'ebyon* should be paid his wages each evening because he depends on them for his very sustenance. From this we learn that the *'ebyon* were employed as hired wage earners and that they led a hand-to-mouth existence, having no resources or surplus to fall back upon.

Finally, Exodus 23:6 guarantees the *'ebyon* fair legal process. Being poor, of course, it was likely that justice would not be done for them. Although the law protected their legal rights, what actually happened was quite another story—as Amos 5:12 testifies.

We could look yet at the use of *'ebyon* in Proverbs and Job, but since it would not add significantly to what we have already found, we can consider ourselves to have completed the first stage of the investigation: we have seen the distribution of *'ebyon* in the Bible, and have looked at its various contexts. In the economic sphere we have seen that it is used for those who have no land, need to borrow money and may not be able to pay it back, and work for wages. As such they are powerless and consequently require their legal rights to be singled out for special mention and protection.

Our next step (clue 3) is to define how the word *'ebyon* is different from other words in Hebrew for poor or needy people. We know what these other words are, because we find them used with "needy" in the references we have just looked at or we find them in the concordance under the entry for "poor" and "needy."

Dal, meaning poor or weak, is a term used by Amos four times, in 2:7, 4:1, 5:11, and 8:6. Next to *'ebyon*, it is his most popular term for poor. In 4:1 and 8:6 it is used as a parallel to *'ebyon*. These two words are obviously closely related. *Dal* occurs 48 times in the Old Testament. Its distribution pattern is different from *'ebyon's* as the following chart illustrates.

Law	4 times	Exodus 2 times; Leviticus 2 times
Narrative	5 times	
Prophets	14 times	
Psalms	5 times	
Wisdom	20 times	

Dal is used, in contrast to *'ebyon*, in narrative, more frequently in wisdom, and much less frequently in Psalms. It would thus seem to be a more "secular" term.

If we look at the environments in which *dal* occurs, we can see some immediate differences from *'ebyon* (clue 3b). First, *'ebyon* only refers to people, while *dal* can be used of animals as well, as in Genesis 41:19. Second, *dal* is used frequently as the opposite of "strong" (*gadol*) and "rich" (*ashir*) as in Ruth 3:10, while *'ebyon* is not (with one exception). As such, the term can be used of the population left behind in the land after all the powerful and wealthy people have been deported into exile, as in 2 Kings 24:14, 25:12, and elsewhere. This same contrast is also found in the laws. In Exodus 23:2 and Leviticus 19:15, judgment is to be just regardless of whether people are *dal* or powerful *(gadol)*. In the bringing of sacrifices the *dal* do not need to offer as expensive an offering as do the wealthy *(ashir)*, Exodus 30:15 and Leviticus 14:21. However, *dal* does occur in some environments very similar to those of *'ebyon*. For example, in Isaiah 10:2, Proverbs 14:31, and in Amos, the *dal* are the victims of oppression. In summary, *dal* is a more general term than *'ebyon;* it can be applied to both people and animals; it seems to refer to the poor and powerless in general as the opposite of the rich and powerful. The emphasis in *dal* is on their poverty or poor condition, rather than on their condition of oppression. The *'ebyon* may of course be found among the *dal* and the *dal* certainly were the objects of oppression.

Another word for poor is *rash*. This word is used differently than either *'ebyon* or *dal*, as its distribution pattern shows.

Law	0 times
Narrative	4 times
Prophets	0 times
Psalms	1 time
Wisdom	16 times

The majority of uses are in Proverbs, fourteen times, for those who are paupers and the opposite of those who are rich as in Proverbs 10:4, 13:8, and elsewhere. In 2 Samuel 12:1, 3, and 4 likewise it is used as the opposite of rich. Thus *rash* seems to have a very similar meaning to *dal*. It occurs in very similar environments, being the opposite of rich, but has a very different distribution in terms of the type of literature it occurs in. The explanation of this phenomenon is presumably that *rash* was a wisdom term being used especially in that type of literature, while *dal* was a term used more generally in the language. This is a type of complementary distribution, the type of literature being the determining factor as to which word would be chosen in a given case (clue 2b).

An example of this same kind of distribution pattern would be swine and pig in present-day English. In normal language, most people use the word pig, but in agricultural books and between and among farmers, the term "swine" is used when talking or writing about the business of pig raising. Thus, pig and swine have a complementary relationship, with pig having a much wider distribution, while swine is the

more technical term, although both are synonymous in most of their occurrences. This seems to have been the same situation with *dal* and *rash*
in Hebrew.

Finally, the most frequent word for "poor" is *'ani*, a word which as
we have seen is used along with *'ebyon* in several passages. *'Ani* occurs
74 times and like *'ebyon* it occurs most frequently in the prophets and
Psalms, while it does not occur at all in narrative.

Law	7 times	Exodus 1 time; Leviticus 2 times; Deuteronomy 4 times
Narrative	0 times	
Prophets	25 times	Amos 1 time (?); Isaiah 13 times; Jeremiah 1 time; Ezekiel 4 times; Zephaniah 1 time; Zechariah 4 times
Psalms	30 times	(Including 2 Samuel 22:28; Habakkuk 3:14)
Wisdom	12 times	Proverbs 5 times; Job 6 times; Ecclesiastes 1 time

Like *'ebyon*, *'ani* has a very definite religious meaning in the Psalms, as
well as a social-economic sense in the prophets, law, and wisdom. It is
also used frequently with the other terms for poor which we have just
studied. It seems to share most of the environments in which they occur.
The *'ani* are the object of social oppression, for example, in Isaiah 3:14,
15; 10:2; and elsewhere. They are paupers as in Isaiah 10:30, Zephaniah
3:12, and elsewhere. The term can be used of animals, as in Zechariah
11:7, 11, like *dal* in Genesis 41:19.

In the legal material, however, *'ani* occurs in several laws which do
represent something of a new environment. From Exodus 22:25, "If you
lend money to any of my people with you who is poor [*'ani*], you shall
not be to him as a creditor, and you shall not exact interest from him."
We see that interest is not to be taken from them (also Ezekiel 18:17)
and their pledged garments are to be returned to them in the evening.
This latter regulation is also found of the *'ani* in Deuteronomy 24:12-13,
where the widow is also mentioned in 24:17; no pledge is to be taken
from her.

In Leviticus 19:10 and 23:22, the law requires the gleanings to be left for them and the alien *(ger)*. However, in Deuteronomy 24:19-21, where the gleaning laws are again found, the *'ani* are not mentioned, but instead the widow and orphan besides the alien *(ger)* are allotted gleaning rights. Orphan and widow would seem to have replaced *'ani* in this passage. Following this line of thought, in Leviticus the *'ani* is used as a general term for Israelite poor as opposed to the alien, the non-Israelite. In Deuteronomy, on the other hand, who these poor are is spelled out in more detail—the orphan and the widow.

We may conclude from our study so far that *'ani* is a general term for poor or oppressed, being used often with the other words for poor and includes widows and orphans. *Dal* has more the connotation of being weak, poorly, in a sorry state. As such it is used for both people and animals, and is the opposite of being powerful and rich. *Rash* is very similar to *dal*, but its use is restricted largely to wisdom literature, being a special term in this material. Finally, *'ebyon* also means poor and oppressed people, but ones who are the object of and who are to profit from regular economic readjustments as stipulated by the provisions of the sabbatical year. These provisions involve the use of capital goods, money in Deuteronomy, and land in Exodus.

There is yet one set of terms for poor people which we have not yet examined, the ones designating specific classes of poor people—widows, orphans, and aliens. These three groups of poor people often occur together in the Old Testament. These groups are different from the general terms at which we have been looking because they are terms designating natural statuses—women whose husbands have died, children who are fatherless, and residents who are not citizens (aliens). Their rights too are protected by law and those who disregard their rights were also rebuked by the prophets. This class of people forms a distinct complementary group to *'ebyon*. For example, in Deuteronomy 14:28-29 provision is made for the Levite, the alien, the orphan, and the widow by allowing them the tithe of the produce of the land every third year. What joins these four natural groups together is that they all lack direct access, by ownership rights, to the land—as it is specifically stated about the Levite. If we look at the provisions made for this group, beside the third-year tithes which is repeated again in Deuteronomy 26:12-13, we find that they are to share in the feasting of the festival of weeks (Pentecost) and of the festival of booths, both of which celebrate the productivity of the land. Likewise, as seen above, provisions are made for them to glean (Deuteronomy 24:19-22) at harvesttime.

We might cast the difference in economic provisions made for the *ebyon* as over against the widow, orphan, and alien as follows. First, the widow, orphan, and alien are the subject of welfare laws—a certain amount of the productivity of the land was to be given to them. They were to share in the consumption of the products which were produced by the land through sharing in the tithes, festivals, and gleaning. The *ebyon*, however, was not the object of such welfare laws, but of capital reform laws. That is, the *ebyon* was to be given access to the capital goods of the community—land and money—as legislated by the sabbatical year laws. Second, in contrast to the orphan, widow, and alien, the *ebyon* could own land, was of the same class as those who did in fact own land and possess monetary capital. Thus *ebyon* was not a natural class, but an acquired social class. The status of *ebyon* came about either through loss of capital resources or through lack of access to the capital resources, the means of production and wealth. Following this he either needed to become a wage earner (Deuteronomy 24:14) or he needed to borrow money. The *ebyon* were consequently the economically dispossessed, those who had no access to their own capital resources. The legislation of the sabbatical year was to put them back in command, at least temporarily, of capital resources. This understanding of *ebyon* explains the distribution of *ebyon* in the legal material and the prophets, and sets *ebyon* clearly apart from the other terms for poor which we have examined.[15]

The following two charts summarize these distinctions we have seen from the distribution.

	human	nonhuman	opposite of rich/ powerful
'ani	+	+	+
dal	+	+	+
rash	+	−	+
'ebyon	+	−	−

	own land	work for wages
'ebyon	+	+
widow/ orphan	−	−

Coming back to the book of Amos, as seen above, Amos's two most-used words for poor are *'ebyon* (5 times) and *dal* (4 times). In contrast to this, Amos never mentions the orphan, widow, or alien. Hosea, Isaiah, Jeremiah, and Ezekiel mention them in contrast to this omission on the part of Amos. Keeping with our understanding of *'ebyon,* Amos is focusing on the oppression of those who could and ought to share in the economic resources of the society, but for one reason or another have been dispossessed. This notion fits well with the specific acts of oppression Amos mentions. In 2:6 they are sold into slavery, presumably for debts, rather than having their debts forgiven by the creditor as Deuteronomy 15:1-11 stipulates. In 5:11 they are denied justice contrary to Exodus 23:6. Finally, they are victims of market exploitation in Amos 8:4—subjects of exploitation in the sale of food. Since they had no land, and were evidently not given use of the land in the seventh year for their sustenance as Exodus 23:11 requires, they have no alternative but to buy food in the marketplace with their wages, which they had earned perhaps by working on the land for these same farmer-merchants.

In summary, we can see that a thorough investigation of the word *'ebyon* leads to not only an understanding of the particular significance of the word, but provides us with an invaluable insight into the message of Amos. Amos was not necessarily talking about poor in general, but about a certain class of poor. To miss this point is to miss, to a greater or lesser extent, Amos's real concern.

Matthew 5:38-42

In Matthew 5:38-42 we will look at two terms: "resist" and "right." The word "resist" is used in Jesus' teaching: "Do not resist one who is evil." This saying may seem strange to us: what is wrong with resisting evil? In fact, isn't that what we are supposed to do? To help with this difficulty the term "evil" in this passage is often translated or understood to mean "evil person." Either, of course, is a possible understanding of the Greek, which is ambiguous at this point. The advantage of translating the word "evil" as "evil person" is that from such a translation it is implied that it is all right to resist evil, but not the evil person. This is probably too fine a hair to split, since resisting evil usually involves resisting the one doing the evil deeds.

By looking in a concordance we discover that the Greek word used here for "resist" is *anthistemi,* which occurs twelve times in the New Testament. Among these occurrences we find both commands to resist evil and examples of people resisting other people. "Resist the devil" is found in James 4:7 (see also 1 Peter 5:9), or in Ephesians 6 we are told to put on the whole armor of God "in order to resist in the evil day" (Ephesians 6:13). In the same way, Paul writes in Galatians 2:11 how he "resisted" Peter to his face in Antioch. All these passages seem to contradict the notion that we should not resist either evil or the person who does evil.

However, in addition to these references where "resist" (*anthistemi*) has the sense of to oppose or go against, or to withstand, it also occurs in passages which are connected with court scenes or legal proceedings. For example, in Acts 6:10, we read how Stephen's adversaries were not able to "resist" him, so they brought against him false witnesses to convict him before the court. Here "resist" has the sense of "refute" or "show to be in the wrong." Likewise, Luke 21:15 predicts that when Christians are charged and brought before the government officials, none will be able to refute or show them to be wrong. In the Greek translation of the Old Testament *anthistemi* is used in a legal context in Deuteronomy 19:18. Again, the context is concerning a witness whose evidence is able to convict—to show the other party is in the wrong—although in this case, the testimony is false (clue 2c).

A further bit of evidence along this line is that *histemi*, a word related to *anthistemi* (resist), which usually means "stand," has a similar legal sense as well—as in Acts 6:13 and 22:30. Thus, we can conclude that "resist" (*anthistemi*) had two senses in Greek—a general one, meaning to withstand or oppose, and a legal nuance meaning to oppose, to show to be in the wrong.

This understanding of "resist" (*anthistemi*) in the legal sense is further supported by the fact that the Greek word *anthistemi* was also used to translate the Hebrew word *amad*, which also meant to "stand" or "withstand." More importantly for us here, *amad* (stand) was also used in the phrase "to stand on one's rights or dues." The rabbis taught that it was a virtue to be compliant, to not always insist on the full measure of the law being applied literally. Thus it was said that one should not always stand (insist) upon his rights.[16]

That resist is being used by Jesus in this legal sense in Matthew 5:39 is what we might expect from the context (synthesis). "Eye for an eye, tooth for a tooth" was a principle of law, taken from Exodus 21:23-24 (also Leviticus 24:20). At the heart of this principle of law, which is sometimes referred to by its legal name *lex talionis*, is the idea that punishment should be equal to the crime—not more and not less. This rules out vengeance (inflicting greater punishment) and privilege (getting by with less than just punishment). Jesus' teaching was different— don't demand exact reciprocity for wrongs done.

We have seen that the word "resist" *(anthistemi)* in a legal context means to oppose or to show to be wrong or, perhaps influenced by the Hebrew expression, to insist upon one's exact legal rights. This latter sense fits well with the context in which the phrase is found in Matthew 5:39. Therefore, we conclude that Jesus was talking here specifically about "resisting" in terms of legal action, and not necessarily about resistance generally.

This conclusion is in accord with a general line of teaching in the New Testament against Christians pursuing their rights through legal proceedings. It is echoed in the teachings of Jesus in the Sermon on the Mount in the first antithesis (Matthew 5:25-30) and in Luke 12:57-59, as well as by Paul in 1 Corinthians 6:1-8. In this latter passage, Paul indicates that it is better to be defrauded by another than to insist upon one's rights in court. This legal understanding also shows this passage to be in harmony with the commands and examples of positive resistance found elsewhere in nonlegal contexts in the New Testament.

The second term we will examine is the phrase "right cheek" which occurs in the first focal instance that Jesus gives to illustrate his new teaching. In specifying the right cheek, Matthew seems to have some deeper significance than just a simple slap on the cheek, since Luke has only "cheek" (Luke 6:29) (clue 1). In rabbinic law, a slap in the face was the prime example of a personal insult in which no actual physical damage was done and consequently there remained no evidence of the insult for proof in court.[17] Such violations were, of course, punished, but this was done on the basis of a violation of a person's rights, rather than on the basis of any actual physical damage caused. It has been argued that, contrary to later Jewish law on such insults which was based on Deuteronomy 25:11ff., Jesus includes such insults under the class of injury covered by "eye for an eye" *(lex talionis).*[18] This is not necessarily the case, since in Matthew this case is meant to be an illustration not of what is meant by "eye for an eye" but of a new principle of "not resisting." This is certainly the case in the following examples, since they are not connected with "eye for an eye," having nothing to do with bodily injury at all. Rather, Jesus is teaching that in the case of such insults, one should allow oneself to be insulted rather than pursue litigation for the recovery of damages. This illustrates Jesus' new principle of positive reciprocity (respond in new and different ways) which is opposed to the old principle of tit for tat *(lex talionis)*. Jesus is illustrating and contrasting general principles in these focal instances, not specific classes of law.

What is the sense of "right cheek" in this context? Assuming that most people are right handed, a blow on the right cheek would be given with the back of the hand. It was exactly this type of blow which carried with it a greater penalty—a double fine over being struck with the palm of the hand.[19] Thus, Jesus has picked the most severe case of insult. Even when struck with the back of the hand, you do not sue your opponent in court. Rather let him commit a lesser offense as well—a slap with the palm of the hand.

It is evident that the context of this focal instance, as well as the second, is law and actions governed by law. This lends added support to our conclusion above that Jesus was speaking about the Christian's use of the law to enforce his rights in saying "do not resist the evil person."

Jesus however extends this principle beyond the law as can be seen in the final two focal instances which speak of lending and borrowing. Since in these last two cases the other party is no longer a powerful aggressive opponent as in the first three, but a supplicant for a favor, the attribute of "evil person" does not seem at all applicable. Although these last two cases appear to be exceptions, the first example shows clearly that Jesus was speaking to situations regulated by law and taught that Christians should not avail themselves of the law to enforce their rights over against their adversary.[20]

Romans 13:1-7

In Romans 13:1-7 we will look at three words, "submit" *(hypotasso)*, "powers" *(exousia)*, and "sword" *(machaira)*. But first a general observation about the language of this passage: as has been pointed out, Paul in this passage uses words which are correct technical political expressions. In writing about the state, he seems to be choosing his words carefully with a regard to their secular political sense, rather than using them in a broad or general sort of way.[21]

The word "sword" *(machaira)* occurs in the phrase, "They bear not the sword in vain" (v. 4), a phrase which has been understood to mean that states have a right, in fact, almost a divine mandate, to exercise capital punishment.[22] Is this, however, what "sword" and "bearing the sword" mean in this context? A concordance can tell us that *machaira,* which Paul uses here, is the most common word for sword in the New Testament, occurring 29 times. The only other word used for sword in the New Testament is *hromphara*, which occurs seven times, six of these in the book of Revelation. There is, however, another word for sword in Greek, *xiphos*. It was this word, *xiphos*, which was used when talking of the power or right of the state to wield the sword in capital punishment.[23]

On the other hand, *machaira* was used of police who used force to obtain compliances with the law. In fact, beginning in Egypt, the police were called "sword bearers," using the same words as Paul uses here when speaking of not bearing the sword in vain.[24] Assuming that Paul was choosing his words carefully, it would seem that by using *machaira* instead of *xiphos* for sword, he is referring to the civil police function of the state and not to the right or duty of the state to exercise capital punishment. Paul is saying, then, that the state uses force to maintain order, to uphold laws, in the society. If you would not fear the state, do not disturb the order. This illustrates how knowing to what group a word belongs and how its usage (distribution) is different from other words in the group leads us to an understanding of the meaning which the word has.

There are differences of opinion as to the meaning of "submit" (*hypotasso*). Some hold that there is a distinction between "submit" and "obey" (submit does not include obey),[25] while others contend that submit is, in fact, a stronger word than obey (for example, stronger than the Greek words *hypakouo* or *peithomai*).[26] *Hypotasso* occurs 37 times in the New Testament, 23 times in the same type of construction as found here: that is, where someone is to be subject to someone else.

To whom are we to be subject? The word occurs with quite a range of people as the following chart shows:

To God, God's will	1 Corinthians 15:28; Romans 8:7; 10:3; Hebrews 12:9; James 4:7
To Christ	Ephesians 5:24
To disciples (said of demons, not of people)	Luke 10:17,20
To fellow church members or church leaders	Ephesians 5:21; 1 Corinthians 14:32; 16:16; 1 Peter 5:5

To husbands	Ephesians 5:22; Colossians 3:18; Titus 2:5; 1 Peter 5:5
To parents	Luke 2:51
To masters	Titus 2:9; 1 Peter 2:18
To secular authorities	Romans 13:1; Titus 3:1; 1 Peter 2:13

Mainly it is used of Christians in their relationships to other people, usually people with a specific social status such as husband, church member, parent, or slave. The command to submit is addressed to the one in the subordinate position—to wives, slaves, church members, and citizens. Thus, it is a term which regulates the behavior of a social subordinate to a social superior. Addressed to the subordinate person, it means, "Allow another to have authority over you." In this broader context it can be seen that Paul, in asking Christians to "submit" to the state, is not calling for any special allegiance to the state as opposed to other social relationships, but only that the same social deference should be shown to the state as to fellow Christians and church leaders.

What does this evidence imply as to whether *hypotasso* means to obey or something stronger or weaker? It would seem that obey would be included in the general sense of "allowing another to have power over you" since to disobey is a sign of the rejection of another's power and authority. In Romans 8:7, *hypotasso* which occurs with "law of God" is taken most naturally as meaning "obey," submitting to the regulations of the law of God. Second, *hypakouo* (obey) and *hypotasso* (submit) are interchangeable in some contexts. Titus 2:9 and 1 Peter 2:18 exhort slaves to submit to their masters; Ephesians 6:5 and Colossians 3:22 ask them to obey. These contexts are so similar, that there must be an overlapping of meaning here. We must conclude, therefore, that the evidence does not allow a sharp distinction between submit and obey. Submit *(hypotasso)* would seem to be the broader term, regulating a wider range of social relationships and responsibilities, including that of obedience. Obey *(hypakouo)* more characteristically describes a response to a verbal communication, such as a command or the Gospel (as in Mark 1:27; 4:41; Romans 10:16; and 2 Thessalonians 1:8.)

As in the case of submit, so with "powers" *(exousia)* there has been a division regarding its meaning in Romans 13:1. Some have argued that "powers" here refers to spiritual forces behind the state, or to both the spiritual forces and their earthly representatives, the governing officials.

Others have seen in the powers here only a mention of the human rulers or governing officials of the Roman Empire.

Those who argue that spiritual forces are meant, base themselves on two lines of evidence.[27] The first is that in the Bible there are spiritual powers directly related to nations. In the Old Testament we find occasionally the mention of other divine beings, as in Psalm 82 (also in Psalm 29:1, 89:6-7; 1 Kings 22:19; and Exodus 15:11). In addition to this general notion of a divine court or assembly of spiritual beings, there is also the idea that these divine beings have a relationship to the pagan states round about Israel. Here the Greek translation of Deuteronomy 32:8-9 is important: "When the Most High gave to the nations their inheritance, when he separated the sons of men, he fixed the bounds of the peoples according to the number of the sons of God. For the Lord's portion is his people, Jacob his allotted heritage." This same idea that the pagan nations have been allotted certain "gods" occurs again in Deuteronomy 4:19 and 29:26. At the end of the Old Testament period, as reflected in the book of Daniel (10:13, 20, 12:1) there were specific angels, which were the angels of specific countries or empires. This evidence from the Old Testament shows that in Paul's time Jewish people could have viewed the state as an earthly political organization, behind which stood a heavenly being, each nation having its own heavenly being.[28]

The second line of evidence is that Paul himself uses the word "powers" *(exousia)* for precisely these heavenly, divine powers standing behind the earthly rulers and governments. References like 1 Corinthians 15:24; Ephesians 1:21; 3:10; 6:12; and Colossians 1:16; 2:10, 15 are cited in support of this assertion. In fact, it is claimed that everywhere when Paul speaks of the powers in the plural *(exousiai)* or with "all," these angelic beings are meant. (This is with the exception of Titus 3:1). In particular, 1 Corinthians 2:8 ("None of the rulers of this age understood this; for if they had, they would not have crucified the Lord of glory") and 1 Corinthians 6:3 ("Do you not know that we are to judge angels? How much more, matters pertaining to this life!") are cited as passages which clearly show an intimate relationship between the earthly and heavenly powers. The first passage shows how difficult it really may be to decide whether Paul is speaking of earthly or heavenly rulers; in fact, they argue, he has both in mind since they are inseparable in his thought. In the second passage (6:3) the Christian's judgment of the angels is evidence that the church should settle its own disputes internally, rather than taking them before the secular authorities. Since we will judge the angels and these stand behind and support the existing earthly order and authority, Christians therefore are superior to the existing earthly authorities and systems. That the angels stand behind the present cultural arrangements is further shown by 1 Corinthians 11:10, where Paul supports a cultural convention by mentioning the angels.[29] In light of this evidence, in Romans 13:1, we expect Paul to be consistent and to use powers *(exousiai)* as elsewhere to refer to the "national angels."

Against this view, the following can be argued.[30] The plural "powers" *(exousiai)* is construed most naturally in Titus 3:1 as referring to the governing earthly authorities. This is in keeping with New Testament usage elsewhere, such as in Luke 12:11, where actual government officials are clearly meant by "powers." Second, the phrase as used here, "ruling powers" (verse 1) and "rulers" (verse 3), is in a specific political context, and as such most naturally refers to the higher officials of the Roman empire, the "imperia" and "magistratus" to which these Greek words are the equivalent, and which they translate.[31] Third, in the actual context of the passage it would seem that Paul is concerned with specific government officials, as verse three shows. In this verse "power" *(exousia)* is used, in the singular, and clearly refers to actual Roman rulers. Since this is what "power" means in verse 3, it is likely that this is what it means in verse 1 as well.

From its various political contexts it would seem that powers *(exousiai)* has two meanings. In uses mainly in the Pauline writings and in the plural, it can focus on spiritual powers, rulers, or forces which may be in league with earthly rulers. On the other hand, it can also mean, in both the plural and singular, earthly government officials. Which of these meanings the word has in Romans 13:1 must be decided on the basis of its context in the passage. In light of the content of the entire passage, Paul's use of specific political language which refers to the Roman state of that time and his use of "power" in verse 3 to refer to Roman officials, it seems probable that Paul was also speaking of Roman government officials in 13:1.

4.10 *Summary*

This last example of word analysis illustrates two principles which are important to keep in mind as you study the meaning of words, and which have been demonstrated in most of the above examples. One is that words have a variety of meanings and nuances. Consequently we should not try to force them to mean the same thing throughout their distribution. Second, the context is finally determinative for meaning. This is true both in determining the senses of a word in its range of distribution and in determining which sense is appropriate in the passage under study.

It is important to investigate the various meanings of a word or expression in various contexts. From its usage we infer the rules regulating a word's occurrences. Second, we must see a term in the context of its word group. How does its distribution differ from those of its associates? The difference in distribution patterns gives the most specific meanings of a word.

Since words have a range of meaning, the context of the passage being studied is crucial. A firm grasp of both the passage's structure and its form is necessary in order to understand how a word is being used in this particular occurrence. Thus, the preceding two steps, the analysis of structure and form are a prerequisite to word analysis.

Part II
THE CONTEXT

Chapter 5

From Context to Composition:
Tradition Analysis

5.00 Traditions

When we think of an author today, we think of someone sitting at a table with pen and paper in hand, writing down something new which he wants to say. A bit more modern view would perhaps substitute a typewriter for a pen. In either case, the author is a creative person, someone who comes up with new ideas or stories.

But where does the writer get his material, the themes, plots, and the phrases he uses to express himself? They are by and large drawn from the culture and language of the author. Just as an author does not invent his own words, grammar, and forms, but draws on his linguistic tradition for these, so also an author does not necessarily invent his own metaphors, plots, or themes, but draws them from his cultural tradition.

Even the modern author who we think of as operating very creatively, is actually operating within limitations. These limitations are both linguistic (set by the language in which he is writing) and cultural (the themes, motifs, and phrases which are drawn upon are part of the furniture of a culture). In order to fully understand an author, we must see how he works within these limitations, what new combinations of traditional material are made, or perhaps how the limitations are broken in the composition.

What we have just said about modern authors is even truer of many biblical writers. They wrote, not so much with a view to saying something different and creative, but rather to transmit the traditional, to communicate the heritage of the past to their present. They often function more as transmitters of traditions, as channels of transmissions, than as original creative authors. On the other hand, part of what they did was creative and original. Thus, in studying the work of an author, we need to observe both

141

what is traditional and what is new and creative. We need to note especially how an author uses traditional material creatively in composing a unit.[1]

In this stage of study, we will discover the roots of a passage, its prehistory, so to speak. From where did the material, ideas, and expressions in the passage come? We want to study both what an author selected from his heritage and how he combined these traditions in novel ways. We may also at times see what an author has chosen to omit. This may be as important a clue to understanding a passage as what is chosen.[2]

In studying a unit with a view to finding what traditional materials an author has selected and how he used them in composing a unit, we can make a difference between an author drawing upon a stream of tradition, and drawing upon material which is already formed. In the first case, the author uses material which is "in the air," part of his culture. In the second, the author takes up literary compositions, either oral or written, into his work. We will discuss each of these aspects of tradition analysis in turn.

First, it is clear that various biblical authors wrote as they did because they were drawing upon a distinctive theological tradition. Their experience with a particular tradition has shaped their language and perspective. In order to understand why they wrote as they did, we need to analyze the ideas which lie behind their work and interpret them accordingly.

A vivid illustration of a theological tradition shaping an author's presentation can be seen in the difference between the synoptic Gospels (Matthew, Mark, and Luke) and the Gospel of John. The differences in their presentation of Jesus' ministry are obvious and striking. In John, words like "truth," "life," and "light" abound, occurring much more frequently than in the other three Gospels combined. On the other hand, the word "parable" never occurs in John; instead, Jesus teaches in long discourses in a kind of dialogue with the Jews. Likewise, in contrast to the synoptic Gospels where Jesus' ministry is characterized by the proclamation of the coming or present kingdom of God (or heaven), the term kingdom of God (or heaven) is almost absent from John, occurring only two times (3:3, 5).

Not only in vocabulary, style, and concept is John different, but he also depicts the events of Jesus' life differently. The cleansing of the temple, for example, comes at the beginning of John's gospel, rather than at the end of Jesus' ministry, as in the Synoptics. In John, Jesus seems to be in constant movement between Galilee and Judea. Indeed, much of his ministry in John takes place in Judea and Jerusalem. In the Synoptics, by contrast, Jesus appears to have had an early Galilean ministry, a journey to Jerusalem, and a final brief period of ministry in and around Jerusalem.

To understand why John's Gospel is shaped as it is, why he uses the vocabulary, motifs, and plots he does, it is necessary to probe into the intellectual circle within which he stood or to which he was speaking. In this particular case, ideas which are also found in later gnosticism seem to have influenced John and explain much of his language and presentation of Jesus.[3]

We can also investigate an author's use of fixed expressions or stereotyped word groups to see if they are a clue to a particular theological or social group. These expressions have been noted in the previous chapter. "Thus says the Lord," for example, we found to be a "message formula." The question is now what view of prophecy does this represent and who in Israelite society regarded the prophet as God's messenger.[4] Figures of style can also be analyzed for their roots. The poetic sequence of numbers in the phrase "for three transgressions . . . for four . . ." is found most often in Proverbs. Thus this figure of style has been taken to link Amos with the wisdom tradition or circle in Israel.[5]

Thus far we have been discussing an author's use of traditions in a fairly broad and indirect way. We were not assuming any specific direct literary dependency. This has been called "standing in a tradition" (drawing on ideas and expressions which are part of the author's environment). However, the link can be closer and more direct. Two passages may be so closely related that an actual literary dependency may be assumed, with one author borrowing material composed by another.

Sometimes, indeed, the biblical authors tell us that they are relying on older sources which they name. For example, in the Old Testament as far back as the Pentateuch, sources are cited from which material was taken. In Numbers 21:14b-15, *The Book of the Wars of Yahweh* is mentioned. Likewise, in Joshua 10:12-13, *The Book of the Upright* is cited. In writing of the kings of Israel and Judah, the author frequently refers to the books of the acts of the kings of Israel and of the kings of Judah (1 Kings 14:19, 29, for example). Even where sources are not cited, we can often tell that an author was in fact following a source. For example, large sections of Chronicles agree with Samuel and Kings, which must have served as a source for the former.

It is the same in the New Testament. Luke 1:1-4 tells us that he was relying on reports which had been given to him and he now was arranging the material in an orderly account. The fact that Luke used written

sources is borne out by the close verbal agreement which often exists
between Matthew, Mark, and Luke, and which sometimes exists just
between Matthew and Luke. This agreement in wording makes it
evident that Luke was directly dependent on Mark and on material
which Matthew also used. Thus, from an analysis of Luke's material as
well as his own testimony, it would seem that Luke drew upon literary
sources when he composed his Gospel.

In tradition analysis we not only need to practice literary ar-
chaeology by finding what borrowed material lies behind the passage, but
where appropriate we also want to link the materials under study with
others from the same source. That is, we not only want to find the
literary roots of a passage, but also their literary connection with the
other passages in the book belonging to the same source. This is possible,
of course, only where an author has used sources.

In this phase of tradition analysis we check to see if the borrowed
material in a unit may have formed part of a literary composition before
it was taken up into the unit where it is now found. To do this we need to
find other material which belonged to this previous collection. In the
book of Luke, for example, the material which Matthew and Luke have
in common is assigned to a source called "Q." The similarities in Matthew and Luke are explained by saying they both took material from this
common source. Thus in tradition analysis we want to discover if the material was once a part of a separate collection of units (like Q) before being incorporated into a unit. Such collections or cycles of units which
existed independently before being absorbed into another literary work
are often referred to as "sources."

Perhaps the following will help you visualize this process:

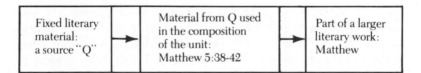

Fixed literary material: a source "Q"	Material from Q used in the composition of the unit: Matthew 5:38-42	Part of a larger literary work: Matthew

If the unit is not a combination of materials but it seems to belong
almost entirely to a single source, then the traditions behind the composition of the unit in the source need to be studied here. But the transmission and use of the unit will be studied in the next chapter.

For example, the Lord's prayer occurs in both Matthew and Luke.
We thus assume it comes from Q. In tradition analysis we would study

the ideas, motifs, and sources used to compose the prayer. The present wording of the prayer, however, is different in Matthew than in Luke. The change of wording could have occurred either in the period of time between Jesus' giving of the prayer and Matthew and Luke's writing it down or it could be due to changes made by Matthew and Luke when they incorporated the prayer into their gospel. Both of these possibilities will be studied in the next chapter. The first will be studied in the step called transmission analysis, while the second possibility will be our concern in redaction analysis. Since at times it will be difficult to know just where to study what, the following diagram should help you grasp more clearly the difference between tradition analysis (this chapter) and transmission and redaction analysis (the next chapter).

1. *Tradition Analysis: Pre*-composition

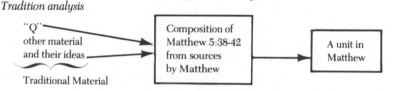

2. *Transmission Analysis: Post*-composition

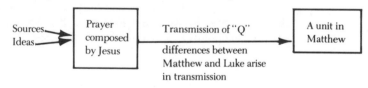

3. *Redaction Analysis: In*-corporation

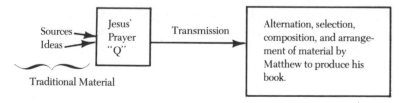

Where the author of the unit and the redactor of the book are the same (as in diagram 1 above) we will focus on his compositional activity as it relates to the unit in this chapter and his redactorial activity in the next chapter. The results which we gain from analyzing his compositional activity in the unit should support what we will discover in redaction analysis.

In addition to the use of sources, we also find biblical writers quoting material. For example, in Philippians 2:6-10, because of its style, it is thought that Paul has taken up into his letter a hymn of the early church.[6] Sometimes a quote is directly acknowledged, as in Titus 1:12.

In this stage of study, then, we are interested in finding what roots from his literary and intellectual heritage an author drew upon in the composition of a unit. This is important for two reasons. First, the way an author draws on a theological tradition or shapes a literary one often shows his point of view or what he is intending to emphasize. Second, an author may use or quote only part of what is in a tradition because he assumes the remainder is known. By knowing this tradition, we can understand the author's words in light of this wider context. In addition we also need to determine if material in our unit is part of a larger source or literary layer which the redactor or editor used to compose the book as a whole.

5.01 Axiom: All writing involves the creative utilization of materials from the literary and intellectual heritage of an author. How an author shapes and draws on this heritage in composition points to the meaning of the composition.

5.02 *Procedures*

The question, now, is how do you proceed to analyze the material for its traditional material? How do you determine what traditions an author drew upon and whether or not fixed literary material has been taken up into the composition of the passage? The method is largely comparative: you compare the unit or item under study with other units of material which are similar. To explain these similarities you must determine if a connection exists between the passages. The connection may be of two types. They may share a common intellectual tradition or outlook, or they may share a common literary tradition. The Gospel of John, discussed above, is a good example of a work shaped by a theological tradition, while the use of Mark or of Q by Matthew would be examples of a shared literary tradition. These two types of links, literary and intellectual, are, of course, closely related since expressions, phrases, motifs, and themes may indicate both a conceptual tradition and a literary source. Likewise they both can point to a social setting for the traditions and the composition of a unit.

In the following steps of tradition analysis, you should compare the unit under study not only with the material found in the Bible, but also with material from the surrounding cultures as well. Furthermore, it is often necessary to look at other material written by the same author to get clues as to the traditions which have influenced his writing. From an author's work as a whole you may find evidence for traditions which lie behind a unit, but which may not be very obvious in the unit itself.

In cases where the unit is reporting an event or speech, as in narrative material, the intellectual and literary background of the events or speech can be traced.

A. *Analysis*
  1. Determine if the passage is *related* to other material.
     a. Does the passage contain set phrases or expressions, characteristic word clusters or vocabulary?
        (1) Can you trace these to a certain literary body or school of thought? From the study of words and expressions just completed it will be clear if words or phrases in a passage cluster in a certain type of literature such as Deuteronomy, Proverbs, or Psalms. If so, then this provides a clue as to the theological and literary home of the passage.
        (2) Do these phrases or word clusters give insight into the social situation or roles presupposed by the unit? (See also form analysis above.)
        (3) Are there images or metaphors which likewise can be traced to a certain body of literature, a particular type of material, or social situation?
     b. Are there elements of style which are characteristic of a tradition? Is the form or genre of a passage characteristic of a certain school of thought or milieu? For example, proverbs belong to a wisdom tradition.
     c. Are there ideas or concepts, a certain viewpoint, which reflect a particular intellectual tradition? Often in order to understand the concepts of a passage adequately, it is necessary to know their roots, what they are built on, and with what other ideas they are associated in their intellectual tradition.
     d. Is the *theme*—the basic topic—found elsewhere in the literature? An example in narrative would be the theme of a universal flood

for the destruction of mankind. In legal material it might be the topic of just and unjust weights.
e. Are the *plot* and its traits also found in other passages? The plot is the actual skeleton of the story; it is the outline of how the theme is realized. *Traits*, on the other hand, are the characteristic ways in which the plot is carried out or developed. For example, in the flood story, the plot revolves around the survival of life by the building of the ark. Traits in the story would be the landing of the ark on top of a mountain, plans for the ark which are revealed by God, the sending out of the birds, sending three times, and the sacrifice at the end, and finally God declaring that never again would there be such a flood and the placement of the rainbow in the sky as a sign of this pledge.[7]

2. Are the similarities close enough that they are evidence of direct borrowing? Have sources or quotes been used by the author in composing the unit?
   a. Is there a literary dependency of one biblical passage on another:
      (1) Is the actual wording so close between passages compared that some form of literary dependency of one on the other or both on a third source is to be assumed?
      (2) Are the variations so significant that a direct literary link seems to be excluded?
   b. Where such parallel accounts do not exist, the clues to literary material being used by the author may come from the unit itself.
      (1) The first clue is the presence of material which is different in style, perhaps being in tension with the unit as a whole. These differences may exist within a passage even after material has been separated out of a passage during structural analysis. This is because we often find that an author has used his sources to weave an organic whole, but the threads of the warp and woof may yet show glimmers of the raw materials that have been used. An example of such material in the letters of Paul would be Philippians 2:6-10, which seems to be a quotation from a hymn on the basis of its hymnic style.[8]
      (2) The second clue does not actually arise from the text itself, but rests on a presupposition about the text. It is presumed that some material represents the fruit of a long oral tradition. The biblical authors, it is assumed, have composed many passages largely on the basis of what they have received from oral tradition. The question is, what was the oral form of the unit which the authors used? In addition, some would seek the various developmental stages in the growth of the unit during its period of oral transmission. As this reconstruction is often highly speculative, it is usually not very profitable in interpreting the present unit to pursue the issue of previous stages of the passage beyond the oral state which may have been the im-

mediate predecessor of the present unit.[9] An example of where we know there was an oral stage between composition and the present written stage is the teaching of Jesus. In fact, Jesus' teachings were originally spoken in one language, Aramaic, but eventually written in another, Greek.

   c. Where fragments and quotes have alrady been analyzed under structural analysis, their traditional background can be sought. However, material that has been added to the passage subsequent to its initial composition in a form similar to what we now have in the text will be studied in the next chapter.[10]

3. Did the unit once belong to an independent literary cycle before being absorbed into a larger literary work?
   a. Does the work as a whole show within and between the units signs of composite authorship? (See 2.42 for clues.)
   b. Is there a common viewpoint or threads which link a series of units or parts of units together?

B. *Synthesis*
1. Having completed the analysis of a unit for traditional material, you need now to synthesize your results. You can do so around four basic considerations:
   a. First, state with what literary or intellectual traditions the unit is linked, where the concepts of the unit are at home. This result will help you see the unit in its wider context. This perspective is necessary for a proper understanding of the ideas, themes, and traits which you find in a unit.
   b. Second, determine whether or not fixed literary material has been taken up into the composition of the unit. Reconstruct as far as possible the shape of this material before the author used it. This allows you to understand what the author did with what he had at hand.
   c. Does the unit belong to a source? If so, give the reasons for this judgment. Characterize the source. (You may wish to delay this at least partially until redaction analysis if you treat the source as the primary literary context for understanding the passage.)
   d. Third, you now can state how the traditional materials were used. What was taken over, what changes made, how do these function in the context of the passage? Also, you can see perhaps where the unit stands in the development of its tradition—is it an initiator or a consumer? Does it make a radical shift in the use of the traditions? All these results help you understand the purpose of the author, by seeing how he used his traditions.

2. Conclusions
   a. What can you now state about the author's purpose from the use of traditions in the unit?

b. How does this purpose help you understand the passage?
c. How does the perspective of the wider tradition background aid your understanding?
d. How does the unit's membership in a source (if relevant) aid your understanding?

5.03 *Illustrations*
Genesis 12:10-20

In Genesis 12:10-20 we have a story that appears quite similar to two other stories in Genesis where the patriarch claimed that his wife was his sister: Genesis 20:1-18, again about Abram and Sarai, and Genesis 26:1-11, where the figures are Isaac and Rebekah (clue 1e).

These three stories all seem to have the same theme, which we will refer to as "the endangering of the matriarch," since in two of the stories the wife of the patriarch is taken into the harem of a foreign king, where it appears that she will be lost forever (12 and 20). In the third variation, chapter 26, the stage is set for this loss, but events do not develop to this state of affairs, since the lie is discovered before events take their usual course.

The plot in all three stories seems to be similar (clue 1e). First, there is a deception on the part of the couple, for it is pretended that the wife is really a sister. This is followed by the actual or potential loss of the wife. Finally her actual status is discovered, the patriarch is summoned and scolded, and his wife's status is restored.

Many of the traits of the plot are shared (clue 1e). In each instance the story takes place in "foreign" territory. The one taking the matriarch is the king. Usually it is stated that the wife is beautiful (12 and 26), and for this reason the patriarch fears for his life and acts to deceive others as to his wife's status. Because of this deception, the patriarch prospers materially. The deception is always discovered by the foreign king, usually because of a loss or damage to the king's estate (12 and 20).

From all these correspondences it looks very much indeed like we have three variations on a single theme (clue 1d). However, each story also has its own individuality.[11] We will concentrate on the story in Genesis 12:10-20 to draw out its uniqueness against this background of the common tradition (clue 2a). Only this story begins with a conversation between Abram and Sarai. The other two accounts simply report that the patriarch called his wife his sister. Only in Genesis 12:10-20 does the patriarch ask his wife to practice the deception; in the other two stories it is just reported that the husband says, "She is my sister." In contrast to the other two stories, however, the actual lie itself is not reported in Genesis 12:10-20. Instead, there is a good deal of emphasis on Sarai's desirability; the courtiers see her, praise her to the Pharaoh, and Pharaoh then takes her. This is in contrast to the extremely brief and stark report in Genesis 20:2b of Sarah being taken by Abimelech. Likewise, only here does Abraham obtain wealth as a result of the lie, before its discovery. In the other two stories, wealth comes after the uncovering of the deception. Finally, only in Genesis 12:10-20 is the couple expelled as a result of their deception. In the other two accounts the patriarch is either entreated to stay (20:15) or given protection for his continued stay, which is assumed (26:11).

Since the wording too appears individual, the likenesses between these three stories is not due to actual literary dependency one upon the other, but rather each story appears to represent its own unique permutation of the plot and its traits which cluster around the theme, "the endangering of the matriarch." That is to say, while these stories are not directly dependent on each other, one serving as a source for the other, they do share a common literary tradition.[12]

Besides the specific related material shared by the three stories in Genesis, there are also more general relationships to other stories in the Bible. These relationships may help us understand the more general tradition within which our story in Genesis 12:10-20 might have been understood. The motif of famine and the seeking of help or refuge in another country is found again in the book of Ruth and in the Joseph stories.[13] It would not surprise the audience that Abraham would likewise seek aid in a foreign country.

Another parallel to our passage may be found in the Exodus story. Gunkel has pointed out how the outline of our story is similar to Israel's experience. Famine leads the family finally to Egypt. In Egypt they suffer danger from which God saves them by afflicting Pharaoh.[14]

Weimar relates Genesis 12:10-20 to several other stories. One of the closest parallels is to be found in Exodus 1:15-20. This unit begins with a speech, a speech by Pharaoh to the midwives of the Israelites. He commands them to kill all the male babies born to the Hebrews. The unit also has a speech at the end, again by Pharaoh in which he reproaches the midwives, as he does Abraham in our story. Also the expression "to be good for" occurs there as in Genesis. The midwives, in contrast to Abraham, are positive examples of trust in God. What a startling turnabout—the man of faith, faithless, while two Egyptian women exercise faith in a life and death situation. Seeing this contrast helps us gain a dimension of depth in our story which we would otherwise overlook.[15]

Can we now proceed from step one, finding the traditional elements in our unit and its connection with similar elements in other units, to discovering the oral form of the story previous to its present written form in the text (synthesis 1b)? Probably not very clearly or completely, but the following might be suggested. The beauty of the wife was probably an essential part of the tale, since it is mentioned or presupposed in all three accounts. Furthermore, it is foundational to the plot since this is the problem to which the deception is the solution. Furthermore, the fact that it is always the king who takes the wife into his harem further accentuates her beauty and desirability. Thus, it seems probable that the beauty of the wife was a fundamental aspect of the story in the oral tradition. Since all three stories have their location in a "foreign" urban environment, this too was probably a part of the tradition. At a minimum, the traditional plot seems to have revolved around the danger to the beautiful woman and her husband when entering into foreign territory. Since in connection with this plot the patriarch enriches himself in the end, this, too, may have been part of the tradition. Thus, it would be a story of how the husband of a beautiful wife not only copes with the danger of having a beautiful wife, but does so very successfully, becoming rich in the process.[16]

Since in terms of history the patriarchal period is usually assigned to the Middle Bronze Age (somewhere around 1800 BC or before) while the written form of the story which we now have is commonly dated at the earliest to the tenth century, a span of about 900 years would separate the events from the writing of them in the Bible.[17] This common tradition was thus presumably an oral tradition, since so many centuries separated the actual events from the time of their composition in the written form which we now have in the text. So the unit in Genesis 12:10-20 is apparently a written form of an orally transmitted tradition about the patriarchs.[18]

Was this unit composed by itself, or was it part of a larger cycle of materials which were later taken up into our book of Genesis (clue 3)? Scholars have found in Genesis signs of composite authorship. From these signs, three cycles or strands of material have been reconstructed. The letters, J, E, and P have been used to designate these three strands. Our passage, Genesis 12:10-20, has been assigned to J (it uses Yahweh as the name for God) while the parallel account in Genesis 21 belongs to E (Elohim being the name for God there).[19] Thus, we consider our story to be part of a larger cycle.

As we have seen above, this particular story in Genesis 12:10-20 is a result of the casting of a traditional theme, plot, and traits into the literary form of a speech-fulfilling narrative. If this act of composition was done by J, the author or collector of the J document to which this story belongs, then there was no literary transmission of this unit before J. What any previous literary form of this story was, we do not know.

Some, however, consider Genesis 12:10-20 to be an interruption of the main thread of the story of Abraham, which begins at the end of chapter eleven. According to this understanding, Abram moves to Canaan, travels about in the land, and following a dispute with Lot he splits with him and ends up at the oaks of Mamre (13:18). Thus, his detour to Egypt is a digression from these travels in Canaan and forms an intrusive addition. Furthermore, Lot is not mentioned in our story. If this tack would be taken, then Genesis 12:10-20 would have had an independent existence before being incorporated into the J material.[20]

The evidence, however, does not seem to make such a conclusion necessary. First, such an argument seems to be based on a prescriptive notion of what the plot should be rather than on a descriptive assessment of what the plot is as it now stands. Without other types of supporting evidence, such prescriptive judgments are weak, especially because the very reasons that can be given for eventually placing 12:10-20 where it is would also serve for its placement there by J in the first place. Thus the simplest hypothesis would be that J composed this story in its present form from traditional material to fit this place in his cycle of stories about the patriarchs of Israel. This explanation has the advantage of avoiding the knotty problem of why a compiler would insert a story which already had parallels in two other contexts and which created such a digression in an otherwise admirably straightforward narrative.

Turning now to synthesis, how do we account for or explain how the author of the unit Genesis 12:10-20 has selected, shaped, and added to his tradition (synthesis 1d)? Most of the features found to be unique to this story are explained as a result of the genre in which the unit is now cast. As seen above, Genesis 12:10-20 is a speech-fulfilling narrative. It begins with a speech, here between Abram and Sarai. This unique feature of the story is explained by its present form. Likewise, the unique length spent describing Sarai's beauty is also in accord with the structure of the form, since it is here that Abram's speech receives its narrative fulfillment.

Finally, God's intervention, which is reported in very brief form (compare this with the lengthy account in chapter 20), leads to the final denouement, the expelling of Abram and Sarai, and after her restoration, their return to Canaan, the land of promise. This unexpected outcome, as we have seen above, is in accord with J's use of the pattern of speech-fulfillment narrative to present the plans of man in contrast with the providence of God. Thus, we see here a close fit between the genre used, the purpose of the unit, and the author's use and transformation of the tradition. This comparative tradition analysis has served to confirm and sharpen our previous steps in analysis. Furthermore, it raises and under-scores a theological principle of the author—how God's providence is related to human endeavor. This is an element to keep in mind as we study this unit further.

Amos 2:6-16

The passage Amos 2:6-16, as we have seen, is a messenger speech of doom. Since we have focused on verse 6b in our previous steps, we will continue our examination of this line, "because they have sold the righteous for silver, the needy for a pair of shoes." Our first question in tradition analysis is, on what tradition is Amos basing himself in making this accusation? The assumption is that there is some criterion of right or wrong which Amos is using and that the crimes he mentions are judged wrong by this criterion (clue 1c). Furthermore, since he holds the people accountable for their deeds, there must be some consensus among the people about the wrongness of the deeds he describes.

As we have seen above, two unique features emerge with Amos's accusations: an emphasis on social sins, such as oppression of the eco-nomically dispossessed rather than on moral or religious sins; and a shift in audience, from addressing the king to addressing the population. When we inquire about the traditions behind Amos, we will want to ac-count for these shifts in his audience and message if we can.

What appears striking in Amos is that he does not appeal to the very traditions which we might assume he would in order to justify his accusations against the people. He does not appeal to the laws in the Old Testament, although in 2:4 he makes the general charge that Judah has not kept God's law and statutes. In specific cases, however, he does not mention that such actions are a violation of God's laws. It has been thought that he appealed to a certain class or genre of law, but this cannot be maintained consistently.[21] Likewise, he never speaks of Moses or calls the people to remember Mount Sinai. Indeed, from the book of Amos we would never know that Israel had a law which was given by God at Mount Sinai through Moses. It does not appear, at least explicitly, that Amos is basing himself on Mosaic legal tradition.

Likewise, it is striking that the word "covenant" never occurs in Amos in the sense of God's covenant with Israel, nor do the literary types which Amos uses seem to presuppose a covenant. (Amos 4:6-12 may be an exception.) On the basis of Amos's message alone we would be entirely ignorant of the whole covenant motif and theology found in the Old Testament. Of course, it might be argued that both of these traditions, law and covenant, were so intimately related and indeed united in Israel, that they were assumed by all to be the basis of Amos's charges against the people. That is, when they heard Amos's accusations, since they too would immediately recognize them as valid on the basis of law and covenant, Amos did not have to mention this. While this could be true, it is only a possibility; the problem remains that much of what Amos accuses the people of doing wrongly is just not covered by the laws which we have, or at least not covered explicitly. Indeed, what he accuses may even be *allowed* by the law. In the case in 2:6b, the selling of an Israelite into slavery for debts seems to be allowed in the laws (the law speaks of one selling himself). Amos appears to be condemning things which were not illegal. Consequently, the law does not seem to form a helpful background for explaining why Amos brought the charges he did.

Wolff has argued that Amos was in fact not speaking from these religious traditions of Israel, but was basing himself on the wisdom traditions.[22] He argues this from two major blocks of evidence as well as from several minor considerations which arise from the language and content of the book of Amos. First, there is the variety of speech types which Amos uses and which are also characteristic of the wisdom literature, such as Proverbs and Job. For example, Amos has a series of leading questions which teach in 3:3-6, 8. This is a favorite device found in wisdom, as in Job 6:5-6 and 8:11. Likewise, Proverbs 1 and 2 employs the numerical pair 3/4 used in Amos, as well as other number pairs of a like sequence (n/n + 1).

In addition to such features of style, Wolff points to certain themes found in Amos which seem to have their home in the wisdom tradition.

This is especially true of the fundamental assumptions which lie behind Amos's social critique. For example, in Amos 3:10a, the word *nekoha,* "straight," is used. This word occurs in neither the covenant tradition nor in the legal tradition but does occur several times in wisdom literature—Proverbs 8:8; 24:26. Likewise, the basic concepts of "justice/ righteousness" (*mishpat/sedaqa*), which lie at the foundation of Amos's message (Amos 5:7, 24; 6:12), are also found together in wisdom literature (Proverbs 16:8), but never in the legal or covenantal texts (clue 1c). In addition to this, some of the specific crimes which Amos mentions are paralleled by the same concern in the wisdom tradition. For example, compare Amos on false weights and measures in 8:5 with Proverbs 16:11 and 20:23, or Amos's evaluation of worship in 5:21-24 with Proverbs 21:3; 15:8; and 21:27 (clue 1d).

Finally, Wolff points out that Amos was from Tekoah, the very place from which Joab recruited a wise woman to trap king David into allowing Absalom to return home (2 Samuel 14). Amos could have come into contact with a wisdom tradition which was at home there. Wolff therefore concludes that Amos drew from the oral tradition of ancient Israelite tribal wisdom.[23]

It is striking that the words which Wolff singles out as characteristic of Amos's basic concerns and which he suggests link him with wisdom, could also tie Amos to Israel's royal ideology. That is, these words are political words. For example, *nekoha* (Amos 3:10a) is connected with the court in Isaiah 30:10 and 2 Samuel 15:3. The last reference is especially instructive in this regard, as Absalom pronounces the case right (*nekoha*) of those who are coming to the king to receive their due justice; but unfortunately for them, there is no judge from the king to hear their cases. By such judicial discernment and alacrity, Absalom shows himself worthy to be king instead of his father David. By presenting himself as a champion of justice, Israel is won over to his side.

Likewise, justice and righteousness are most frequently found in connection with the king, as for example 2 Samuel 8:15; 1 Kings 10:9; Psalm 72:1; and Isaiah 9:6; Jeremiah 23:3, 15; 33:15. The terms "justice" and "righteousness" express the epitome of what kingship was to be about, what it was that kings do when they exercise their power appropriately. It would appear, consequently, that Amos stands firmly within Israel's political tradition when he calls for the nation or the power elite to seek justice and righteousness.[24]

That it is exactly these two political words, justice and righteousness, which in fact do sum up Amos's message, can be seen from those statements in which Amos is calling the people to act positively. Justice and righteousness are his positive program for the nation (see 5:15, 24). As such, they form the positive antithesis to Amos's negative statements, his accusations like 2:6b. The crimes that Amos attacks are an indication of the absence of justice and righteousness.

Taking our clues from this, we need to investigate the background of the terms "justice" and "righteousness" in the political tradition in order to gain a proper perspective on Amos's accusations (clue 1c). First of all, in the Old Testament "righteousness" (*sedaqa*) has the connotation of being in accord with the proper norm. Thus, it is used for certifying that things are as they should be, that the proper order exists. For example, the term "righteous" is used to speak of weights and measurements which are "correct": this is, they conform to the norm (Leviticus 19:36; Deuteronomy 25:15). Likewise, in a legal context it means "innocent" or as a verb "to declare innocent" (Exodus 23:7; Deuteronomy 25:1). Again, to be "innocent" is to be in accord with the legal norms.

While "righteousness" has to do with being in accord with the norms, "justice" (*mishpat*) seems to indicate implementing or bringing about the right order, bringing things into line with the proper norms. For example Exodus 21:1 refers to the following laws ("These are the *mishpatim*—the laws"). The individual laws, if followed, will bring about the proper order. As such, then, the two terms often occur together as an expression for both right norms and proper implementation of these norms. In this usage as an expression of both proper goals and actions, the two terms together serve admirably as a catch phrase to summarize the internal political responsibility of the king, since the king is responsible to strive for a properly structured or ordered society through the appropriate means. Thus, the expression serves as a summary statement in 2 Samuel 8:15 which indicates David as being fully established as king and functioning appropriately as one. Likewise, in 2 Samuel 15:1-4, Absalom's not so indirect attack on his father's kingship strikes at the very heart of the responsibility and exercise of kingship by claiming David to be derelict in this matter.

That the matter of justice and righteousness was not only rhetoric in the sense of being an expression for "ruling," but goes to the very core of the political tradition and exercise of kingship can be vividly illustrated from ancient Near Eastern texts relating to kingship.[25] In the Mesopotamian political tradition, kingship was a gift of the gods, "They (the gods) had not yet set up a king for the beclouded people, no headband and crown had yet been fastened, no scepter had (yet) been studded with lapis lazuli ... scepter, crown, headband, and staff were (still) placed before Anu in heaven ... then, kingship descended from heaven."[26] The institution of kingship was a blessing bestowed by the gods on mankind, for it was kingship that enabled people to become truly civilized, since the time before kingship was a time of barbarism. "The men of early time knew not to eat bread, knew not to wear clothes, mankind went on hands and feet, ate grass as sheep, drank water from the ditches."[27] This early time was the time when the "crown was not worn."[28]

Not only was the origin of kingship a divine gift, but present kings were called by the gods to assume their thrones; they were called by divine grace to become king. Urukagina of Lagash writes, "... when Ningirsu, the foremost warrior of Enlil, gave the kingship of Lagash to Urukagina, and his hand had grasped him out of the multitude; then he (Ningirsu) enjoined upon him the (divine) decrees of former days."[29] Lipit-Istar says, "When An and Enlil had called Lipit-Istar, the wise shepherd, whose name had been pronoucned by Nunamir—to the princeship of the land, in order to establish justice in the land, to banish complaints, to turn back enmity and rebellion by force of arms, and to bring well-being to the Sumerians and Akkadians...."[30] Likewise Hammurabi, "... Anum and Enlil named me to promote the welfare of the people ... to cause justice to prevail in the land, to destroy the wicked and the evil, that the strong might not oppress the weak.... When Marduk commissioned me to guide the people aright, to direct the land, I established law and justice in the language of the land, thereby promoting the welfare of the people."[31]

Note that the call to be king was not for the self-aggrandizement of the person called, but to implement the proper order. Because of this responsibility, the kings were quick to point out that they had discharged the divine obligation of kingship to promote order and justice. As these quotes illustrate they testify of themselves that they did in fact carry out their responsibility to promote justice and to provide equity for the oppressed.

Hammurabi writes again in his law collection, "That the strong may not oppress the weak (and) so to give justice to the orphan and the widow, I have inscribed my precious words on my monument ... to judge the judgment of the land (and) decide the decision of the land

(and) so to give justice to the oppressed."[32]

Urukagina writes, "He (Urukagina) amnestied the 'citizens' of Lagash (literally, "the sons") who (were imprisoned because of) the debts (which they) had incurred, or (because of) the amounts (of grain claimed by the palace as its) due...."[33]

Lipit-Istar in his law code, "I Lipit-Istar ... established justice in Sumer and Akkad in accordance with the word of Enlil. Verily, in those days I procured ... the freedom of the sons and daughters of Nippur.... Verily in accordance with the true word of Utu, I caused Sumer and Akkad to hold to true justice. Verily, in accordance with the pronouncement of Enlil, I, Lipit Istar, the son of Enlil, abolished enmity and rebellion; made weeping, lamentations, outcries ... taboo; caused righteousness and truth to exist; brought well-being to the Sumerians and the Akkadians."[34]

Note how the theme of justice and truth or righteousness runs through the statements quoted above. In Akkadian, this was expressed by the two words, *kittum u misharum*. *Kittum* was the proper order or the norms to which things on earth ought to conform. This is much like *sedeq/sedaqa* (righteousness) in Hebrew. *Misharum* was justice, the proper implementation of these principles.[35] This is the counterpart of mishpat (justice) in the Bible.

It is also striking in these quotes how the treatment of the dispossessed and the oppressed is the sign that justice is being done, that indeed the king is carrying out his responsibilities. Note in particular the mention of the orphan and the widow as the epitome of this class. These too occur constantly in the Bible's calls for social justice.

This political tradition is also found north of Israel along the coast of Syria at Ugarit. In the *Aqhat Epic* we find the following picture of the king: "Thereupon Danel the Rephaite ... raised himself up, and sat at the entrance of the gate beside the corn-heaps which were on the threshing floor; he judged the cause of the widow and tried the case of the orphan."[36] Here judging the widow and orphan is the sign that the king is ruling as he ought. Again, in the *Keret Epic* we find the same ideology, although in slightly different guise. Here the crown prince Yassib wants his father to abdicate the throne, so he, Yassib, might be king instead. "The lad Yassib departed to (the presence of) his father, he entered (and) lifted up his voice and cried: 'Hear, pray, O munificent Keret, hearken and do thou lend an ear: as when raiders (?) make a raid (?) thou shalt be carried away and shalt dwell in the pit. Thou art brought down by thy failing power; thou canst not judge the cause of the widow, canst not try the case of the wretched, canst not put down them that despoil the children of the poor, canst not feed the orphan before thy face and the widow behind thy back, when thou art brother to a bed of sickness, friend to a bed of plague? Come down from the (throne of thy) kingdom that I may be king, from (the seat of) thy dominion that I may sit on it.' "[37] Yassib's argument is clearly that his father no longer deserves to be king since he can no longer do what a king needs to be able to do, namely, promote justice and equity for the dispossessed. Note the great similarity between this argument and that of another crown prince, Absalom, discussed above (2 Samuel 15:1-4).

From this very brief survey of some ancient Near Eastern material we can see, first, that the concept that the king was to promote a proper order in his society was at the heart of kingship ideology. To be a legitimate king meant to promote justice, so the king gave an account to the gods that indicated his dedication to the cause of the poor and oppressed. Likewise, when this was not being done, kings were called upon to resign. Second, whether this was in fact being done could be measured against the lot of the poor and dispossessed, such as the orphan and widow. This class was the test of the king's success or failure as a ruler. Therefore, they played a major role in the political tradition and their treatment became the key for an assessment of how a particular government or society was doing in terms of justice.[38]

Having seen what lay at the core of the king's domestic duties and how his performance was judged, what tools did the king have to discharge his responsibilities? How was he expected to promote a just order for the oppressed? There appear to be three major ways which kings had to bring about social change or to promote the cause of the oppressed in order to establish a more equitable state of affairs.

The first law, which seems the most obvious, is in some ways also the most problematical. The king obviously had the major responsibility for both the formulation and propagation of laws and their enforcement. While law seems to us today as the normal, legitimate avenue open to governments for the regulation of society, it is not entirely clear what the purpose and status of legal collections were in the ancient Near East. This is for several reasons. First of all, taking the law collection of Hammurabi as a case in point, this law collection seems to have been almost entirely ignored in the actual practice of law. In the day-to-day regulation of affairs as we see them reflected in the contemporary legal documents, the law collection was neither particularly followed, cited, nor appealed to. What its actual status and authority were for practice is uncertain.[39] Likewise, in Israel it has long been noted that the practice of the people as reflected in the narrative texts does not follow the prescriptions of the legal material. There appears to be a gap between the law collections and the actual norms of practice.[40]

Second, the laws were evidently deposited in the temple, rather than placed in open public places. As such, they appear to be an attempt to show the gods that Hammurabi, for example, is discharging his divinely appointed duty of providing equity for the citizenry. They may be viewed more as royal apologia to the gods, than as legal programs to be promulgated or enforced in the social realm. It is probably in this light that we are to judge the lines of the code (see above) which say that people may come and read the code to see how their case ought to be decided. That this was in fact ever done, we have no evidence. The claims made by Hammurabi in his law collection notwithstanding, his laws were probably never intended to provide for the oppressed.[41]

Besides the sponsoring of law collections, the king could actively enter into day-to-day governing through the legal system. He could do this on an *ad hoc* basis, so to speak. People with cases would write to him directly or indirectly, asking him to settle their cases for them. For example, we have many letters addressed to Hammurabi requesting his decision in a matter. Likewise, in the Bible kings are sought to provide legal decisions, especially in cases where the poor are being oppressed by the powerful as in 2 Samuel 12, where Nathan presents the case of a poor man whose single sheep was taken by a rich man with a large flock. Or the king was sought where the application of the law would lead to injustice since the law may work against the dispossessed. In 2 Samuel 14, the woman of Tekoa presented such a case to David. The case involved a widow and the murder of one of her sons, which might lead to the loss of her lone remaining son. Thus, the king was sought as one responsible to uphold equity for the poor against both the rich and powerful and the rote application of the law.[42]

While by becoming involved with actual cases the king could actively promote equity, the effect of this would only extend to the limited number of cases he could actually adjudicate. Also, the king was only treating symptoms rather than the disease, since deciding cases involved no change of structure to alleviate the causes of social oppression. The king, however, did have at his disposal a legislative means of promoting equity in the society as a whole, the *reform act*. The king in Mesopotamia could decree a reform (*misharum* or equity, also later *andurraru*, decrees) which released debtors from debts, freed slaves, returned property to previous owners, fixed prices for commodities. The text of several of these reform acts are not only known, but from contemporary economic and legal documents we know that they actually went into effect. The reform act thus appears to have been the major policy instrument which was available to the king for the regulation of society and for the promotion of equity. By these acts the king was moving society toward the social norms which were to be realized—that is, justice and righteousness. The significance of these reform documents as compared with the law collections is that they had the force of law, they actually regulated practice at least for a while—and thus were regarded as having authority and binding force.[43]

While we have no actual descriptions of a king instituting such a reform in Israel, it has been suggested that several kings in fact did just that.[44] This has been inferred from the phrase, "they did right in God's sight," as applied to Asa (1 Kings 15:11) and Jehoshaphat (1 Kings 22:43). Since Asa and Jehoshaphat did not abolish the high places, this phrase cannot refer to that act of religious reform; instead it applies to implementing a social reform act. These two kings ruled about a century before Amos. The phrase is also used of Hezekiah (2 Kings 18:3) and Josiah (2 Kings 22:22).

In the legal material of the Bible we find Israel's own reform legislation—the sabbatical and jubilee regulations. These two economic reform acts appear to have important parallels with the Mesopotamian material just mentioned above. As such, they embody the same political traditions. As reform acts they intend to establish a more just order, especially to promote the welfare of the poor and of the oppressed. This general ideology of the reform acts would appear to serve as Amos' criterion of what crimes to mention. Since it is exactly the *'ebyon* (needy) who are both the concern of Amos and of the reform texts, Amos focuses on crimes which oppress those whom reform legislation was to protect.[45]

The plea of Amos for justice and righteousness is a positive plea to provide equity for the dispossessed; it is a plea to promote the norms which kingship through reform legislation was intended to promote. We can see how in the political tradition both his negative judgments and his positive exhortations form two sides of the same coin—they are based on the political ideology of the reform documents. Given this background in the political tradition, the reason why Amos does not seem to draw in any extensive way on Israel's religious traditions in his critique of the nation is apparently because his critique is political, being based on the dominant social-political ideology.

Placing Amos in this common political tradition of Israel and the ancient Near East may also explain some of the affinities between Amos and wisdom, since the wisdom material is itself identified with the court and political thought. Wolff's notion that Amos represented ancient tribal wisdom has indeed been criticized for this very reason; the concerns of wisdom literature do not seem to be tribal or agrarian, but rather are those of the court and urban society. Consequently, we find a common emphasis on justice and righteousness in both Amos and wisdom, where wisdom is concerned exactly with the exercise of kingship (see Proverbs 16:12; 20:28; 29:4, 14).[46] The fact that Amos is from Tekoa places him near Jerusalem since Tekoa is only some 10 to 12 miles from the ancient capital city. If, in fact, there was a wisdom tradition at Tekoa as Wolff surmises, this would link Tekoa even more closely to political interests and circles.

In summary, from an examination of the conceptual tradition behind the key terms in Amos, justice and righteousness, we are led to a political tradition in which these concepts were deeply imbedded. This finding further substantiates the results of our lexical analysis of "needy" ('ebyon) and places Amos's message in a much broader context. In this context, Amos appears as one who calls for changes on the basis of well-recognized political and social norms. Since these were generally recognized norms, Amos could assume that the wrongs he mentions would be immediately recognized as contrary to what society should be promoting. Amos's critique must be seen as primarily a political and social one. He stands within the political tradition and is in agreement with its basic norms.[47]

Matthew 5:38-42

As we have seen previously,[48] much of the material we have on this fifth antithesis is also found in Luke 6:29-30. Luke has three instances which are the same as in Matthew—being struck on the cheek (Matthew, right cheek), being sued for one's cloak, and being asked to loan something (clue 1d). Luke has one additional case, the one concerning someone carrying off something belonging to you, while Matthew has two cases not in Luke, being forced to go one mile, and lending to one asking. Due to the close similarity in wording, it is generally assumed that Matthew and Luke shared a common source whose wording was fixed (clue 2). The name given to this source is Q from the German word *Quelle* which means "source." Q was evidently a collection of the sayings of Jesus. Thus, in our unit, Matthew 5:39b-42, the author was dependent on a fixed source which he had before him and from which he copied these sayings.[49]

Now attempts have been made to go behind the text to ask what tradition or streams of material were taken up and incorporated into Q (clue 3). In embarking on this hypothetical journey of literary and tradition reconstruction, it is noted that the cases in 39b-42 do not appear to be all of the same kind. Verses 39b-41 belong to one group, while verse 42 with its two sayings seems to belong to another. These two groups can be distinguished in three ways. First of all, the situations in the two groups are really quite different. In verse 39b-41 the person addressed is in a subordinated inferior position. In each case someone does something harmful to him—a blow on the cheek, a lawsuit, or forced labor. In verse 42, however, the addressee is in the superior position; the other person comes as a supplicant. The supplicant effects no injury; he merely asks for something. Now while the first three examples are thought to illustrate the principle of not taking revenge, the last two clearly do not—what is there to revenge in these two cases? Thus, the last two cases appear to be out of harmony with the other three cases and clash with the principle supposedly being illustrated.[50]

The two groups also differ slightly in form, the last two cases being briefer. Finally, while the first three examples seem to differ from both ordinary common sense and Jewish tradition, the last two seem to be related to both Jewish tradition and secular wisdom; see, for example, their parallels to Proverbs 28:27 and Sirach 4:4-5 and 29:1-2. They lack a unique quality.[51]

The validity of reconstructing originally separate origins for these two sets of examples hinges on the argument that verse 42 does not illustrate the principle of not taking revenge while 39b-41 does. The question, however, is whether this is the principle being illustrated in 39b-41.[52] We have seen above that it is more likely that Jesus is teaching a new kind of reciprocity, that is, not responding as people normally would do in these cases. The cases in verse 42 do illustrate this principle well. It would seem, then, that verse 42 rather than being a disturbing element serves as a very valuable clue as to the meaning of the passage.

The passage is not really about revenge, but about the reciprocity of love.

The fact that verse 42 finds an echo in the Old Testament and the Jewish tradition should not surprise us in the teachings of Jesus. Jesus was a Jew who lived his whole life in the context of the Jewish nation and religion. Almost all the people he associated with as well as the people he taught were Jewish.

Likewise, Matthew seems to reflect Jewish tradition in his use of his sources. In the list of examples given in this passage, Matthew has kept the teaching of going the second mile, when forced to go one, while it is absent in Luke. This is probably because this example, at home in Palestine, communicated to Matthew's audience or was in line with his viewpoint, while it would not have been understood by Luke's audience. Again, in the example of being struck on the cheek, Matthew specifies right cheek, while Luke only has cheek. Here again the right cheek would have meant something to Matthew's audience acquainted with Jewish law, while it would not have done so for Luke's.[53]

A further problem is raised by verses 38-39a, the antithesis proper. Since this saying did not occur in Luke (Q),, the issue is, did Matthew inherit this antithesis or did he formulate the saying as an antithesis (clue 2). That is, is the antithesis formulation the result of Matthew's editorial activity, or did he take it over from his tradition? This question is disputed. One view holds that antitheses 1, 2, and 4 (verses 21, 27, and 33) were in the tradition which Matthew received. That is, Matthew found some teachings of Jesus already in the antithetic form which we find today in the New Testament. To these three antitheses Matthew added three more by combining originally independent sayings, with an antithetic teaching (as in verses 38-39a).

Why do scholars divide the antitheses into two sets, with antitheses 1, 2, and 4 in one group and 3, 5, and 6 in another? There are three major reasons which have been given for this division. First, the formulation of the first group is different: the thesis is negative and the antithesis extends what is prohibited by the thesis. For example, in the first antithesis; thesis—you shall not kill; antithesis—you shall not even be angry. In the second group, however (3, 5, and 6), the thesis is stated positively like "an eye for an eye" and the antithesis is negative, "do not resist evil," being an abrogation of the law cited. Thus, in the first group, Jesus could be seen as extending the law, but in the second group, he appears to be annulling the law.[54]

Second, it is argued that the antitheses in the first group could not have stood by themselves as independent teachings since they make sense only in relationship to the thesis. In the second group the antitheses could stand by themselves as independent teachings.[55] Third, it is claimed that in the first group the antitheses do not have the proverbial form of the second group.[56]

Against this others have argued that all of the antithetic formulations were joined together by Matthew.[57] That is, the antitheses even in the first group could have been independent of their thesis at one time. In number four this is particularly clear, since James 5:12 has the same teaching about swearing oaths, but without the antithetic formulation of the teaching as here. Thus we may assume that there is no clear criterion for deciding which antithesis Matthew received from tradition and which sayings he cast in that form. Conversely, they all could have been received by Matthew from the traditions available to him.[58]

Wherever in the chain of tradition one places the formulation of 5:38-39a, what does seem evident is that Matthew did not receive 5:38-42 as an antithesis plus focal instances, but rather combined two separate traditions to compose the unit as we have it today in the text. Operating on this assumption we can infer that Matthew joined these two together either to make the antithesis clearer or to give the rule behind the examples. This reconstruction of what Matthew did with his traditions confirms and emphasizes what we have already seen—the examples are to illustrate what is meant by "not resisting the evil (one)." To not resist means to respond to wrongs not by the reciprocity of justice (tit for tat) but by the reciprocity of love—even if it is to your own loss and injury.

Romans 13:1-7

Romans 13:1-7 is a passage which has suffered misinterpretation because it has not been understood within the tradition in which Paul is writing. Although these words may appear striking, in fact Paul is presenting a traditional view of the state, a view which has its roots in the Old Testament (clue 1c).

In the Old Testament we find rulers called the servants of God; they are his instruments which carry out his plans upon the earth.[59] That a king like David should be regarded as God's servant (see for example 2 Samuel 3:18) does not surprise us. However, it was not only the Israelite kings but also foreign kings who were called servants of God and regarded as the instruments of his purposes. This was so even though these kings were destroying God's own people. Thus we find Nebuchadnezzar called "servant of God" in Jeremiah (25:9; 27:6; 43:10). The destruction he brings on Judah is consequently seen as an act of God, as in Jeremiah 21:7, 10. Earlier, the Assyrian king was regarded as God's instrument in Isaiah (10:5-6). The Persian king Cyrus even receives from God the title of "messiah" (Isaiah 45:1).

This is part of the general belief that God allots the rule of mankind to whom he wills. The kings that be, owe their thrones and success to God. This is clearly stated in Daniel 2:21: "He changes times and seasons; he removes kings and sets up kings; he gives wisdom to the wise and knowledge to those who have understanding." (In 2:37-38 the same idea is expressed.) That God allots political dominion to whom he wills runs like a litany through Daniel 4 (see verses 17, 25, and 32). This same idea is expressed again in the Wisdom of Solomon 6:1-11. In the Old Testament we have, then, a tradition that political power was exercised under the sovereignty of God, and specific kings as a result owed their kingship and their success as kings to God's favor.

This notion that God is sovereign over the political process is a part of a larger picture which sees God as ultimately sovereign over all realms of human existence. As Isaiah 45:5-7 states, "I am the Lord, and there is no other, besides me there is no God; I gird you, though you do not know me, that men may know, from the rising of the sun and from the west, that there is none besides me; I am the Lord, and there is no other. I form light and create darkness, I make weal [shalom] and create woe [evil], I am the Lord, who do all these things." Political power would be a specific example of God's general providence.

Now, it is not necessarily thought that God ruled over the nations directly, but rather there were intermediaries between God and the nations. These intermediaries take two forms. In the older form the idea is that God has allotted to the nations other gods—as in Deuteronomy 32:8, "When the Most High gave to the nations their inheritance, when he separated the sons of men, he fixed the bounds of the peoples according to the number of the sons of God." This same concept is found again in Deuteronomy 4:19 and 29:25. In later times the intermediaries became angels; and each nation seems to have had a divine being which represented it. These angels also fought among themselves. The outcome of these battles is reflected in the varying fates of their nation on earth. Daniel provides us with this view of the matter, "The prince of the kingdom of Persia withstood me twenty-one days; but Michael, one of

the chief princes, came to help me, so I left him there with the prince of
the kingdom of Persia.... Then he said, 'Do you know why I have
come to you? But now I will return to fight against the prince of Persia;
and when I am through with him, lo, the prince of Greece will come' "
(Daniel 10:13, 20). When Michael, who has charge of Israel, becomes
dominant, then Israel too will also experience a change in its fortunes:
"At that time shall arise Michael, the great prince who has charge of
your people. And there shall be a time of trouble, such as never has been
since there was a nation till that time; but at that time your people shall
be delivered, every one whose name shall be found written in the book"
(Daniel 12:1).[60]

Now the fact that kings owe their political power and prosperity to
God's providence, even though perhaps indirectly through intermediaries, does not mean that they were immune from God's judgment. Because they were kings, they received the responsibility of kingship, to
govern justly and remain humble. They themselves were responsible for
their office and its conduct; they were not autonomous. This responsibility of kingship meant accountability for how that responsibility was
manifested. Thus, in the very passage where Assyria is singled out for
mention as God's instrument, God's judgment against her is also mentioned (Isaiah 10:12, 16). Likewise, the divine beings will be judged because they too did not promote justice and righteousness with their
power (Psalm 82). This concept that political leadership given by God
brings accountability before God is perhaps best expressed in the
Wisdom of Solomon 6:1-11.

> Listen therefore, O kings, and understand; learn, O judges of the ends of the
> earth. Give ear, you that rule over multitudes, and boast of many nations. For
> your dominion was given you from the Lord, and your sovereignty from the
> Most High, who will search out your works and inquire into your plans. Be-
> cause as servants of his kingdom you did not rule rightly, nor keep the law, nor
> walk according to the purpose of God, he will come upon you terribly and
> swiftly, because severe judgment falls on those in high places. For the lowliest
> man may be pardoned in mercy, but mighty men will be mightily tested. For
> the Lord of all will not stand in awe of any one, nor show deference to greatness;
> because he himself made both small and great, and he takes thought for all
> alike. But a strict inquiry is in store for the mighty. To you then, O monarchs,
> my words are directed, that you may learn wisdom and not transgress. For they
> will be made holy who observe holy things in holiness, and those who have
> been taught them will find a defense. Therefore set your desire on my words;
> long for them, and you will be instructed.

That divine power or will stood behind the throne of the ruler was of course not a unique idea to Israel. As discussed above in connection with Amos and the political tradition in Mesopotamia, it was held that the king owed his throne to the favor of a god or gods. Likewise, he had responsibilities to carry out as king, to do justice and righteousness. Kingship was viewed as embedded in a wider cosmic setting, so that what happened on earth was a reflection of what happened in the heavens amongst the gods. The ascendance of Babylon, for example, was the result of the dominance of Marduk, the god of Babylon, among the gods. The rise of Assyria, meant the hegemony of Asshur, the god of Assyria, in the divine pantheon.

This close connection between the affairs of the gods and the fates of men led naturally to the notion that rulers lived under the shadow, so to speak, of the gods or a god in particular and represented this divine will or order on earth. This resulted in a chain of command or pyramid of power, with the king under the gods, the government officials under the king, and the subjects under them. In this view of things, the emperor and his agents would be the agents of the god or gods to bring about the divine order on earth.

This political tradition, which has its roots in the ancient Near East, was taken over and incorportaed into the Hellenistic view of government and spread through the Roman Empire. By the time of Paul, both Jew and Gentile would have acknowledged that the government operated under divine authority; that the rulers which were, reflected the divine arrangement; and that their officers were agents of the divine will to institute the appropriate order.[61]

Paul seems to have taken this tradition up into his own thought. This apparently is what he means when he speaks of the powers (see chapter 4 for a discussion of this word). For Paul, however, the powers are seen as negative, as being in rebellion against God. He speaks of powers as ignorant in 1 Corinthians 2:6-8, "Yet among the mature we do impart wisdom, although it is not a wisdom of this age or of the rulers of this age, who are doomed to pass away. But we impart a secret and hidden wisdom of God, which God decreed before the ages for our glorification. None of the rulers of this age understood this; for if they had, they would not have crucified the Lord of glory." Here the very close connection which exists between "powers" and human government is clear. Indeed, it is difficult to distinguish whether Paul has primarily in mind the earthly authorities or the divine powers which stand above them.

In 2 Corinthians 4:4, he speaks of the god of this world which blinds people to the gospel. Colossians and Ephesians especially speak of the powers as the opposite of the Christian realm, as in Colossians 1:13: "He has delivered us from the dominion of darkness and transferred us to the kingdom of his beloved Son." The word translated "dominion" here is really the word "power." Here powers are negative, the controllers of the realm from which the Christian has been transferred. Likewise, Paul sometimes speaks of the "elemental forces" as forces which control people's lives outside of Christ (Galatians 4:1-11; Colossians 2:8).[62]

For Paul, although these powers seem to act independently and are opposed to the gospel and the kingdom of Christ, yet paradoxically Christ is the head of the powers. Philippians 2:9-10 testifies to the exaltation and preeminence of Christ in these terms, "Therefore God has highly exalted him and bestowed on him the name which is above every name, that at the name of Jesus every knee should bow, in heaven and on earth and under the earth." (See also Colossians 1:15-17; 2:15-23; Ephesians 1:21-23). Christ's victory over the powers, however, is not complete, since Paul depicts the struggle as yet continuing in 1 Corinthians 15:24-28. The present can be seen as a time in which the struggle with the powers is in process although their defeat is sure.

Since the battle is now, Christians and the church are exhorted to be vigilant and to stand firm (Ephesians 6:12 and 3:10). In 1 Corinthians 6:3 Paul reminds the Corinthians that they will some day judge the angels. Since this is the assured future, Christians in the present are to live in light of this future. In Corinth this means that the church should settle disputes internally rather than taking them to the secular law courts.[63]

In summary, for Paul the present situation of the Christian seems to be a situation of struggle, but with ultimate victory assured. The powers still function and have authority, but they are on the wane. Over against them stands Christ, the head of the church, who leads the struggle against them and will emerge victorious. It seems that in light of Christ, Paul has relegated the powers to a largely negative role, one which sees them in opposition to Christ and in rebellion against God. This would in turn mean that earthly governments too would share in this estrangement from God. As a result for Paul these spiritual powers cannot legitimate government, as they would have done in the Hellenistic tradition. On the contrary, since the state stood under these estranged powers, they also stand under God's judgment, perhaps even in a heightened sense.

Finally, we should look at the parallel passages to Romans 13:1-7 in the New Testament (clue le). Three passages to seem to form clear parallels: 1 Timothy 2:1-2; Titus 3:1; and 1 Peter 2:13-17. All four passages recommend submission to the governing authorities. First Peter 2:13-17 is set in the context of a series of rules for behavior, for citizens toward government, slaves to masters, wives to husbands, and husbands to wives. In both 1 Peter and 1 Timothy there seems to be a missonary motive, since by being obedient citizens, evil reports about the Christians will be squelched.

Romans 13:1-7, however, is unique in one regard: it enjoins the paying of taxes. The other passages talk in general terms of being submissive to government, but in Romans, Paul makes a very specific application to the paying of taxes. This modification of the tradition by the introduction of taxes would seem to indicate Paul's main focus. Paul is using a broad tradition about government, in order to support a specific practical action, tax payment. This finding reinforces what we have noted before about the importance of taxes in the passage.

To summarize, what can we learn from the tradition and Paul's use of it which will help us interpret Romans 13:1-7 more accurately? First, we have seen that appointment by God also places responsibility on the government; God's raising of a ruler to power does not mean that whatever the ruler does is God's will, but rather that government is seen as an instrument of God's providence and at the same time responsible to God's judgment. Since Paul is not addressing government officials in Romans 13, but Christian citizens, he does not mention government's responsibility.

This notion of the government's responsibility and accountability to God leads naturally to the idea, as we have seen, that rulers and government are judged by God. Since they do not necessarily obey God's will, God's judgment will come to rest upon them. Paul extends, as does the Old Testament, this judgment beyond the earthly government to the divine realm. These powers too live under the judgment of God. In short, in the context of his political tradition Paul would say that government operates under God, but what they do may in fact be against God. In the end they will be judged on the basis of their rebellious deeds (see the Old Testament examples quoted above.)

An analogy may help us understand this way of thinking. Accord-

ing to the Bible (Genesis 1), God created the natural order good and
declared it good. Yet not all that happens in nature is good; floods, earth-
quakes, volcanoes, and other natural disasters may be very evil things, by
taking the lives of many innocent people and causing great human suffering. Nor is this natural evil to be seen necessarily as the expression of
God's will, although he created nature and his providence overarches all.
Likewise, government may be good, rulers may come to power by divine
providence. But how governments operate, how rulers rule, may indeed
be evil and against the divine will. Thus, when Paul says that the powers
are appointed by God, he says only half of what can be said; the other
half is that they also do evil and they will be judged by God for this. We
must keep this part of Paul's tradition in mind when interpreting
Romans 13:1-7.

In applying this to "submit," we can infer that Paul intended this
conditionally. For the Christian, furthermore, an appeal to the spiritual
powers does not legitimate the state nor its actions, since these powers
themselves are in rebellion against God and under divine judgment. If a
Christian participates in those deeds which will bring judgment upon
the state, he will share in that judgment.[64]

Chapter 6

From Composition to Collection: Transmission and Redaction Analysis

6.00 Transmission

In our age of mass publishing we do not think a great deal about how written works are transmitted or how they survive. These seem like such easy and natural processes. An author writes something down, copy is prepared, the work is published by the thousands of copies, and many of these copies find their way into libraries, both public and personal, where they are preserved.

Transmission in biblical times was quite different in several respects. First, of course, all documents had to be copied by hand. There were not as many copies and they were not as widely distributed as today. Their existence was more precarious than today's works.

Second, there were not many libraries or archives in which documents of a literary nature could be placed for safekeeping. Outside of the royal court (which kept the annals of the kingdom) and the temple (which kept the scrolls of the law), documents probably faced an uncertain future.

Third, and this is the major emphasis of this phase of analysis, many of the books of the Bible are a result of collection rather than the original work of a single author. Just as we saw in the last chapter that the author of an individual unit may have taken up into his composition several documents, so also the "author" of a biblical book may have drawn either on a whole collection of units (a "source") or on individual independent units which he then arranged to form the present book.[1] Thus, when we talk about "authorship" in biblical times, it can have at least two senses; the author of the orginal unit, or the author of the completed work of which the unit is now a part. In this latter sense authorship may be mainly a process of collection and arrangement. An illustration would be the "author" of the book of Psalms or the book of Proverbs.

This means that before these original units were taken up into the books in which we find them, they circulated either independently or in small collections or cycles of stories. It is this period in the life of a unit which transmission analysis investigates: what was the journey of a unit from its composition until its integration into the larger work in which we find it today?

That indeed there is a process of transmission behind the biblical materials can be seen from Luke 1:1-3, which we have examined above. Luke received his materials from others, from eyewitnesses, and those who had set down accounts of Jesus before him. He then took this material, organized it, and from it fashioned the book of Luke. But who were those who transmitted the material, where was it transmitted, and how was it used before Luke? These are the questions to which we seek answers in this phase.

Likewise, behind the book of Amos, there must have been a similar process. Amos spoke his words in a variety of contexts and occasions. But the book as we have it today is the work of later collectors who edited and arranged his speeches. For example, Amos 1:1 was added by a later editor to place the words in their historical setting. Most prophetic books begin in the same way by identifying the king or kings during whose reign the prophet was active.[1a] Likewise, in Amos 7:10-17, we find biographical material about Amos written by another. This material was obviously joined to the words of Amos by an editor or collector.

How the prophet's words were preserved and transmitted we do not really know, but from Isaiah 8:16, "Bind up the testimony, seal the teaching among my disciples," we get a glimpse perhaps of what might take place. A prophet may have had followers or disciples.[2] It would be among these that the prophet's teachings would be preserved and transmitted. Finally, the book of the prophet's sayings would emerge with additional material as we find it today in the Bible. It is this process of transmission, from the prophet to book so to speak, which we analyze in this step of our study.

When we probe the transmission history of a unit, we do so in order to discover the various ways in which the material was used and understood—what did the unit mean to the people who transmitted it? In searching for answers to this question, two ideas need to be kept in mind. First, what is used is not lost, but what is not used is lost. Therefore, we must speculate on how the material functioned for the transmitters, how did they use it? Second, people retain things in which they have a stake, things that are important for them and their interests. Thus, by inferring who would have been interested in this material, we can gain a glimpse of who was responsible for the unit's transmission.[3]

In order to interpret a passage properly it is important to understand the transmission history for several reasons. First, how the passage was used and what it meant to its carriers is a valuable clue as to the meaning of a passage when it was taken up by the author responsible for the total work where the unit is now found. Second, passages were not only transmitted but also were shaped in the process, since the use to which the material was put as well as the interests of those who handed it on could result in changes and additions to the unit over time. These changes may have alrady been discovered in compositional analysis, where additions and glosses were found in the analysis of a unit's structure. This material, which accrued to the basic unit during its period of transmission, should be fitted into the history of transmission. These additions also preserve valuable clues for the why and who of transmission.[4]

Since transmission analysis investigates the processes and developments which fall between the composition of the individual unit and its final placement in its present larger literary context, in cases where the author of the unit and of the entire work are the same, we have no transmission history. This means, in practice, that for many passages, indeed even for whole books, the question of transmission does not arise.

6.01 **Axiom:** **Since the author of the unit may be different than the author of the work where it is now found, we need to trace the history of the unit from time of composition to time of incorporation into the work. Knowing this journey allows us to understand the significance of the material when the author incorporated it.**

6.02 *Procedures*

What are the signs which point one to the transmission history of a unit? First of all, of course, it must be determined if this is an appropriate question—is the author of the unit different from the author of the work within which the unit stands? If so, then there is a period of transmission; if not, then there was not.

The following clues are the signs that point to the unit's history of development:

A. *Analysis*

1. Was the passage as a whole part of a source or layer of tradition (such as Q) which has now been taken up into the book? If so, then the history of the transmission of this source needs to be reconstructed. This can be done using clues 2-4 below, but applying them to the source as a whole rather than to the individual passage only.

2. Are there internal tensions within the unit which indicate the history of the unit's transmission by pointing to compositional stages through which the unit passed? You have already collected the data for this assessment in the analysis of the unit's structure under compositional analysis.

3. Compare the unit with other units of the same form; differences may indicate changes made during transmission. These changes may signal how the unit was used, since the form of language is very closely related to how it was used or what it was intended to accomplish.

4. Compare the unit with other passages having similar material; do differences here indicate different transmission histories? Differences in content may well suggest the outlook of those transmitting the material (the omission of the Bathsheba story in Chronicles, for example).

B. *Synthesis*

1. What changes took place during transmission? Did the changes take place all at one time?

2. From the above clues focus on answering the following general questions. How did the unit manage to survive—why did changes take place? Specific questions may help to focus observations here:
   a. What forces or values are reflected in the changes? What can be inferred from this about its transmission?
   b. Who would have had an interest in its survival? Why would they value it?
   c. Why would they have preserved it; how would they have used the unit?

6.03 *Illustrations*
Genesis 12:10-20

This story is usually seen as part of a much larger strand of material which was taken up in the formation of the first four books of the Bible. This strata or cycle of stories is usually called "J" after the name Jahwe, which is the German form of Yahweh (used in English). Jahwe (or Yahweh) is the name used for God in these stories. Two other strands of tradition are also found in Genesis through Numbers: P which stands for a priestly source, and E for material which is named after Elohim, the word this source uses for God in Genesis.[5] The J strata of material is obviously not the final form of the Pentateuch. Thus, we need to consider the transmission of this J strata until the end of the processes of the composition of the Pentateuch, until its combination with the other sources.

In brief, the usual sketch of J's transmission history goes something like this.[6] J, as an independent source, was first combined with the E material. This JE combination served as the basic Israelite narrative of its past. Later, Deuteronomy was added, which while possibly affecting the end of the JE story, assumed JE's account of the patriarchs. Finally, the basic document JE with Deuteronomy was supplemented with the P material. This priestly material sometimes was amalgamated with J material, sometimes supplemented it with additional information, and sometimes added new information and stories. With this recasting of the material the Pentateuch reached its final form. Genesis 12:10-20 seems to have been left largely untouched by these later transmission and editorial stages. At least there does not appear to be any material within the story which is the result of this process of transmission, addition, and adaptation.[7]

This transmission history gives us little additional information which helps us interpret the story of Genesis 12:10-20. There are several reasons for this. First, the J material seems to have provided the basic outline for our present Pentateuch. Later editions have not modified this plan greatly, at least in Genesis. Second, the J material has come down to us in relatively organic form which, along with E material, still retains its basic outline and purpose.[8]

Amos 2:6-16

This oracle forms the last in a series of oracles addressed to various nations, all of which follow the same pattern: "Thus says Yahweh, for three transgressions of . . . (nation's name), because of four, I will not turn it back." This beginning is followed by the mention of a crime: "because they. . . ." In Hebrew this phrase is an infinitival phrase. However, Amos usually begins his citation of crimes with participles—as in Amos 4:1, for example. This modification of his language is due to fitting this saying to the set structure of the series of oracles which, as we have just noted, begins with an infinitival phrase. Was this adaptation done by Amos or by a later editor who took an originally independent oracle of doom against Israel and placed it in this series of oracles against foreign nations? There is no necessary reason to suppose that it was not Amos himself who formed this messenger speech of doom to fit this pattern.[9]

However, within the speech itself, in verses 9-12, the problem is more acute. As we have observed above, the interjection of a historical résumé into an oracle of doom is without parallel elsewhere in Amos (clue 3). On the other hand, we have seen that in Kings, the oracles of doom did have a historical flashback enumerating the acts of God's grace to the addressee of the oracle. The purpose of these, as also apparently here in Amos, was to intensify the accusations.

In any case, the grammatical changes and the backtracking in the historical sequence which begins in verse 10 leads us to consider that these verses might be a later addition which was inserted in the course of transmission by an editor in order to expand on the historical flashback in verse 9 (clue 2). To substantiate this point of view, we need to look elsewhere to see if there are links between verses 10-12 and another circle of tradition. If there are, we need to search elsewhere in the book to see if there are other examples of editorial activity which are parallel to what we find here (clue 1).[10]

It has been argued that these verses are related to the Deuteronomic circle of tradition.[11] The basis of this argument is that the vocabulary of these verses is much like what we find in Deuteronomy and the Deuteronomic history. For example, in verse 10, "bring up" (*'alah*) is used for the Exodus from Egypt. It is used in a similar manner in 1 Samuel 8:8, where the gift of the land is included, and in Deuteronomy 20:1 and 1 Samuel 10:18, where the Exodus is linked with conflict against Israel's enemies. These contexts and connotations are also what we find here in Amos. Likewise the phrase, "I led you forty years in the wilderness," is identical to Deuteronomy 29:5a (see also Deuteronomy 8:2). "To possess the land" is a Deuteronomic cliché (Deuteronomy 2:31, 9:4-5, 11:31, etc.). The use of the verb, "raise up" (*qûm*) for a prophet (verse 11) is found also in Deuteronomy 18:15, 18. Amos himself uses another verb when speaking of himself in 7:15. There he says that Yahweh "took him" (*laqach*).

Others have objected to these arguments, pointing to what is unique in these verses: nowhere else are prophet and Nazarite joined together. Also, that "bring up" is Deuteronomic is disputed, since it also occurs in Exodus 20:2, Micah 6:4, and Amos 9:7. Likewise, Hosea has the notion of a succession of prophets (see Hosea 6:5 and 12:10). These elements, it is argued, could all come from the time of Amos. These arguments against Deuteronomic connections are not as strong as those for it. Uniqueness does not provide any evidence of relationships one way or the other; the use of "bring up" in its particular nuance here does seem Deuteronomistic;[12] and Deuteronomy also expresses the notion of a succession of prophets in chapter 18.

Can we find other examples of Deuteronomistic editorial activity in Amos? There do in fact seem to be such examples. Amos 1:1, which must surely have been added by a later editor in its present form, shows a dual dating of the kings of Judah and Israel which we also find in the books of Kings. Since this history is considered as the work of Deuteronomistic redactors, the heading here in Amos is also considered to have come from this circle.[13] If this is accepted, then it would appear that at some time in the history of the book of Amos it was transmitted in Deuteronomistic circles. Did this stage of transmission leave other marks on Amos's message? Many scholars believe so. For example, in Amos 3:7 we find a straightforward declaration, "For Lord Yahweh does not do anything except he has revealed his counsel to his servants the prophets." This statement interrupts a series of rhetorical questions and thereby appears intrusive in its present context. Its language appears related to Deuteronomic literature in some respects. "Servant" is a familiar title for Yahweh's prophets in the Deuteronomistic literature (see, for example, 2 Kings 17:13, 23; 21:10; 24:2).[14] Furthermore, the idea expressed here is very Deuteronomic: a prophet gives an oracle which is then fulfilled in history. This is the function of prophecy, to relay God's plans to mankind and thereby warn them.[15] We see this pattern in 2 Kings 17:12 and following verses. The evidence of a literary break coupled with a linguistic and theological connection to the Deuteronomic literature seems to warrant the conclusion that here again we find traces of a Deuteronomistic editing of the material in Amos.

Returning to Amos 2:6-16, it would seem probable that the verses 10-12 bear witness to a stage of transmission in Deuteronomic circles. In this stage of transmission, the words of Amos found an audience in the Southern Kingdom of Judah. Thus the words of God to the Northern

Kingdom of Israel also became applied to the Southern Kingdom of Judah and took on a renewed vitality in this new context. Since on account of these sins God's judgment had come upon Israel, would not the same fate befall Judah because of these same sins? Because of this continued relevancy, the words are used and thus preserved.

Matthew 5:33-42 and Romans 13:1-7

Because these two units, in the form we now have them, came from the authors of the work as a whole, they do not have a transmission history. The traditions which do lie behind these units were used by the authors of the total work to compose the present units in their present place in the work. The study of these traditions is included in tradition analysis.

6:10 Redaction

We now come to the final literary step in the analysis of a passage—redaction analysis. We have studied the traditions which lie behind the composition of a passage, and we have looked at the journey, if any, from composition to collection. Now we will look at the final stage, the function of the unit within the book.

At this level of analysis, we want to understand both the design of the work as a whole and how the individual unit functions within this. Just as we have seen earlier that words and sentences within a unit do not occur in random fashion but are patterned, so also units themselves do not come one after the other in a sort of jumble. Rather, each book has a design and units are ordered or arranged in accordance with this design. They have meaning based on their participation within this structure.

In speaking about the arrangement of material within a book, we have two styles of "authorship." On the one hand we have the book of Romans written by Paul. Here the author of the individual units and the book is the same. On the other hand, in Matthew the situation is different. In this case the composition of the units may be due to a variety of people, including Matthew, while the present arrangement of the material in the book is due to Matthew. Matthew appears to us to be more of a collector or editor than an author like Paul. For this sort of writer the word "redactor" is commonly used.

A redactor not only collects, but also transforms the material which he takes up into his work by integrating the parts into a whole. A redactor works differently from the editor of an anthology, who takes materials over as they are and is limited by and large to arranging them according to some logical order and providing them with an introduction. A redactor is much more actively engaged with his material and his influence can be seen within the units themselves; he integrates. This may be done in a variety of ways, such as presenting the material in a new form (antithesis), or changing the wording to make it communicate better, or composing bridging passages. An editor of an anthology produces a collection of isolated pieces, a redactor an integrated whole. This being the case, redactor and author form two halves of a continuum, their activities shading into each other. This is why it is not inappropriate to speak of redactors as "authors." In any case, in studying the final phase of the unit in its final literary context, we need to note not only the arrangement or design of the book, but how the individual units are composed or fitted to carry out the author's overarching purpose which lies behind the work.[16]

The fact that the materials in the Bible have been arranged by the various authors is clear if we compare Matthew with Luke. For example, the Sermon on the Mount in Matthew 5—7 consists of material which is scattered throughout Luke.[17] This means that different principles have guided these two redators in gathering together material about the life and teachings of Jesus as well as in their organization of the material. Consequently, we must regard the arrangement of the units in a book not as a given necessity, but as the result of choice. The arrangement of material is due to the interests of the author, and reflects the purpose of his writing.

Discovering the larger literary context and its design helps us to understand the individual unit in a variety of ways which we otherwise might miss. First, it aids our understanding of how an author used the traditions available to him, and why the traditions are shaped as they are. Seeing this shaping as part of a larger process which gives coherence to the work as a whole enables us to put the proper emphasis on what the author has done in a particular passage. For example, the cleansing of the temple which occurs at the beginning of the Gospel of John has one meaning in this context. It has another meaning in the synoptic Gospels where it comes at the end of Jesus' ministry.

Seeing the overall design of a work and the function of a unit in it allows us to appreciate the purpose or intention of an individual unit. This means that we can set limits as to how wide a scope a passage ought to have. By ignoring this context, we may appropriate the passage for uses quite inappropriate to its original literary setting. Romans 13:1-7 is a good example of a passage which has largely been interpreted out of its immediate literary context and the context of Paul's thought as a whole.

Further, the larger context of an author's work may allow us to see implications in what is said that would not be apparent from focusing on the individual unit in isolation. The reverse is also true; we might read some implication into what is said, which is really illegitimate in light of what the author writes elsewhere. Putting a unit in this larger perspective can prevent us from going off on exegetical tangents, since by seeing the unit as a harmonious part of a larger context, certain interpretations are excluded while others are brought to the fore.

Sometimes, on the other hand, it is as important to know what a redactor has *omitted* from his sources or traditions as it is to know what has been done with what was retained. For example, the Chronicler, the "author" of 1 and 2 Chronicles, used the books of Samuel and Kings as sources for his history. Knowing this we can see how he has selected from these sources. For example, he has omitted the entire Bathsheba episode from the story of David. He apparently wishes to present David in a much more favorable light than this story does. This is in line with his glorification of the Davidic dynasty, especially its founder, David. Thus, an author's point of view can come through as clearly by what he doesn't say as by what he does say.

Redactors may compose as well as arrange. However, the compositional work of a redactor is studied under tradition analysis. There, for example, we studied Matthew's composition of the unit 5:38-42 from older traditions. In redaction analysis we will look at how Matthew used this unit within the book as a whole. Alterations (of the type studied under transmission analysis) which an author makes in fixed units in order to fit them into the book and its perspective are also studied in redaction analysis. There should be a dovetailing between an author's redactional aims and his compositional activity. This means that the findings of the previous stage of analysis will be drawn upon and extended in redaction analysis.

6.11 **Axiom: Since passages occur as integral building blocks in a larger literary structure, to understand their intention and function it is necessary to understand the larger design and their part within it.**

6.12 *Procedures*

What are the clues which will guide you to the function and meaning of the individual passage in its present place within the larger literary context? These clues will focus around two operations of the redactor on his material. The first is how the work is structured and the place of the unit in this structure. The second is how the point of view of the redactor has also influenced the selection of material and how the material selected is reworked to fit the work's structure and perspective. The clues are grouped around three focal points which should help you see the perspective of the author. These are (1) the organization of the work, (2) the selection of material, and (3) the adapting or editing of the material.

While the focus is on understanding an individual unit, the aim of this stage of study is to examine the author's literary technique and theological perspective as it is found in the book and his work as a whole. Material from other parts of the work which points to the author's activity in the book needs to be used. These serve as points of reference for the study of the author's redactorial techniques.

A. *Analysis*
  1. Selection
     How has the author used his sources in constructing his work? (You may have already studied the author's use of sources under tradition analysis. Here you will extend it to the book as a whole.)
     a. What material has been omitted?
     b. What principles are at work in the process of selection?
     c. What new material has the redactor added to his sources?

  2. Adapting
     a. How has the author adapted literary types to suit his purposes? (You will have already traced changes in type under form analysis. Here it is necessary to build on those results.)
       (1) How do changes in form fit the unit to its present context?
       (2) Is this type of modification consistently typical of the author or redactor?
       (3) How has the author used literary conventions and style of language to fit the passage to its position and function in the work?
     b. How has the author adapted the treatment of the subject to fit his purposes? (This builds on tradition analysis already completed.)
       (1) Do differences or changes made in the unit relate to its function in its present context?
         (a) Changes/differences in the text, in wording, and phrasing.
         (b) Additions and deletions within a unit.

(2) Are there consistent changes which indicate the author/redactor's outlook?

3. Organization
   What is the unit's position in the structure of the work?
   a. How is the unit integrated into its immediate context? What links connect it to the units on either side of it?
   b. Is it part of a block of material, a story cycle, or a cycle of sayings? Look for headings in the text which point to a collection of materials or to groupings within the work.
   c. What is the structure of the work? How does the unit fit into this larger whole?

4. Viewpoint
   a. How does the subject treated here link with other passages in the book?
   b. Does the passage fit into a major theme of the book?
   c. How does material that is unique to the author point to his main ideas?

B. *Synthesis*
   1. How does the redactor's compositional activity give you clues as to the purpose or the perspective from which he wrote? Draw upon the findings you have made under tradition analysis.
      a. What is the meaning or significance of the way the author has combined sources?
      b. What is the significance of the way he has added to units or deleted from them? What is the significance of new material?
      c. How do the differences in wording found above point to the meaning of the passages?

   2. From the above clues, what seems to be the major theme or perspective of the book or work? What seems to be the theology of the book? State how these illuminate the meaning of your passage. How does your passage fit the theme and structure of the book?

6.13 *Illustrations*
Genesis 12:10-20

This story seems only loosely related to its present context (clue 3). In fact, some have suggested that the passage seems like a detour since it interrupts the main thread of the story of Abram. According to the main story line, Abram travels to Canaan, journeys about in the land, has a dispute with Lot, and divides the land with him. Finally, he comes to the oaks of Mamre (13:18) which serve as something of a headquarters. His trip to Egypt is a digression from these travels in Canaan which bring Abram to Mamre. The story thus appears to be an intrusion. (See page 150) under Genesis 12:10-20.)

As we have seen (2:12, Genesis 12:10-20), the beginning of the story is quite abrupt, seemingly unconnected with what has gone before. Perhaps the way for the descent into Egypt has been prepared by verse 9 which records the travel of Abram to the southernmost part of the country, the part nearest to Egypt.[18]

At the end of the story (Genesis 13:3, 4), Abram is near Bethel again where he was in 12:8, before the episode in Egypt. Verses 13:1, 2 seem to form a transition to this following story, especially the mention of Lot at the end of 13:1. Lot, of course, is not mentioned at all in 12:10-20. We can see that although this story has been worked into its present context, it appears to be different from the stories immediately surrounding it.[19]

As we probe the contribution which this story makes to the Abram cycle of stories, we may become clearer about why J has positioned this story where he has. In order to do this, it will be helpful to begin from the compositional end: what is it about the form of this narrative that is appropriate to its function in the story cycle? If we can discover its function in the cycle, we will be in a position to determine why this particular location in the cycle is appropriate.[20]

The form of this story, as analyzed above, is a speech-fulfilling narrative. This same type of narrative occurs again in Genesis 16, as well as elsewhere in J (clue 2a). Thus, Genesis 12:10-20 does not represent a unique form or genre within the J material. What is it about this story form which makes it appropriate for the J's purposes? The major theme and tension running through this cycle of stories (clue 4) is promise— promise of descendants, fame, land, and blessing by God to Abram.[21] Already before Genesis 12:10-20 we have two such texts of promise, Genesis 12:1-3 and 12:7.

Genesis 12:1-3 is a heading for the Abram stories and perhaps for the history of Israel, and as such its emphasis on promise casts the mood for the whole story.[22] Likewise, 12:7 is an affirmation of this promise. After the story we find promises in 13:14-17, in chapter 15, in 16:10, and in 18:10. By a simple reading through these chapters, one senses the amount of emphasis placed on promise. This is shown not only by the frequency of this theme, as just suggested, but also by the positioning of these elements within the narrative.

A tension runs throughout these stories, the lack of fulfillment in spite of the constant promises. At the beginning of the Abram and Sarai stories we are told two things which appear to make the promises impossible of realization. In 11:30 we read that Sarai was barren. How could the barren be a mother of a great nation? How could she even be the mother of a single child? As Sarai grows older and older, it appears less and less possible that the promises of God will be realized through her. The second tension revolves around the land, since in 12:6 we find that when Abram arrived in Canaan, he found others in possession of it. Yet in spite of present reality, God promises in the next verse (12:7) this very land to Abram's descendants. How incongruous this all appears. Thus the major tension of these stories is the promises of God versus the reality of the situation in which the promises do not appear to be coming true.

Genesis 12:10-20, by its very form, as we have observed above, revolves around the plans of man. Usually speech-fulfilling stories report the plan and then narrate its realization. Abram is the planner here. Abram is realistic. Given reality, this is what it is necessary to do to get along. The problem with Abram's planning is, of course, its unforeseen results, the loss of Sarai. This is exactly the point at which the author departs from the conventions of the form in order, in a quite shocking and striking way, to drive home the lesson of the break between the well-conceived plan and the actual outcome (clue 2a). Abram cannot plan adequately enough. With the loss of Sarai it does indeed appear as if God's promises will not be realized through her. Here then Abram's own plans have the totally unexpected consequence of apparently thwarting the plans of God. This story, therefore, forms a counterpoint to the theme of promise. In living by plan rather than by promise, Abram threatens the promise. The story heightens the tension of the gap between promise and reality, a gap which is only increased when Abram takes matters into his own hands.

By its very setting this story also is a counter to the theme of promise (clue 3). In verse 6 we find that the Canaanite is in the land. In verse 10 Abram, on account of the famine, leaves the Promised Land. Is there no room in the land for him? Can he not find a toehold in the land of promise? Both history and natural events seem to conspire against the promise. Thus, in this story a double blow apparently has been dealt to the promise. We not only have the loss of the matriarch and consequently a defeat for the promise of offspring, but also a vacating of the Promised Land itself.

Now the loss of Sarai did not necessarily mean that Abram could have no offspring. Abram could and did have other wives by which he could have children. But 11:30 which announces Sarai's barrenness alerts us to the fact that the children of promise were to be Sarai's children; this is an important point which we must not miss in our story.

In chapter 16 where the same story form is used, we see a similar tension developed between God's providence and human plans. This time it is Sarai's plan. She wants Abram to impregnate her servant Hagar, so that through this she may have a child. Her plan is an attempt to circumvent God's preventing her from having her own children, but her scheme was not to be. God intervenes and offers a promise to the child, but not the promise of Abram. The child of promise is to be Sarai's child.

The writer of these stories, then, uses the speech-fulfilling narrative (as in Genesis 12:10-20) to put in tension the plans of man and the promises of God. In fact, there is not only a tension, but man's plans may even jeopardize the promise. Divine providence will be worked out not only in the face of a contradictory reality, but also in spite of the plans of men and women.[23]

Having seen now how this story functions with regard to the major theme and tension of the Abram cycle of narratives, we need to probe the reasons for placing this story here in a place which seems to interrupt Abram's journeys in the land of Canaan (clue 3). There are two considerations which shed light on the placement of this story here.

First, both the Abram and Isaac cycle of stories have a word of promise at or near their beginning (Genesis 12:1-3, 7 and 26:1-5). This promise is in both cases closely followed by a story built on the theme of the endangering of the matriarch. This pattern may have been imbedded in the tradition, or conversely, J may have arranged the material in this fashion in order to increase the tension between promise and reality; specifically to point out the gap between divine promise and human action.

A second reason for the story's placement is that it best fits the larger story line here. In the Abram cycle, as we have suggested, there are a series of stories which seem to tell not of the realization, but the unfulfillment of the promise. In chapter 13, following the quarrel between the servants of Lot and Abram, the land of promise is divided, with Lot, not Abram, getting the best share. In chapter 16 as we have just noted, there is an attempt to realize the promise by a child other than from

Sarai. Finally, in chapter 18 there is a promise of a child, but long after Sarai's childbearing years are past. These stories point quite vividly to the lack of the fulfillment of the promises.

Genesis 12:10-20 stands at the beginning of this sequence, because here the clash between promise and reality is harshest. In this story Abram leaves the land and as a result of his own initiative loses the matriarch as well. At least in chapter 13 he is left with a part of the Promised Land, while in chapter 16, although the plan did not work, there is no real loss or danger to the partners of the promise. In chapter 18 it is nature which is against the promise, not Abram himself. Thus Genesis 12:10-20 comes early in the Abram stories, immediately after the promises of 12:1-3, 7, in order to sharpen the tension, to make the stories more gripping as they unfold the working of divine providence against the variety of impediments which these stories relate.

A final question is why this story of Sarai's endangerment is placed here, while the parallel account is found in chapter 20. According to the usual source divisions, our story in Genesis 12:10-20 belongs to the J material while Genesis 20 belongs to E. Thus the redactor who joined J and E together could have omitted one of the parallel accounts or perhaps even switched their sequence. We have just indicated why we believe 12:10-20 belongs where it does. Likewise, there appear to be good reasons for retaining and placing chapter 20 in its present location.

As it now stands, the story in chapter 20 follows the Sodom and Gomorrah episode. Abram's part in this story was at the beginning in the poignant bargaining scene, where Abram plays on the theme, "Will not the ruler of all the earth do justice?" (verse 25). In the end, Abram reaches the limit to which God will allow himself to go, and in spite of these efforts, the city is destroyed.

Now in chapter 20, after Abimelech has taken Sarai into his harem, God appears to him and speaks words of judgment. But Abimelech protests; he did what he did innocently. Should the unknowing suffer for the fault of another, in this case Abram, who had, in fact, deceived him? The tension around the theme of justice links this story to the Sodom and Gomorrah episode. God instructs Abimelech to return Sarai to Abram and have Abram intercede for him, since Abram is a prophet. Here Abram is once more cast in the role of an intercessor for the innocent. Likely because of the links which exist between chapters 18—19 and 20, the redactor of the JE material placed this story where he did.

Thus even though 12:10-20 and chapter 20 are parallel in basic theme, in their literary formulation, their form, and in their function within their wider literary context, they are quite different, and thus functionally not parallel at all. It is through the study of these stories in their literary context, their present redactional/authorial setting, that we can begin to appreciate their meaning as they now stand in the Bible.[24]

Amos 2:6-16

The book of Amos is of quite a different sort than Genesis. Here we find no plot, no story line, no development of a theme. Instead, we seem to have a jumble of sayings and stories without any apparent order or structure. Usually in the prophetic books we find three types of material, the speeches or oracles of the prophet, prayers and hymns, and stories about the prophet. In Amos we find all three of these, but without any seeming order.[25] Indeed, the prayers and hymns seem to promote disorder rather than order. For example, the hymn in Amos 5:8-9 seems to interrupt the continuity between verses 7 and 10 (note how the *NEB* has rearranged these verses).[26] Indeed, it may be helpful to look at the book of Amos as sort of an anthology, a collection, without any particular plan or organic unity.

Amos 2:6-16, however, is found in a quite definite setting within the book—at the end of a series of oracles against the foreign nations. This positioning seems to say that just as God will bring punishment on the foreign nations because of their wrongs, so also will God bring judgment upon Israel. Indeed, the opening verses (3:1-2) of the following chapter emphasize this. Exactly because they are God's people, Israel can expect to be judged. In this same vein the deeds of God's election are used to intensify Israel's guilt (2:9-12) rather than offer her the solace of God's favor in spite of her deeds. Her election, then, instead of exempting her from judgment, makes judgment for her injustices all the more certain.

In this light, the digression in 2:9-11 which we have discussed above is both pertinent and appropriate to the speech's present place in the book and its function (clue 3). Thus, in this present location, the judgment speech against Israel at the end of the judgment speeches against the foreign nations would seem to mean a leveling for Israel, a placing of her among the nations. Likewise, as mentioned, the following speech, 3:1-2 reinforces exactly this point. Thus, within the collections of sayings, Amos 2:6-16 seems to gain a wider definite meaning as a result of its placement.[27]

When we come to the larger context, however, things are not quite as clear. The structure of the book appears to consist of a series of smaller collections which have been put together, one after the other. Following the collection of sayings in 1:3—2:16, there is a collection of three prophecies beginning with "hear" 3:1-15, 4:1-12, and 5:1-17. But these three are obviously collections of sayings, since they contain a variety of material. Then there are two "woe" sayings, 5:18-20 (21-27) and 6:1-14. Chapters 7, 8, and 9:1-4 contain reports of a series of visions which Amos received. This series is interrupted in 7:10-17 with the biographical account about the prophet's conflict with Amaziah and by 8:4-14 which contains another oracle of doom beginning with "hear." Finally 9:7-15 contains both judgment sayings and a prophecy of future restoration. From this it can be seen that all apparently similar material is not grouped together and even what is grouped together may be quite varied, as in chapter 3 for example.

Kaufmann has argued that the book of Amos has a three-part structure.[28] The oracles against the foreign nations (1:2—2:3) and prophecies of consolation (9:11-15) form the frame for the book. The filling which is placed between these end pieces is the oracles against Israel. As support for this thesis he points to Joel 3:16-18, which is very much like Amos 1:2 and 9:13. He argues on this basis that these verses once formed a connected text which Amos took up and used as a frame for his prophecies of judgment. As further evidence, he points out that events spoken of in 1:3—2:3 happened before the time of Amos.

This threefold division of the book, however, divides the material awkwardly. It separates sayings which it would seem are intended to go together, like 1:3—2:3 and 2:4-16. While older ninth century traditions perhaps do lie behind these sayings, it is best to see them as later formulations. Likewise, there is a break between 1:2 and 1:3, so that it is not clear that 1:2—2:3 was ever a traditional unity. In summary, it seems that the book of Amos is a collection of oracles and other materials loosely connected together. While there do appear to be some subsections, an overall arrangement or structural development is not obvious beyond the progression Kaufmann points to: (1) sayings of judgment against the nations, (2) against Israel, and finally (3) hope for Israel. Chapter 2, verses 6-16 would then serve as a bridge between sections one and two (clue 1).[29]

The form and content of the prophecy in 2:6-16 is very similar to what we find elsewhere in Amos (clue 2a). Amos speaks more often in the form of the oracle of doom than in any other form. The content of the accusation in these speeches is almost exclusively concerned with social justice. In these respects what we find in 2:6b, the accusation we have focused on, is very representative of the message of Amos. In terms of the larger tradition, we found above that Amos represents a shift in the tradition of these messenger speeches of doom, in that he addresses the powerful groups within the nation, or the nation as a whole, instead of individuals. Here again, the speech in 2:6-16 is typical, being addressed to the nation. That Amos addresses himself to the powerful groups within the nation is due to their responsibility for justice and righteousness, which is Amos' central concern. Likewise, if justice and righteousness are not found in a nation, it will be destroyed. Our passage is in accord with this theme of the book of Amos. As a typical passage, then, it can be used as a window into the world of Amos and his message.

Matthew 5:38-42

This passage is a part of the Sermon on the Mount which extends from chapter 5 through chapter 7. The antitheses, of which this unit is a part, are linked with what immediately precedes them in 5:16-20 by being examples of what Jesus meant by the higher righteousness of verse 20. Jesus' teaching on this higher righteousness continues up to 7:13. From that point on, until the end of the sermon, there are warnings of the judgment which will come if this higher righteousness is not manifested.[30]

The teachings that we find gathered together in Matthew to form the Sermon on the Mount were evidently given at various times and places in the ministry of Jesus since we find them scattered throughout Luke. For example, our antithesis is parallel to Luke 6:29-30, but the Lord's Prayer comes in Luke 11:2-4 in quite a different context. The saying about salt (Matthew 5:13) occurs in Luke 14:34-35, while the saying on lack of concern about material goods (Matthew 6:25-34) is found in Luke 12:22-31. Even Luke 6, which has more parallels to the Sermon on the Mount than any other chapter, has a different setting; it is a sermon on the plain! It seems clear that Matthew has collected, arranged, and set the material here in chapters 5 to 7 according to some reason or purpose. Our task is to discover this purpose and in light of this to evaluate the meaning of 5:38-42.[31]

We will begin this search with an analysis of the structure of Matthew (clue 3). Matthew has traditionally been divided into five major sections, which contain both teachings and stories of Jesus. These five divisions are: chapters 3—7, 8—10, 11—13:52, 13:53—18:35, and 19—25. These divisions are marked by the phrase, "And it was when Jesus finished..." (see 7:28 and 11:1, for example), so that it looks as if Matthew consciously indicated the end of each section. Further, this view would see in these five sections a parallel to the five books of the Torah (law) in the Old Testament. In these five sections Matthew is presenting the Torah of Jesus for Christians. Each of these sections is patterned after the five law books in that each of them consists of both teaching and narrative, just as do the books of the Torah.

However, objections have been raised to this division of Matthew.[32] The birth and passion of Jesus do not figure into this structure; this seems strange to say the least. There seem to be more than five discourses in Matthew. Chapter 11 seems to stand out as a separate discourse, and there is a break between chapters 24 and 25. In fact, we might consider there to be seven divisions of teachings in Matthew. The parallel to the Pentateuchal books is unfounded, too, since one may have only narrative and no law (Genesis), while another may be mainly law (Leviticus). Finally, the function of the phrase used to mark the divisions, "And it was when Jesus finished..." is really a sign that Jesus has finished a particular discourse. It is not the heading of a new section since it contains no theme or topical heading for the next section of material.

Instead of this fivefold division, a threefold one has been suggested.[33] These three sections would be 1:1—4:16, the person of Jesus the Messiah; 4:17—16:20, the proclamation of Jesus the Messiah; and 16:21—28:20, the suffering, death, and resurrection of Jesus the Messiah. In this schema the phrase "from that time Jesus began ...." in 4:17 and 16:21 serves as a sign marking the turning points in Jesus' ministry and a superscription for the new section which it begins. Matthew 1:1 serves as the introduction to the first section. In this outline, the Sermon on the Mount is Jesus' initial proclamation of his messianic teaching (clue 3). This threefold division seems superior to the traditional fivefold one and will be assumed below.

Having looked at how Matthew has arranged and organized his material, we can now examine his use of sources (clue 1). First of all, Matthew not only follows the order of Mark, but also includes most of Mark in his Gospel. Of a total of 661 verses in Mark, 606 of these verses occur in Matthew. This comprises about half of Matthew. Into this Markan order and material, Matthew inserts at logical places additional teachings of Jesus. Many of these teachings, as indicated above, he got from another source, Q, which was a collection of Jesus' teachings. Thus, the activity of Matthew may be seen at least partly as the combination of Mark with the additional teachings he found in Q. This is the case with the Sermon on the Mount in general and of our antithesis in particular. Matthew has placed the sermon between Mark 1:39 and 1:40. Mark 1:39 reports a teaching ministry of Jesus in Galilee, following the selection of the first disciple, as does Matthew in an expanded form in 4:23 and following. Likewise, after the Sermon on the Mount, Matthew 8:1-4 resumes with Mark 1:40-45. It seems, then, that Matthew has taken this opportunity to spell out what was the content of Jesus' teaching as he went about in Galilee at the beginning of his ministry.[34]

As we can see from Matthew's selection and arrangement of material, the teachings of Jesus are of paramount importance for him.[35] This leads to a major question in Matthew: what is the relationship between the teachings of Jesus and the law?[36] Within Matthew there appears to be a tension as to their relationship. On the one hand, it is clear that the law has abiding validity. Matthew 5:17-20 is eloquent testimony to this: "Think not that I have come to abolish the law and the prophets; I have come not to abolish them but to fulfil them. For truly, I say to you, till heaven and earth pass away, not an iota, not a dot, will pass from the law until all is accomplished. Whoever then relaxes one of the least of these commandments and teaches men so, shall be called least in the kingdom of heaven; but he who does them and teaches them shall be called great in the kingdom of heaven. For I tell you, unless your righteousness exceeds that of the scribes and Pharisees, you will never enter the kingdom of heaven." This material does not occur in any of the other Gospels. Matthew's unique inclusion of it underlines the importance of this statement for him. Or again the passage in Matthew 23:2-3: "The scribes and the Pharisees sit on Moses' seat; so practice and observe whatever they tell you, but not what they do; for they preach, but do not practice."

In the same way Matthew's concern for the continuing validity of the law extends even to wording. For example, in Matthew 11:13 we find, "For all the prophets and the law prophesied until John," while in Luke 16:16-17 we read, "The law and the prophets were until John; since then the good news of the kingdom of God is preached, and every one enters it violently. But it is easier for heaven and earth to pass away, than for one dot of the law to become void." In the Luke passage it could sound like the law has been superceded by the gospel, "the law and prophets were until. . . ." In Matthew's wording such a possibility has been removed.

On the other hand, we find passages which seem to suggest that Jesus and his teachings run counter to the teaching of the law. In Matthew 19:3-9 (Mark 10:2-9) Jesus seems to repeal to some extent the Mosaic statute which allowed divorce for a cause (see Deuteronomy 24 for this law). Likewise, in Matthew 15:1-20 (Mark 7:1-23) Jesus calls the religious leaders blind guides and seems to denigrate traditional washing of the hands before a meal. However, he does not go as far as Mark, who states that "thus he [Jesus] declared all foods clean" (Mark 7:19). These two cases, then, at least to some extent, point to a tension between Jesus and the law as understood and practiced by his religious contemporaries.[37]

This same tension can be seen in the antitheses. For example, in verses 33-37 Jesus rejects the swearing of oaths altogether. This goes far beyond what we find in the law, which directly allows swearing by God's name, as in Deuteronomy 6:13 and 10:20. It appears that this antithesis is in fact repealing a law rather than extending it. The same appears to be true with the last two antitheses in 5:38-48. Here, again, what is taught in the law is contrasted with a new way of acting. No longer is it to be an eye for an eye, but a new way of reciprocity. The key to this tension is Jesus, who is the fulfillment of the law and the prophets (Matthew 5:16-20). The law points to Jesus, but Jesus now himself takes the center of the stage, "*I* say. . . ."[38]

This raises the question of how Jesus is presented to us in Matthew's Gospel. First, there can be little doubt that Matthew presents Jesus as the fulfillment of the Old Testament. No Gospel quotes the Old Testament as often as Matthew (more than sixty times). From the time of his birth on, Jesus' life is presented as a constant sequence of acts which fulfill the Scriptures.[39] (See, for example, Matthew 2:5-6, 15, 17-18, 23.) Since Matthew places so much emphasis on the theme of fulfillment, we would expect, then, the teachings of Jesus likewise to fulfill the Torah.

Second, in Matthew Jesus is Lord for his disciples. In this gospel the disciples always address Jesus as Lord, while in Mark they call him teacher or rabbi. (Compare Matthew 8:25/Mark 4:38; Matthew 17:4/

Mark 9:5; Matthew 20:33/Mark 10:51.) For Matthew to be a disciple was not to follow in a literal sense so much as to come under the lordship of Jesus.[40]

That this theme of discipleship is central to Matthew's Gospel is witnessed to by the constant call to obedience and the indication of future judgment on those who are not doers of the word.[41] The end of the sermon is an eloquent passage on this theme (see 7:13-27). The central theme of obedience and discipleship also emerges at the very end of Matthew's Gospel, where Jesus charges his disciples to "make disciples, teaching them all I have commanded you." But the question yet remains: how do the teachings of Jesus, the Lord who fulfills the Old Testament, relate to the teachings of the Old Testament?

This is resolved by a third way in which Jesus comes to us in the Gospel of Matthew. He appears as widsom.[42] The saying in Matthew 11:28-30, "Come to me, all who labor and are heavy laden, and I will give you rest. Take my yoke upon you, and learn from me; for I am gentle and lowly in heart, and you will find rest for your souls. For my yoke is easy, and my burden is light," has its background in wisdom literature. Wisdom makes an appeal to people in a similar way in the book of Sirach:

> Listen my son, and accept my judgment; do not reject my counsel. Put your feet into her fetters, and your neck into her collar. Put your shoulder under her and carry her, and do not fret under her bonds. Come to her with all your soul, and keep her ways with all your might. Search out and seek, and she will become known to you; and when you get hold of her, do not let her go. For at last you will find the rest she gives, and she will be changed into joy for you. Then her fetters will become for you a strong protection, and her collar a glorious robe. Her yoke is a golden ornament, and her bonds are a cord of blue. You will wear her like a glorious robe, and put her on like a crown of gladness (Sirach 6:23-31; see also Sirach 51:26-27).

Wisdom is also identified with the law or Torah (see Sirach 24:3-4, 7, etc.). This identification of the law and wisdom was easy in Israel, because the law was regarded as Israel's wisdom (Deuteronomy 4:6-8).

In the Matthew passage, however, Jesus places himself in the place of wisdom and the law. As such, then, when Jesus speaks, he is speaking for the law. What he says is the proper understanding or interpretation of the law as against its possible misunderstanding. In the "I say . . ." of the antitheses, Jesus rather than repealing the law is in actuality giving the real meaning or intent of the law. Even though it may appear that

Jesus is voiding the law, the authority of Jesus, as normative for the interpretation of the law, is bringing out its true intent. It is because of this authority that the people marveled at the end of the sermon (7:28-29). Jesus was Lord of the Scriptures in the sense that he had the key to their interpretation. Because of this, true obedience to the law was true obedience to Jesus' teaching of the law. Thus in 5:20, the antitheses are prefaced by the saying that Jesus' disciples must be characterized by a higher righteousness than that of the scribes and Pharisees: they are to be obedient to the teachings of Jesus, the true interpretation of the law.

But how can teachings which seem to go directly against the law really be a true interpretation of the law? To understand this, we need to see the key which Jesus used to get from the letter of the law to his new teachings on the higher righteousness. This key is love, for in this is the fulfillment of the law.[43] This is how the teachings in the sermon are summed up in 7:12, "So whatever you wish that men would do to you, do so to them; for this is the law and the prophets." Likewise this is his answer to the lawyer's test question concerning the greatest commandment in the law, "You shall love the Lord your God with all your heart, and with all your soul, and with all your mind. This is the great and first commandment. And a second is like it, You shall love your neighbor as yourself. On these two commandments depends all the law and the prophets" (Matthew 22:37-40). Thus, the fulfillment of the law was love. Seen in this light, in 5:17, where Jesus talks of *fulfilling the law*, love is meant (cf. Romans 13:8-10; Galatians 5:14).

The teachings of Jesus were related to the law as its authoritative interpretation, which meant that they fulfilled the law. This interpretation was based on love. Since obedience to Jesus' teachings fulfilled the law, this obedience established what the law was meant to establish, the higher righteousness of Matthew 5:20.

In returning to our antithesis we can see that this is quite true here. Instead of an eye for an eye (justice), the response of Jesus' disciple is the reciprocity of love. This explains why the illustrations seem so radical; it is because love is so radical in comparison with normal human justice. The next antithesis (vv. 43-48) clearly points as well to love as the proper basis of the disciples' actions. These two antitheses coming at the end of the antitheses, in which Jesus' teaching is contrasted to the old, point unmistakably to why Jesus' teachings here are in tension with the law. They are based on the concept of love instead of justice.

This means that Jesus by his teaching a new reciprocity in human relations is aiming at what the law was also aiming at—to establish righteousness. The way to this, however, is not by justice, but by love. Thus Jesus does not do away with the law. It yet has validity in promoting a just order. He rather goes beyond this means to another—love.

It has been noted that while mercy and faith play a part in Matthew, justice does not. This might be seen as surprising given the prophets' stress in particular on justice along with faithfulness and mercy. It is doubly surprising seeing Matthew's great use of the Old Testament, using it at every turn to show Jesus' fulfillment of it. This apparent lack of concern with justice on Matthew's part has been attributed to his situation; the church was not in a position of authority and so justice was not a central issue in it.[44] However, there may be a more significant reason. "Regular" righteousness was based on just laws which were equitably implemented (see the discussion of justice and righteousness above). Here justice is the way to righteousness, and by acting in accordance with what was just, one was "righteous" or innocent. Jesus, however, teaches another way—a righteousness based on love. It is love which is the way to righteousness and it is by acting in accordance with love that one is "perfect" (Matthew 5:48), and a true disciple (Matthew 19:21). This is the higher righteousness, a righteousness beyond justice.

This idea illuminates our antithesis, because here Jesus is really contrasting justice—fair dealings with another based on the law (eye for an eye)—with love, responding to people not on the basis of what is just, but what shows love. In this contrast we have the heart of Jesus' teaching about both the fulfilling of the law (5:17), which is love, and the "higher righteousness" (5:20), which is the order or arrangement which love brings about.[45]

Romans 13:1-7

This passage is often understood apart from its present context in the book of Romans. One reason for this may be the apparent loose connection of 13:1-7 with its immediate context, since what goes immediately before and after would seem to fit together quite well, being an exhortation on love, while 13:1-7 seems to be concerned with quite another topic, submission to the state.

Looking first at the structure of Romans as a whole (clue 3), the book can be divided into two major parts, chapters 1—11 and 12—15 (16). The first part of the book is largely a theological exposition while

12—15 contains practical material, exhortations, and advice on Christian living. Our passage obviously occurs in the practical, ethical part of the book. However, as Furnish has pointed out, we must not separate too sharply between these two sections of the book. Indeed, he sees in 12:1-2, which is the heading for the teachings in chapters 12-15, a recapitulation of the theology of the book.[46] Romans 12:1-2 talks of being transformed; this is the power of the Gospel mentioned in 1:16-17. Just as a lack of knowledge of God led to the dishonoring of the body (1:18 and following), here knowledge and offering of the body to God are mentioned together. Romans 13:1-7, then, is practical advice based on the gospel and its implications for discipleship (12:1-2).

The immediate context in which 13:1-7 is found is a series of exhortations and admonitions found in chapters 12 and 13 which form a unit, since chapters 14 and 15 treat another topic. This section 12-13 has been divided in various ways, and perhaps the following division is as accurate as any:[47] 12:1-2, forms a preamble; the rest of the passage comes under the general principles set forth here. Romans 12:3-16a deals with Christian behavior in the Christian community. Here there are a series of teachings about *charismata* (gifts) and about manifesting these in love. This section begins and ends with sober thinking about oneself and others. Romans 12:16b—13:7 gives advice about Christian behavior in the world. Romans 12:16b-21 advises nonretribution as a private citizen and the giving of good, instead, while 13:1-7 advises subordination to the governing officials. Finally, 13:8-10 forms the conclusion and summary of both parts (12:3-16a and 16b—13:7). Seen in this light, the theme of these chapters is discipleship which expresses love in service toward others, both those inside and outside the church. Paul's emphasis is active, what the Christian ought to be doing in these areas of life.

Since the words of our passage are found in the context within which Paul wrote them and assumed they would be understood, they are no longer abstract unconditional words, but rather words which are meant to express Christian obedience in the world. Thus, from the immediate context, the interpretation of Romans 13:1-7 must be consistent with Christian discipleship, love and service, since these instructions are meant to be an expression of these. This means they are limited by what constitutes Christian obedience and discernment of God's will (12:1-2). Consequently, as Kasemann writes, "Christian obedience can and must end at the point where, because of the nature of the existing political authority, service, though still possible as an act of the individual, is yet robbed of all meaning within the total context of the life of a given community."[48] Paul himself sums up his teaching here with the words, "Owe no one anything, except to love one another" (13:8), which is a direct play on the words in 13:7, "give to all what is owed."[49]

When we look at Paul's writings on this theme elsewhere, we can see even more clearly within what limits Paul meant his words to be understood. As we have discovered in tradition analysis, Paul regards the powers in a largely negative fashion. They are ranged in opposition to God and lack knowledge of God and what his purposes are (1 Corinthians 2:6-8). This means that the wisdom and knowledge of God is to be found not in the state but in the church. This is why Christians ought to settle their affairs among themselves, rather than take them to the state authorities for adjudication. For the Christian the state has been superseded by the new community, where the law of love should reign (1 Corinthians 6:1-8). Indeed, as we saw, Christ will dethrone the powers and they will acknowledge his lordship, which is now a fact which the powers do not recognize (Philippians 2:10-11; 1 Corinthians 15:24-27; and 2 Corinthians 4:4). In the present, the church is to stand fast and, like its Lord, live in victory over the powers. In terms of a Christian's relationship to the state, Paul does not dissolve the tension which exists between Christ's kingdom and this world order. Rather, the Christian is called to live as a member of Christ's body who also lives in the world. Thus, any view of the state and the Christian's responsibility to the state must be compatible with Paul's view of the church and the regenerate Christian's life and responsibilities in it. Romans 13:1-7 must not be interpreted so as to negate either 12:1-21; 13:8-10, or Paul's high view of the church where God's will and purposes are known.

Caird[50] mentions three ways in which Paul suggests Christians are to live in the present as responsible members of the church in the world. First, they are to bear witness to God's revelation, for it is the knowledge of God which illuminates the darkness of the present age and its rulers (2 Corinthians 4:4-6). This knowledge shows the powers as they truly are (Galatians 4:9; 1 Corinthians 2:9-12). Second, the Christian is to be identified with Christ (Romans 6:3-9). This identification means putting off the old and putting on the new (Philippians 3:8-12), which in turn leads to freedom from the binding forces of the present age (Galatians 5:1-9). Finally, the Christian is to be obedient to Christ, which is not an outward formalism, but is having the mind of Christ within (Philippians 2:5-7). This stance as servant, as one who is humble and receives wrongs without retribution, is the stance of love. Evil and the powers are thus defeated by Christians absorbing abuse and thus overcoming evil with good. This is the way of discipleship spelled out in Romans 12 and 13.

Practically, this means that for the Christian the discernment of God's will is found through the transformed mind and the committed body (Romans 12:1-2), which expresses itself to all by love. The state is not, therefore, the source of the Christian's wisdom as to what is God's will, nor how it should be expressed. Instead, the state's demands are to be weighed in light of the gospel (Romans 12:1—13:10).

Perhaps an example may help bring this point home. One of the functions of the state is to pass laws to regulate life within its jurisdiction. Once a law has been passed, it may be legal or illegal. The fact that it is a law does not mean that it is automatically right. Rather, the law may be tested in the courts to see if it is right, in accord with the governing legal principles. If it is decided that it is, it is not only a law, but also legal. The fact that a law is declared legal does not mean that it is thus necessarily just or equitable. The law, even legal laws, can be used to harm or take advantage of others or to get an unfair advantage for someone. Likewise, that something is legal does not make it right in the light of Christian morality. Indeed, the state is incompetent to make this judgment; only Christians can as they discern God's will. This is why for Christians the debate on the morality of abortion was not ended with the United States Supreme Court's decision declaring it legal, since for the state to declare something legal does not make it right.

Here, then, is a real limitation of the state—the most it can do is to declare something legal. The Christian, however, cannot assume that whatever is legal is also in accordance with Christian morality. This would be to give to the state powers which it does not have. Rather, it is in the church that God's will is known. In the end there will always be a tension between what is legal and what is right. This does not mean that most laws are wrong or that Christians can dispense with government. It does mean that Christians cannot abdicate to the state their discernment of God's will, nor use Romans 13:1-7 as an excuse to do so.

In Romans 13:1-7, taking it in context, Paul is teaching that Christians should relate to the state as disciples of Christ in love, just as to all others both within and without the church. In this particular case, Paul says that as a practical application this means to pay them their taxes. Why this was an expression of Christian love we will see in the next step, when we look at the historical context for this passage.

Chapter 7

From Author to Audience

7.00 Historical Background

When they think of in-depth Bible study, most people think immediately of digging into the historical background of a passage. Up to now, however, we have focused mainly on the passage itself, although in the last two steps of analysis we have also related some aspects of the passage to the history and culture of the time. In this phase of study, however, we will look at the historical and cultural environment of the composition of the work. A knowledge of the historical situation can guide us to a better understanding of both the point of a unit and its function in the larger work to which it belongs.

This exploration into the historical context of a passage can aid our understanding for two major reasons. First of all, language is not self-contained, but refers to objects, people, events, and processes in history and in the experience of people. Language is used as a sign to point beyond itself to what is being talked about. This means that often in order to understand what is being said, we need to know the topic of conversation. We have all had the experience of coming into the middle of a conversation and not being able to make heads or tails out of what is being said until we ask, "What are you talking about?" Once we find this out, the pieces of conversation fall into place and we understand what was said. Thus, while we have spent a good deal of time studying the language of a passage in the past stages of study, we must go on to learn the context in which this language was used and about which it is speaking in order for us to understand it accurately.

The second reason for needing to know the historical circumstances of a work is because of the conversational aspect of language. An author in writing to an audience assumes a certain situation or state of affairs. This situation forms the background for what he is saying to them. As a result, many things are left unsaid. They do not need to be expressed since they are part of the shared knowledge on the part of author and audience. However, for an "outsider" listening in or reading the work, this background information may not be known and may cause the words to be misunderstood. Because of this, it is vitally important that the context is recovered so that a more accurate understanding can take place.

These two considerations allow us to reinforce a point already discussed: *when the context of a word, passage, or work is changed, the meaning may also be changed.* Having crossed back and forth between the United States and Canada, I have discovered that some English words do not have quite the same meaning in these two countries, in spite of a common language and a largely common culture. How much more this is true when we think of the vast differences between modern Western culture and the ancient Near East, since in addition to different cultures, we also have a great distance in time. We need to always be on our guard against "westernizing" the biblical authors. We can avoid this by seeing their writings in their authentic historical and cultural context.

To summarize: the books of the Bible were written in specific situations, by individual authors who were often addressing themselves to specific questions or circumstances. In order to interpret their writings correctly, we must uncover these specific historical factors assumed in their writing.

For example, the Gospel of John is written differently from the Synoptics. One of the reasons for this has to do with a different historical and social context to which the book is addressed. By uncovering these peculiarities of the context, we can also then understand the peculiarities of the book. If we ignore these and interpret John as if it were just like the Synoptics, we will misunderstand the book because we are taking it out of its context.

The words of Scripture came to their audience addressed to their situation. By uncovering that specific historical situation, we can begin to catch a glimpse of why the words were written. This will be important in our application of Scripture for two reasons. First, it allows us to see the reason or rationale behind what is written. Why, for example, did Paul command that Christians should greet one another with a holy kiss? Putting this exhortation in its context may allow us to more readily grasp the principle behind these words. It is this principle which we in turn will seek to put into practice in our context.

Second, it allows us to put together the various voices in Scripture on a subject. When we realize how Scripture was written in and to specific historical contexts, and we understand its meaning in those contexts, we can begin to see the strengths and limitations of various passages. For example, notice Jesus' use of Scripture in Mark 10:2-9. Here, Jesus bases his teaching on Genesis 1 and 2 rather than Deuteronomy 24. He does so because he draws out why Deuteronomy 24 was given. Realizing this, he is in a position to understand its relative merits with regard to Genesis 1 and 2. He values the latter more because of the difference in reason or motive behind the text. Thus, the historical situation is invaluable for understanding a passage not only for itself, but for its place within the total context of the Bible.

In discussing the historical context, we can divide it into two major aspects. There is, first of all, the general historical situation within which a work was written and read. This is the general cultural environment against which a passage needs to be seen. For the New Testament the general environment of the first century AD would be important background information. But, of course, cultures are not just general and uniform; they have various streams and circles, subcultures within the larger culture. These are distinct circles of ideas, customs, and traditions. Thus, it is necessary to move from the general to the specific; what was the specific situation of the author when he wrote and who specifically was the audience? This is the second aspect of the historical situation. Here we try to find out all we can about who wrote to whom, when, where, and why. It is this specific information which often gives us the deepest insights into a book or passage.

The historical setting itself can be divided into two major parts. There is first of all the social, cultural, and historical background of a work. In addition, there is the intellectual or theological setting of a writing. Just as we have studied in tradition analysis the thought background for a specific unit, so also we can study the intellectual background of the book as a whole. This builds on redaction analysis just completed: where is the theology of the book as a whole at home in the culture?

7.01 Axiom: Words have a meaning in a given context; since changing the context may change the meaning, a valid interpretation is based on understanding the words within their original context. This is their normative historical sense.

7.02 *Procedures*

What are the clues which will help to reconstruct the historical background? In general, there are two kinds of information to draw upon—internal and external. Internal evidence is what can be learned from the work itself, while external evidence is what you can discover from other sources. The questions you will need to ask usually draw more heavily on internal than on external information. However, it is the dovetailing together of the two sets of information which gives the greatest certainty to the results.

A. *Analysis*
  1. What was the wider historical and cultural context of the work?
     a. What was the political situation of that time?
     b. What was the social context?
     c. What cultural currents or historical events seem to be reflected in the work?
     d. What intellectual or theological currents are reflected in the work?

  2. What were the immediate circumstances of the composition of the work?
     a. When was the work composed?
     b. Where was it composed?
     c. Who was the author and what were the circumstances of writing?
     d. To whom was the work written? What was its immediate audience?
     e. What can be reconstructed as the circumstances of the work? In what context are we to understand the book?

B. *Synthesis*
  1. From the above, what were the major precipitating influences which lie behind the writing of the book?

  2. In what ways is this information useful in illuminating the meaning of your passage?

7.03 *Illustrations*
  Genesis 12:10-20

Setting the general historical and social context of this story in its present written form is not easy to do. There are not many clear clues to guide us here. As we have seen, this story is part of what is usually called the J material. The question is when and in what social context was the J material set down as we have it today. Usually in dating a document, we first try to set the limits before which or after which it must occur. For J we must ask what period of time or events must it come after, that is what events are presupposed in the writing. For example, in Genesis 14:14, we read that Abram followed the four kings as far as the town of Dan, where he then attacked them. In Judges 18:27-29, we read that the name of the city was Laish until the Danites destroyed it, rebuilt it, and then named it Dan. Thus, Genesis 14:14 would seem to have been written after these events which take place in the period of the judges. Likewise, in Genesis 12:6 and 13:7, when it is said that "the Canaanite was then in the land," it seems to indicate that they are not there any longer. This again would be sometime after or during the period of the judges, since we still find the Canaanites around at that time (see Judges 1 and 4-5). Or again, the Philistines are mentioned in Genesis 26:14, 15, 18, and elsewhere. Since the Philistines came to Israel as part of the sea people's migration in the period of the judges, it seems clear that these stories in their present form date from after their migration and invasion of Palestine.[1]

If we look at the laws which occur in J in Exodus, we receive the impression that these laws presuppose a village, agrarian existence, a type of life we likewise see developing in the period of the judges. Similarly, there are passages such as Genesis 49:8-12 and Numbers 24:9, 17-19 which point to kingship.[2] Thus, it seems clear that the J material was written at the earliest sometime near the end of the period of the judges and the beginning of the monarchy in Israel.

Besides this type of evidence, there are certain general tendencies in the Yahwist (J) which seem to point to the period of David and Solomon as the time of composition. First, there is the notion of "all Israel" as being represented in these stories. But the period of the judges reflects a period of tribal independence, and indeed at times intertribal warfare. A united Israel seems to have come about under the monarchy of David. So, too, the people which J talks about are the peoples of David's time—for examples, the Philistines, Moabites, Ammonites, Amalekites are the neighbors and foes of the Davidic kingdom (see 2 Samuel 8). Or again, in Isaac's speech to Esau in 27:30-40b, Isaac mentions that Esau would throw off Jacob's yoke. Some have seen in this an allusion to Edom's rebellion against Solomon and 1 Kings 11:14-22.[3]

In addition, the time of the early monarchy seems to have been a

- time when writing flourished in Israel. It is thought that perhaps three narratives were written in that period about David and the events of his life. There are, the history of the ark (1 Samuel 4—6 and 2 Samuel 6); the rise of David (1 Samuel 16:14 to 2 Samuel 5:12); and the narrative recounting the succession to the throne of David (2 Samuel 9—20 and 1 Kings 1—2). Thus, the soil would have been fertile for putting down into a more comprehensive, connected form the ancient traditions concerning Israel's ancestors. Moreover, definite correlations in writing style, theme, and motifs have been seen between the narratives concerning David and the Yahwist's narratives.[4] Thus, it seems that the time of the united monarchy in the tenth century B.C. would form a suitable environment for the composition of the J material.[5]

What were those times like in ancient Israel? It was a time of ferment, of rapid social development and change. It was the time of the introduction of a new institution into Israel, the monarchy. This had the effect of diminishing the old tribal autonomy and turning Israel into a state with centralized authority. To support this new center of power, there was also a centralized military force which did the bidding of the king. An example was David's mercenary band of soldiers who were loyal to him, supporting him against the Israelite militia in the time of Absalom's revolt. This new institution, monarchy, with its new customs and ideology must have sent tremendous shock waves through Israel.

The king also became the sponsor of religion and of the central sanctuary which he cultivated. David brought the ark to Jerusalem amidst much celebration while Solomon built the magnificent temple in Jerusalem. Thus, religion too came under royal patronage and was influenced by it. The royal psalms in the book of Psalms are one indication of how deeply kingship and religion became intertwined in Israel.

David also created an empire. Israel was no longer an unknown, a little backwater area of village people, but the center of a powerful empire which received tribute from many surrounding peoples. Old enemies like the Philistines had been rendered harmless (2 Samuel 8); glorious days seem to stretch ahead. In this new situation, an international perspective must have spread through Israel. Israel was among the nations.

Also, during this period as the state developed, urbanization must have increased significantly. One thinks of Jerusalem, David's capital and the home of the government bureaucracy. Likewise, in other towns there must have been government officials which increased town populations and commerce. This was a time of prosperity. Income came into Israel in the form of booty from foreign wars, tribute from conquered nations, and the profit from her far-ranging commercial enterprises which seemed to have reached their zenith during Solomon's reign.

New elites arose in order to govern the country, the empire, and the commercial enterprises. This led to a process of social stratification, since the new wealth and power which came to Israel would not have been equally shared by all. New positions were filled by men of cunning, for such were needed to run the new large enterprises. About one of these advisers it was said that his advice was as if one asked an oracle of God (2 Samuel 16:23). This was an exciting new age of opportunity—to make one's way at court or in the field of battle all one needed was clever wits and courage.

There was a more sombre side to these developments, since there was also increasing contact with the pagan religions, both in Israel and in the neighboring countries. Jerusalem, the new capital and religious center, was a Jebusite city with a major Jebusite population. Other Canaanite cities were also incorporated into Israel at this time. Likewise, the free intercourse with the foreign nations meant the increasing awareness of their gods and religions. This was especially so at the court, where the king would take into his harem princesses of foreign nations in order to establish or maintain good relations. These princesses would bring their religions with them. Again, under Solomon, especially, this seems to have had a significant impact on the king and by extension, presumably on the court and country as well.

Exactly the specific situation, the context, within which the J materials were written is unclear, but they do seem to have come from the southern part of the kingdom, from Judah. They may have come from courtly circles who were interested in putting together the traditions of the past. But whatever else may be said, they reflect a strong and vital religious commitment and perspective which has shaped the work. It is from this theological perspective of the material that scholars have tried to determine the specific precipitating processes which lie behind the work.[6]

It has been seen that the J material is addressing the issues associated with the rise of Davidic monarchy—the role of Israel in the world, and of the monarchy within Israel. How does the lordship of God speak to this new situation in which there is great affluence and self-sufficiency? J speaks to this first of all in the theme of promise, for the promises of God to the partriarchs were being fulfilled in the days of David and

Solomon.[7] The promise of land (Genesis 13:14-15, for example) seems to reach its pinnacle of fulfillment as described in 1 Kings 4:24 (English) under Solomon. The great name promised, also, has its fulfillment in the fame of Solomon (1 Kings 1:47 and 10:1-10). Likewise, the prosperity and great nation status, promised at the beginning of the patriarchal stories in Genesis 12:2-3, seems to find fulfillment in 1 Kings 4:20-21, (English) again at the beginning of the reign of Solomon. For the Yahwist, the time of David and Solomon can thus be seen as a time of the fulfillment of the promises of God to the ancestors of Israel.[8]

Second, the promises were to the people as a whole, not to the king as an isolated individual. The king represents the people who are now realizing God's blessing. This is a corrective to putting too much emphasis on kingship and what it means for the prosperity of the people.[9]

For people in the time of David and Solomon, J is thus saying that Israel's successes were not so much due to the crown or to the cleverness of the royal advisers, nor to the might of the army, but rather were a result of God's promise to Israel. The accomplishments of the monarchy were more due to divine grace than to human achievement. This would have been a powerful antidote to the rise of self-satisfaction, not to mention arrogance, which would have accompanied the successes which were taking place under the monarchy. It would be humbling to the monarch to realize that it was God's providence which held the key to the nation's future instead of his own programs, schemes, and wisdom.

In this respect, the anti-theme to promise, the thread of threat and divine deliverance which runs through these stories, is an antidote to placing too much confidence in the plans of man. In Genesis 12:10-20 the threat is the result of human action and human planning. Not only is Israel's blessing due to God's grace rather than to human strength, but human cunning in fact endangers the promise. Rather than human plans implementing or promoting God's providence for Israel, they erected stumbling blocks to its actual realization.

This raises the question of whether the royal plans likewise were not threatening Israel's present destiny. The plans of the king might after all be a detour from the will of God. Empire building, commercial cartels, far-flung diplomatic networks, all so carefully conceived and crafted, may be leading Israel on a path away from her true destiny. The burning question which the theme of promise would pose would be, after the fulfillment of the promise of land, after descendants and wealth, would Israel fulfill her worldwide role, would she be the nation by whom "all communities on earth shall bless themselves" (Genesis 12:3, following Speiser)? This, it seems, was the challenge these patriarchal stories put to the Davidic monarchy.[10]

Genesis 12:10-20 is obviously basic to the theme of blessing/trust and deliverance/planning since it sets the theme forth with such stark clarity. The contrast is between human acts which bring harm, and God's providence which saves. Its call is a call for less reliance on human foresight and greater trust in the divine promise. It represents a challenge to the state which would seek to control its own destiny by political means through its advisers whose advice was like the word of God (2 Samuel 16:22). Its lesson is that the future cannot be calculated by people; but ultimately rests on divine providence. Israel will fulfill the destiny which God has promised her as the people of God by remaining linked in devotion and trust to Yahweh alone.[11]

Amos 2:6-16

The dating of the book of Amos is considerably more straightforward than the Genesis material. From the heading of the book in Amos 1:1, we learn that Amos was active during the reign of Jeroboam in Israel (the Northern Kingdom), and Uzziah in Judah (the Southern Kingdom). Since Jeroboam died about 747 and Amos prophesied his death (7:9ff), the activity of Amos must have come before 747. Uzziah was struck with leprosy during his reign, and so was forced to take his son Jotham as co-regent. This co-regency is mentioned in Hosea 1:1. By implication Amos can be placed before this, perhaps before 755. The victories mentioned in Amos 6:13 seem to reflect 2 Kings 14:25. These successes took place late in the reign of Joash (802-787) and early in the reign of Jeroboam (787-747). If Amos 8:9 refers to the eclipse of 763, and 1:1 to the earthquake dated to 760, this would tie the words of Amos to specific events and would confirm the date of shortly before 760 BC.[12]

To understand the general setting of the ministry of Amos, however, we must begin our story at least a century earlier. After the division of the kingdom upon the death of Solomon, the Northern Kingdom went through an extended period of political turbulence. No ruler was able to establish a dynasty and several reigns ended in bloody coups. This turmoil reached its height shortly before 876, when a general named Omri finally seized power. Omri restored order, built the capital city of Samaria, and established good relations with some of the neighboring states. His son Ahab succeeded him to the throne.

Ahab's reign (869-851), too, was a time of prosperity and increasing political influence. Evidently Ahab was one of the most powerful kings in that region, since he seemd to have been a leader in the coalition of kings from the western fertile crescent which banded together to hold off the Assyrians in the Battle of Qarqar in 853. Ahab's son Ahaziah succeeded him. When Ahaziah died as a result of a fall shortly after taking office, he was succeeded by his brother Jehoram. It appeared that political stability would be established in the Northern Kingdom under the Omride dynasty, as was the case in the south under the Davidic dynasty. But such was not to be.

In 842 a bloody purge of the Omride dynasty took place, instigated by Elisha and carried out by Jehu, a general in Jehoram's army (2 Kings 9—10). In this coup, not only were all the Omrides slaughtered, but also Jezebel, who had been Ahab's wife, and Ahaziah, who was king of Judah and related to Jehoram by marriage. These two murders had far-reaching consequences since they meant a break with Israel's national neighbors: Judah on the south and Phoenicia on the north. This left Israel isolated politically.

Jehu's reign (842-815) was a disaster. As a result of his brutal murders of many of the countries' leaders (2 Kings 10:11) as well as many others, he undoubtedly began his reign with internal tension and hostility. Furthermore, the Arameans of Damascus began to press Israel, and they eventually defeated her. Jehu lost the whole of Trans-Jordan to them (2 Kings 10:32ff.). His son Jehoahaz (815-801) suffered even greater defeats by the Arameans and was stripped of his army. Israel thus sank to a very low ebb. The average Israelite must have suffered greatly in this invasion and conquest by the Arameans.

However, under Joash, the son of Jehoahaz, affairs took a turn for the better. This recovery was in a large part due to a change in the international situation. Assyria, under the leadership of Adad-nirari III, marched west and in approximately 802 conquered Damascus. Fortunately for Israel, Assyria was unable to continue her conquests in the west because she had to turn her attention to a rival power, Urartu. This allowed Israel breathing room. Freed from Damascus and temporarily relieved of Assyrian pressure, Joash was able to reconquer the cities lost by his father (2 Kings 13:25).

Thus, when Jeroboam II came to the throne, Israel was resurgent and prospering. He continued this trend, pushing Israel's border as far north as it had been in Solomon's time (2 Kings 14:25). This event is probably alluded to by Amos in 6:2. Uzziah, who ruled Judah at that time, also expanded his kingdom. First, he extended his control over Edom, ultimately reaching the port of Ezion-geber (2 Kings 14:22). Together these two kings ruled over an area comparable to that controlled by David and Solomon. If that period was Israel's golden age, then the time of Jeroboam and Uzziah was Israel and Judah's silver age.[13]

As in the time of David and Solomon, these conquests and annexations meant prosperity. Amos gives us insights into the luxurious living of the rich in his day (6:1-6; 4:1; and 3:15). But although there was great prosperity, the wealth was not equitably distributed. The peasants who had suffered so harshly during the time of the Aramean oppression did not necessarily participate in the new prosperity. The wealthy in fact seemed to be getting wealthier at the expense of the poor (see Amos 4:1, for example).

The system in fact seemed to operate against the poor, the oppressed, and dispossessed. The economic system did not operate equitably, as Amos 8:4-6 shows, nor were the courts places of justice, according to 5:7, 10. Poverty in the midst of affluence, perpetrated and perpetuated by the social system: this seems to have been the context of Amos's ministry.

Yet the people were not wicked people. They continued to worship Yahweh (Amos 5:20-23; 4:5-6). Indeed, they believed that God must be with them (5:14). Why else would the nation be experiencing such prosperity at home and success abroad?

What had happened that allowed those who were so religious to practice such social oppression? What had happened was that the principles and assumption which promote justice and righteousness were not those on which the social and economic system were based in Amos's time. In fact, the system was operating in just the reverse fashion as shown by the oppression and injustice which Amos decried.[14]

The principles of justice and righteousness are perhaps most clearly manifested in the reform legislation outlined in Leviticus 25, since its purpose was to bring about a more equitable order. Yahweh owned the land, the people were only its users. Thus it was only the use of the land that could be sold (Leviticus 25:23, 14-17). In the time of Amos, however, the land was held as private property by individuals who squeezed the rest of the people off the land (Isaiah 5:8). Further, the reform legislation gave people access to the resources through gleaning, tithes, and the sabbatical and jubilee years. Distribution was based on need (Deuteronomy 15:1-11). In Amos's time, however, there was a market economy where the goal was profit, getting more than giving (Amos 8:4-6). While the goal of the reform legislation was to meet the needs of the poor and the dispossessed (Deuteronomy 15:4, 11), in Amos's time the goal was wealth, storing up the surplus (Amos 3:10). This wealth led to status consumption such as we see described in Amos 6:1-6. The gap between the way of justice and righteousness and the economics of wealth which Israel's powerful few exercised seems to have been the immediate precipitating factor behind the message of Amos. The chart (opposite page) will make clear the difference between the economics of justice embodied in the law and the economics of wealth being practiced.

The message of Amos thus came to a people who were confident, a people who were riding high, a people for whom the future looked bright. The Lord called Amos to bring words of judgment against the social injustice of the people, a social injustice which came from seeking wealth rather than the welfare of the poor and oppressed. It was a socially unjust system which was bound to get worse as long as the people sought ever greater wealth. These factors can be clearly seen behind Amos 2:6b, the callous disregard for human welfare in the search for increased material gain.

One feature of Amos's message for which we have as yet found no explanation is his audience—why did Amos address the people rather than the king directly?[15] This is to be explained against the background of the political situation of that time.[16] With the rise of Assyria a change took place in political accountability between nations. Whereas previously the royal dynasty was held responsible for keeping a treaty with another state, now the whole nation was responsible. This meant that if a nation breached a treaty with Assyria, the people of the offending state would be punished. By analogy, then, the people, not just the king, as accountable to Yahweh, would be responsible for the establishment of justice and righteousness.

This change in accountability also necessitated a change in the function of the messenger for the Assyrian Empire. The messenger now needed to address the king's message to the entire nation. Likewise God's messengers, the prophets, were commissioned to speak to the nation and the leading classes within the nation.

	Justice Economics	Wealth Economics
Ownership of resources	Based on use—Lev. 25:14-17, 25-28, 29-31; Deut. 15:7-8	Title/deed ownership of both consumer and capital goods. Is. 5:8
Access to resources	Open: Lev. 25:1-7; Ex. 23:10f.; Lev. 19:9-10; Deut. 23:25-26; 24:19-22 (gleaning); 15:7-11	Closed: ownership confers exclusive rights. Resource concentration.
Distribution	Need: Deut. 15:1-11; 14:28-29; 16:11, 14. Also the references above under open access—"Eat all you want."	Profit: market economy—getting rather than giving. Amos 8:4-6
Goal	Finite: livelihood of all Deut. 15:4(11) (Acts 2:41-47; 4:33-37)	Infinite: wealth. Never enough, no limit.
Consumption	To meet basic needs	Status expression of wealth, self-aggrandizement. Amos 6:1-6
Result	Peace—based on justice/righteousness. No poor. Deut. 15:4 (Acts 4:32-34; 11:27-30)	Social stratification. Affluence in the midst of poverty; improper social order—injustice and no peace. Amos 2:6-8; 4:1; 6:1-6, etc.

Matthew 5:38-42

To construct Amos's context we were dependent heavily on external sources and archaeological evidence. In Matthew we are dependent on internal evidence. This means that our understanding of the context and aim of Matthew grows out of his message. From our understanding of his message we try to reconstruct a background in which such a message would make sense. It is like having a set of answers to which we are to figure out the questions.

As seen above, Matthew used the sources Mark and Q in the composition of his Gospel. Consequently, much of Matthew can also be found in Mark and Luke. Why then did Matthew write? Why was Mark not sufficient? In answering these questions, we need to determine what about Matthew is peculiar or unique. From these clues, we can draw conclusions as to why he wrote his Gospel. What is unique to Matthew can be seen in Matthew's use of his sources—what he omits and what he changes as he places the material in his Gospel—as well as in the material which is found only in Matthew.

Perhaps one of the most striking features of Matthew is the series of distinctive quotations from the Old Testament which we noted above. These are located in 1:23; 2:6, 15b, 18, 23b; 4:14-16; 8:17; 12:17-21; 13:35; 21:4, 5; and 27:9, 10.[17] These quotations form a series since they all have a similar introductory formula: such and such happened, "in order that might be fulfilled the word spoken by the Lord through the prophet." Since these quotations often seem to be closer to the Hebrew text of the Old Testament than to the standard Greek translation of the Hebrew text, the Septuagint, it is thought that Matthew or his tradition knew Hebrew. In any case, these quotations make it clear that Matthew was concerned to show that Jesus was the fulfillment of the Old Testament Scriptures. This would have been particularly important for a Jewish audience. Thus, it is inferred that Matthew is writing in a context in which either the church had Jewish Christian members or was engaged in dialogue with the Jewish community.

Also unique to Matthew is that only here does Jesus demand "righteousness" of his disciples. This demand, which occurs in several passages, is clustered almost entirely in the Sermon on the Mount: 5:6, 10, 20; 6:1, 33; and 21:32. This parallels Matthew's emphasis on the abiding validity of the law for the Christian community (5:16-20), which we have studied above. This concern with righteousness and the place of the law in Christianity could also reflect a Jewish context.[18]

Several other features of the book affirm this "Jewish" character of Matthew. Questions or conversations between Jewish religious leaders and Jesus are recast in a form which is closer to the rabbinic form of question or argumentation. For example, in the question addressed to Jesus regarding divorce, Mark 10:2 reads, "Is it lawful for a man to divorce his wife?" while Matthew 19:3 reads, "Is it lawful for a man to divorce one's wife for any cause?" Notice how Matthew has "for any cause." Since in Deuteronomy 24 God's law allows for divorce, there was no question about whether or not it was lawful; the question was rather on what grounds it was to be permitted. On this question there was a great variety of rabbinic opinion. Thus, they addressed this question to Jesus to see where he would come out on this disputed point.

Similarly, there are sayings in Matthew which limit Jesus' activity to the Jews, thus laying special emphasis on them (Matthew 10:5, 23; 15:24). Finally, Matthew has systematically changed the expression "kingdom of God" found in Mark and Luke, to "kingdom of heaven," which was the Jewish expression.[19]

Together these features leave the definite impression that Matthew was writing for a Jewish context or at least a context with a strong Jewish influence. While it is possible that Matthew's Gospel could have been written as a missionary effort to the Jewish community in the period when the church and the synagogue were still closely related, the internal evidence seems to indicate that the break between Jewish Christians and the synagogue had already taken place. This is seen from the fact that in Matthew the synagogue is either the place of the hypocrites (6:2, 5; 23:6, 34) or "their" synagogue, as he specifically adds in 12:9 (Mark 3:1; Luke 6:6 do not have "their") and 13:54 (Mark 6:2 without "their"; see also Matthew 4:23; 9:35; 10:17). This clearly puts distance between the church and the Jewish community.[20]

However, Matthew wants to assure Jewish Christians in particular that Jesus is indeed the Messiah promised in the Old Testament. He is the fulfillment of Scripture. In addition, he underscores the fact that being a Christian does not abolish the law, but rather the law remains authoritative as interpreted by Jesus. It is through living according to love that one fulfills the "righteousness" which both Jesus and Judaism demand. We see, then, in Matthew a twofold thrust; first, to define Jesus more clearly as the Messiah, linking him securely with the Old Testament, and second to emphasize the necessity of Christian obedience to the Messiah, who as their Lord gives the true meaning to the law. This

obedience is not contrary to the law but is its true realization even when
it seems opposite to it. It manifests itself in the righteousness to which
Jesus calls his followers. These two emphases would indicate to Jewish
Christians their continuity with the Old Testament and prove how they
are on the right track in following Jesus rather than the rabbinic traditions.[21]

There are also signs that Matthew is not addressed to only a Jewish
Christianity but has a universal aspect as well. This is especially emphasized in the Great Commission at the end of the book, where the disciples are commanded to make disciples of all nations (28:19). Likewise,
in the parable of the weeds in the field, Jesus explains that the soil is the
whole world (13:38), where the Son of man sows the good seed. Thus his
mission would include both Jews and Gentiles. Matthew 22:14 has a
similar statement indicating the universal mission of the church.

The stress on the continued validity of the law (as in 5:17-20),
however, can be seen as addressed to those who might feel that in the
Christian community the law no longer had a place. In light of Matthew
7:13-27, especially verses 20-23, it has been argued that this antinomian
element in the church thought that gifts and spiritual power were the
marks of the Christian rather than discipleship. Against them, Matthew
asserts the basic response of obedience to God's will. Since we know of
this emphasis on gifts in Hellenistic and Gentile Christianity (1 Corinthians), it can be surmised that Matthew was not only addressed to the
Palestinian Jewish community.[22]

Given these aspects of the Gospel of Matthew, what can we say
about the date and place of writing? The date of writing would be after
Mark, since Matthew used Mark. Since Mark is usually dated around
AD 70, this would mean that Matthew probably dates 10 years or so
later, sometime after AD 80. The separation of the Jewish Christians
from the Jewish community and the hostility felt against the Jewish
leaders by the church (as in Matthew 23, for example) would also point
to a date sometime after the fall of Jerusalem (after AD 70), when this
tension would have been intense.

As to place, Syria has often been suggested because it was both
strongly influenced by Jewish Christianity and was also the seat of early
mission efforts. Antioch as the chief church of Syria would then perhaps
be the most likely location. On this, of course, we have no definite information.[23]

How does this reconstructed background help us to understand

Matthew? The major themes of Matthew which we have used to develop Matthew's background are well represented in Matthew 5:38-42. Here, as we have seen, Jesus is presenting a new interpretation of the law, which is to be authoritative for his disciples. He can do this because of who he is, thus the new teaching begins with "I say." This new interpretation is based on love rather than on normal human justice. This teaching of Jesus is central to the new righteousness to which Jesus is calling his followers, so that our passage would have been central to any discussion of what the Christian way was all about. Since Matthew sets forth an expanded Mark by giving more of Jesus' teachings, especially as they related to the demands of the law, we can see that 5:38-42 was one of those added passages which was central to Matthew's purpose.

Romans 13:1-7

Romans 15:22-29 seems to give us information from which we can date and reconstruct the setting in Paul's life for the writing of this letter.[24] In this passage, Paul writes that he wants to visit Rome, but must first go to Jerusalem (v. 25). He also mentions that Macedonia and Achaia have made a contribution to the collection for the Jerusalem church, which was his reason for going there. This description by Paul seems to link it with Acts 19:21-22 and 20:1-3 where, after a long stay in Ephesus, Paul journeys to Macedonia and Greece in order to complete the collection before traveling to Jerusalem.

The three months Paul spent in Greece, mentioned in Acts 20:3 is therefore considered the time of Paul's composition of Romans. Corinth is probably the place of writing, as can be seen from Romans 16:23 where Gaius is mentioned as Paul's host. Gaius was a leading figure in the Corinthian church (see 1 Corinthians 1:14). Also, Romans 16:1-2, where Phoebe, a deacon at Cenchreae is mentioned, supports Corinth as the place of writing since Cenchreae was the port city of Corinth. Phoebe was probably the deliverer of the letter.

When was this stay of Paul in Corinth? This can be dated on the basis of the mention of Gallio, proconsul of Achaia in Acts 18:12-17, when Paul appeared before him as reported in this passage. From Roman documentation we know that Gallio was probably the proconsul in either AD 51-52 or 52-53. Thus, the date of the writing of Romans would be the date of Paul's appearance before Gallio, sometime between 51 and 53 plus the length of time of the events recounted between Acts 18:18 and 20:3, his stay in Corinth. Now most of this time was taken up with a long stay in Ephesus, recounted in Acts 19. This rather long visit of Paul may have lasted for two and a half years (Acts 19:8, 10). Before this visit Paul had stayed on in Corinth after his appearance before Gallio for many days (18:18), journeyed on to Ephesus for an initial brief contact (18:19), traveled to Jerusalem (18:22), and stayed a while in Antioch (18:22-23) before he set out again on his third missionary journey. On this journey he traveled through Galatia and Phrygia strengthening the Christians there (18:23) before he finally arrived in Ephesus for his sojourn there. Following Ephesus, he traveled throughout Macedonia before coming to Greece and Corinth. If we would allow two years or more for all these travels and shorter stays, adding this figure to the two and one half year stay in Ephesus, it would seem that probably five years had elapsed between Paul's first visit to Corinth (Acts 18) and his visit during which he wrote Romans (Acts 20:1-3). This would place the writing of Romans sometime between AD 56 (51 being the earliest date for Paul's appearance before Gallio plus five years) and AD 58 (53 being the latest date for Paul's appearance before Gallio plus five years).

The situation within which Paul wrote this letter has been alluded to above. Paul was now hoping to leave his work in the east and open a new mission field in the west in Spain. Rome would be on his route there, so he hoped to visit the church there on his way. Also, since this was presumably the major church in the west, it would serve him admirably for a mission base, a "home" church, very much like Antioch had been for him in the east. But before Paul could embark on this new program, he had to finish some old business, the collection for the church at Jerusalem. This was the discharge of an obligation which Paul had willingly accepted at the Jerusalem conference (Galatians 2:10). By this act, Paul would show the respect of the Gentile churches for the Jewish mother church at Jerusalem. So too, it might signal the ingathering of the Gentiles to the Jewish community.[25]

When we turn from Paul to the Roman church to ask who were they and what was their situation, things are not as clear.[26] Paul had never visited the church at Rome, although he knew people there (see the long list of names in chapter 16). He had probably met them, like Priscilla and Aquila (Acts 18:1-2), during his missionary journeys while they were in exile from Rome. Thus, while Paul had not visited Rome, he might well have known of events there from these friends.

On the whole the book seems written in quite general terms. There appears to be little in it addressed to specific issues or problems which were current at Rome. Because of this, some have concluded that Paul, having premonitions about his Jerusalem visit, sat down to write out his understanding of the gospel. If anything happened to him in Jerusalem, he would leave behind him this testimony to his faith and understanding of the gospel. In this view of things, the situation at Rome would have little to do with the letter, since it is a general statement of doctrine.[27]

On the other hand Paul Minear has put forward the argument that Romans, like other letters of Paul, was addressed to a specific situation at Rome. The key to this he sees in Romans 14:1—15:13, where Paul is writing about a specific dispute between vegetarians and nonvegetarians. In this dispute, Minear is able to distinguish a variety of positions and parties. He then uses these parties as a key to reconstructing the situation at Rome to which he sees Paul writing.[28]

Outside of 14:1—15:13, however, the focus of the letter seems quite scattered as Paul writes concerning the Jews (especially in 9—11), addresses Gentile Christians (1:5-6. 13f; 11:13; 15:15ff.), and writes against those who have thrown off the law and are now living loosely (3:8, 31; 6:1, 15; 7:7ff.). It looks as if Paul is writing to both Jews and Gentiles, to both legalists and antinomians. Consequently, no consensus has emerged either as to what the context of Romans was, nor as to its importance in understanding the letter, if it would be known.

The truth of the matter is, however, that whatever background has been given in the past for the book of Romans in general, it has not been very helpful in understanding Romans 13:1-7. However, recently a study has been published which sets forth a clear and helpful context for Romans 13.[29]

As is generally recognized, Priscilla and Aquila were in Corinth when Paul met them, because they had been banished from Rome (Acts 18:2). This banishment under Claudius is usually dated to AD 49, when it was reported that a riot broke out among the Jews concerning "Chrestus," usually understood as a corruption of "Christ." This riot caused Claudius to banish the Jews from the city. Under Nero, Claudius' successor, however, they began to filter back into Rome, so that at the time Paul wrote Romans, Priscilla and Aquila were once more back "home" again, with a church meeting in their house.

At this same time, Christianity was beginning to be seen as a distinct religion apart from Judaism. As long as it was seen as a form of Judaism, it had had official status, since Judaism was recognized as legitimate by the Roman government. However, standing alone it was an unofficial religion and thus looked upon with deep suspicion. Suetonius writes of Christianity in the time of Nero as a "new and evil superstition." Thus Roman Christians who had already run afoul of the emperor were also under a cloud of suspicion as being the members of a suspect cult.

But most importantly for understanding Romans 13:1-7, there was a great deal of civil unrest concerning taxes when Romans was written. In Rome, there were two categories of taxes: those whose income was predictable, like the poll tax, which was so much a head; and those whose income was unpredictable, like a sales tax which depended on how much was bought or sold in a given year. Since these latter taxes could not be estimated accurately when setting a budget, they were farmed out to the highest bidder. This gave the government a fixed amount on which it could count and thus it was able to set its budget on assured income.[30]

The tax collectors, however, were prone to extortion and overcollection, and the officials and magistrates very commonly participated in this. One can imagine the resentment felt both toward the large, wealthy, unscrupulous tax collecting firms and toward the system which permitted such abuses to exist. The citizens began to agitate against this unfair taxation, which could become quite heavy. There was even the possibility of a tax revolt. Affairs became so threatening in AD 58 that Nero, faced with this rising protest, decided to reform the tax system. At first, he wanted to abolish some duties, but his advisers were against it. They said if the people got this tax relief they would only want more. In the end Nero listened to his experts and only attempted to see that the tax collectors were regulated more closely.

In this light Paul's advice about the payment of taxes has immediate relevance. Paul saw the payment of taxes, rather than joining the general tax revolt, as the way of love toward the tax collectors. This also is connected with Paul's missionary motivation in writing the letter.[31] A peaceful situation would need to exist between the Roman government and the church if Paul's hopes of using Rome as the base for his western mission were to be successful. Paul's suggestion for the Roman Christians was thus based both on principle—love—and practical considerations—mission. By not aligning themselves with the currently popular tax revolt, both could be realized.

Part III
THE APPLICATION

Chapter 8

From Text to Practice: Making Application

8.00 Making Application

In chapter 1, we discussed several hazards which we need to avoid in going from the biblical text to application today. In this chapter we will concentrate on the positive side, how we can appropriately apply the text to our contemporary context. This process involves two major steps. First we need to state the meaning of the passage clearly in order to have firmly in mind the results of our studies. Once this is done, we then need to apply the meaning by analogy in our context. We will discuss each of these steps in turn.

The previous chapters have presented a series of study steps which have enabled us to examine a unit of Scripture from a variety of angles. Now we need to draw this information together. We must integrate it into a composite picture of the passage. We need to state what we consider the passage to have communicated in its context. In giving the sense of the passage we also want to draw out what are the implicit principles or general presuppositions which lie behind the passage. We need to do this because as we have seen, in moving from the meaning of the passage to application, it is the principle involved that is our best guide to present application (see chapter 1).

Once we have given what we judge to be the meaning of the passage, paying attention to the principles in it, we come to its application. First we begin with a comparison of the passage's context with our own. We try to determine in what ways our context is similar and in what ways different. Having made this comparison, we then take the principle found in the passage and by way of analogy seek to apply it to relevant situations today. There are no set rules for this procedure. It takes a certain amount of insight into the situation both then and now. It takes a certain ability to generalize, to see how different practices can actually be applications of the same principle.

In considering the relevant applications of the passage, we must not only be guided by the individual passage and our present particular context, but we must also consider what else the Bible has to say. We need to consider the entire range of Scripture. We cannot, of course, analyze the whole Bible before we apply a single passage, but we must, to the best of our knowledge, take into consideration other relevant passages when we do make application.

Done this way, Bible study is more like a pilgrimage than establishing resting places. As we come to know more about the Bible as a whole, as well as gain greater insight into individual passages, we continue to increase our understanding and sharpen our insight into how passages apply to our situation. This means we must be open and flexible to new insights. Otherwise we will find ourselves with hardening of the interpretational arteries.

Finally, in application we want to be as specific as we can be. We should try to state the application of the passage as concretely as possible—what would we do specifically if we took the principles of the passage seriously. By being specific, we also have some criteria to determine whether or not we are actually living in accord with the truth as we understand it.

As indicated in the first chapter, the application of Scripture occurs most faithfully in a group setting. The examples below can only indicate the type of considerations which lead to application. These examples, however, must be incomplete where group process is required, as in point 2 under synthesis. Look at these examples as pointers toward a process rather than as offering complete coverage of all the steps listed.

8.01 Axiom: Because of the relativity of cultures on the one hand, and the fact of language being addressed to a specific context on the other, in order to apply Scripture appropriately to our context today we need to be guided by principles which are applied by analogy.

8.02 Procedures

As was stated above, the application of a passage is discovered in two stages. In the first, the meaning, principle, and implications of the passage are set down. This is done on the basis of the previous steps of study whose aim was to enable you to state the meaning of a passage with some confidence and validity. In the second phase, this meaning with its principles and implications will be transferred to a modern setting to see how it can guide you today.

A. *Analysis*
1. Stating the Meaning
   Different forms can be used for stating the meaning of a passage.
   a. Commentary: Give verse-by-verse explanation of the meaning, drawing on the information discovered in your study.
   b. Paraphrase: Express the meaning of the passage in your own words.
   c. Summarize: Give a summary of the main point or the lesson taught. What was the audience to hear or what were they to do?

2. Discovering the Principles
   a. What was the intended function and scope of this passage? What would fall by implication within the range of generalizing from this passage? What are the presuppositions which lie behind the passage?
   b. What general principles, if any, lie behind the passage or are illustrated by the passage?
3. Comparing Other Passages
   What else is there in the Bible which we need to keep in mind when we apply the passage?
   a. Where else is this topic or related ones treated?
   b. How do these passages affect the principle or scope of the passage?

4. Finding the Application
   What in our own situation might be relevant in terms of application?
   a. What is different in our situation which may change the application of the passage?
   b. What is the same about our situation—what do we share in common with the original context?
   c. What contexts or areas of our life and culture are appropriate to the passage?
      (1) What are our cultural or social counterparts to the passage?
      (2) What present-day concerns fall by implication under the scope of the passage?

B. *Synthesis*
1. Formulate active definitions in making application.

    a. What would growth look like in this area?
    b. What would serve as a measure for such growth?

2. Build in accountability: Some group process, a mentor or friend.
    a. Confession and testimony
    b. Discussion and discipling.

8.03 *Illustrations*
Genesis 12:10-20

Since this passage is a narrative or story, most of the details belong to the realm of the descriptive, to the cultural forms of the time. In order to apply this story, we must go behind the events to the principle which we have seen illustrated in the story. This principle or lesson was the tension between the plans of Abram and divine providence: Abram's plans jeopardized the plan of God. We may summarize our story by saying it is meant to teach us to trust God and his providence rather than rely on our own shrewd planning (clue 2). To the contrary, what we regard as shrewd planning may work against us.

The theme of trust and promise is not unique to this story, but as we have seen, it permeates the Abram cycle of stories in Genesis. The stories begin with an act of trust when Abram leaves home and journeys to a new land. Again and again the trust of Abram is emphasized, as in chapters 15 and 22. The lesson of our story receives greater force from this constant repetition. Trust is vital as the whole cycle of stories shows, but planning may lead to ruin (cf. Genesis 16).

The theme of trust is found not only in these stories but elsewhere in the Bible as well (clue 3). In the wisdom literature (Proverbs), which places so much emphasis on planning and understanding, we find a warning, "Trust in the Lord with all your heart, and do not rely on your own insight" (Proverbs 3:5). Here is the recognition of the limits of human understanding and the need for trust.

Likewise, in the New Testament, we can see the same theme in the teachings of Jesus. In the parable of the rich fool (Luke 12:16-21) a man planned wisely, and thought he was well taken care of, but Jesus called him a "fool" because he had not calculated the action of God. Jesus follows this parable with a teaching on trust and not being concerned about tomorrow. (See also the other passages discussed under redaction and historical analysis.)

We know that planning must have its place—we cannot simply live as the birds of the air and the flowers of the field. In fact, we can also find the theme of planning and of carefully considering the future in the Bible. Again in the teachings of Jesus, those who would be his followers are enjoined to count the cost (Luke 14:25-33). They are advised to calculate carefully whether or not they can pay the necessary price. Or again in Luke 16:1-13 Jesus holds up the example of the steward who planned for his future. Thus we can see that planning does have its place in the Bible and people are exhorted to think about the future carefully.

How do we bring together these two threads—of trusting God and not endangering the future by our plans and of needing to calculate the cost and to plan for the future? The answer, it seems, is to plan in the light of God's providence. In Genesis 12:10-20, we saw that Abram did not take God or his promise into consideration in his planning. The implication is that it was his planning from only a human point of view that got him into trouble.

Having drawn out the principle theme of the story, having noted something of its relationship to the same theme elsewhere in Scripture, and having seen how this theme might relate to a countertheme, what specific application might we make to our contemporary context? We do this, as indicated above, by way of analogy. The story itself can be applied at two levels—the individual level and the national. Here we will seek to make an analogy only at the individual level.

How might the principle of planning for the future in light of God's providence affect us in today's world? One answer is in choosing a career. We, like Abram, face an uncertain future. We feel unable in many ways to control our own destiny. We seem to be more victims than initiators. In this situation we are tempted to seek security as best we can by careful vocational and financial planning. Where will there be jobs? Where will we be able to make out best financially? What are safe investments against inflation? Will we have enough to retire on? These are the type of questions which seem often to be on our minds.

It is not that planning is wrong, as we have just seen. It is, rather, that in asking these questions, we also need to ask another set. What is God about in the world today? How can I be a part of this action? Through asking these questions we can plan in the light of God's providence.

Finally, we need to spell this out in specific ways. For example, what choices would I make if I really took God's providence seriously? What career would I choose either when I begin one or change from one to another during my vocational life? What type of investments might I make? It is through wrestling and answering such questions for ourselves that we come to live by trust rather than by plan, to live in the light of providence rather than by our own insight.

Amos 2:6-16

In this passage we have concentrated on the second half of verse 6. We have seen how the practices which Amos denounced here were not specifically forbidden by the law. Rather, they were denounced because they represent the absence of justice and righteousness which was Amos's positive call to the nation (5:24). By way of summary, we can say that Amos is basing himself on the principle that depriving the needy, the dispossessed, of their status indicates a lack of justice and righteousness. Rather than selling the dispossessed into slavery, they should be instituting reforms which would restore their economic freedom.

Having summarized the passage and stated its underlying principle (clues 1 and 2) we can explore this theme or idea as found elsewhere in the Bible. It is a dominant theme in the prophets. It is found in the preexilic prophets as well as in the postexilic ones. (For a brief example, see Isaiah 1:21-23 and Micah 3:9-12 for eighth-century prophets. Jeremiah 21:11-12; 22:1-5, 13-17 for a seventh-century prophet. For a postexilic prophet see Isaiah 58:1-8.) In all of these passages justice and righteousness is central. How the poor and dispossessed are treated is an indication of whether justice and righteousness exist in the society. This is very similar to what we have seen in Amos.

The emphasis on justice and righteousness should not be surprising, because these in turn go back to the very nature of God himself. In Isaiah 58:1-8, we can see how social justice is linked to the worship of God. This is so, because God is a God who does justice, who is concerned for the poor and the oppressed. Indeed, this is a reason we are to praise God as we can see from Psalm 146. The bulk of this psalm is an adoration of God because he is a God who is concerned about the poor and oppressed.

That God is for social justice is perhaps not particularly startling. We would hardly expect him to be against it. However, the theme runs deeper. God is not only for social justice, but his activity for it is part of what it means for God to be God. In Psalm 82, God takes his stand among the divine beings in the council. These other supposed gods are taken to task because they do not promote social justice. In fact, they are doing just the opposite. This shows that they are not gods at all. Yahweh, the God of Israel, is God alone because he is an advocate for the poor and oppressed.

In Psalm 72 we find a prayer for the king, where God is petitioned that his justice and righteousness might be given to the king. This is necessary in order that God's will can be realized on earth. The importance of social justice for the prophets, then, has its roots in the nature of God. It is to be manifested through the rule of the king as he tries to rule correctly.

Given the importance of this theme of social justice, we should not be surprised to find that it dominates the prophets' visions as they look to the future. This is especially true as they look for a future ideal ruler. This ruler will be one who wills God's will, who will bring about justice and righteousness. Again if we look at a sampling of the passages concerning the future ruler we can see that in each one justice and righteousness is mentioned: Isaiah 9:1-7 (English); 11:1-9; 16:5; 32:15-17; Jeremiah 23:5-6; 33:15-16.

Summarizing this material from the Old Testament, we can see that the theme of justice and righteousness as expressed in social justice for the oppressed is a dominant theme in theology, politics, social criticism, and utopian longing. The passage in Amos 2:6-16 stands squarely in this significant theological tradition. In the New Testament we can see the continuation of these ideas in the ministry of Jesus. This is especially clear in the book of Luke where Jesus is presented as one who is good news, literally for the poor, oppressed, and outcast. This topic is too large to be discussed here at length, but an indication of the importance of this theme in Luke's Gospel can be seen by looking at some passages which only occur in Luke. This material, special to Luke, presents the picture of Jesus as one caring for the poor and dispossessed.

When John the Baptist came preaching the good news that those who have should share with those who do not, the people thought that perhaps he was the Messiah (Luke 3:10-18). Likewise, when Jesus began his ministry, he announced that he was to proclaim good news for the poor and oppressed (4:16-30). This agenda was carried out in Jesus' ministry in a variety of ways. First, he was positive toward the outcasts: the Samaritans (10:29-37 and 17:11-19); women (7:11-17, 13:10-17; 8:1-3). He broke down the social rules which bound women, placing listening to his words above domestic duties (10:38-42) and obedience above motherhood (11:27-28). Finally in Luke even the thief on the cross is portrayed positively. The second thief in Luke upbraids the reproach of the first and asks for Jesus' remembrance (23:39-43); this is striking when compared to Matthew 27:44 where both thieves are insulting Jesus.

This picture of Jesus as one caring for the poor and dispossessed reaches its pinnacle in Jesus' teachings concerning wealth and material possessions. He proclaims the poor blessed and pronounces woe on the rich (6:20-26). His parable of the rich man and Lazarus illustrates this principle. The rich man ends up in the fires of Hades, while Lazarus finds his reward with Abraham. The parable of the rich fool teaches the folly of storing up wealth for future benefit (12:13-21). Zacchaeus, when he enters the kingdom, gives half of what he has to the poor (19:10). This is in stark contrast to the rich young ruler, who in chapter 18 was unwilling to make a similar material sacrifice. In Luke, Jesus' disciples are not only exhorted to lay up for themselves treasures in heaven, but are also commanded to sell what they have and give to the poor so that they might have these treasures (Luke 12:33). Only Luke has the parable of the unjust steward (16:1-13) which teaches to use present wealth wisely in order to assure a good future. This parable closes with a challenge for Jesus' followers to choose between wealth and the kingdom. These teachings of Jesus would certainly have been received by the poor and dispossessed as good news.

That this theme was acted on by the early church we can see from Acts 2:41-47 and 4:33-37. There were no poor among the church members because those who had shared with those who did not.

We can conclude that the theme of social justice continues from the Hebrew Scriptures to the life and ministry of Jesus and into the early church in Jerusalem. It is a central theme of the Bible. Therefore the application of the principle which lies behind Amos 2:6 takes on great significance. We are not dealing with a single isolated saying of a single obscure prophet, but with a tune which runs throughout the Bible.

Having placed the passage in its wider context within Scriptures, we need to find an application for this principle. We can begin by seeking out those factors which are the same today as they were in the time of the prophets, Jesus, and the church (clue 4). The most obvious one and probably also the most important one is that the economic situation is similar. In our historical analysis of this passage we saw the conflict between two systems. One was the system of wealth, while the other was that of justice. We today, of course, operate in a context where wealth is the goal, not social justice. So we face the same problems as Amos, Jesus, or the early church did. We are called to practice another way which conflicts with the current economic model.

What is different about our situation which will affect the way we may apply the principle social justice? There are, of course, many things, but perhaps three are among the most significant. First, we have a much more individualistic society. We emphasize personal freedoms, rights, and autonomy. We are very mobile, often uncommitted to where we happen to be at the moment. The social units to which we feel responsible are smaller, often containing only a few other individuals. Second, we have greater information about what is happening at some distance from us. We use expressions like "shrinking globe" to express the fact that we know almost at once what is happening on the other side of the world. We are, consequently, much better informed about the plight of other people. We also live in a more interconnected world. We are dependent on a great variety of people most of whom we will never see. Thus the modern situation is something of an anomaly compared to Bible times: we act more individualistically, but we are dependent on more people at greater distance.

A third difference is the presence of a large middle class. In Bible times there tended to be but two classes, the regular people and the rich. Lines were clearer and the boundaries more easily defined. This situation still exists in many places, but North American society is characterized by a large middle class. The middle class is a group of people who are not poor—although they often moan about their lot—but who are not among the wealthy and powerful either. They do not control major capital resources, but generally work for wages or fees. If we would place them on a continuum it would look like this:

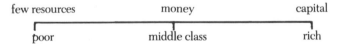

few resources	money	capital
poor	middle class	rich

This new segment of society will affect our conception of social justice and how it is brought about.

Having now seen what are similarities and differences in the two situations, we can turn to application. How might we apply the principle of social justice in our situation?

First we might work for structural change, to change systems so that there is more equity for all. The principle of equity must be interjected into the system of wealth economics in order for social justice to arise. Otherwise, as in Bible times, material prosperity will continue to win out over the treatment of people.

In our times, the *'ebyon*, the dispossessed, might be the dispossessed farmer in Third World countries. Their land is expropriated and used for the production of export crops to countries like the United States and Canada. The dispossessed farmer works on this land for "wages" which are often so low that he can barely buy the food he could have grown on his own land. We who profit from this slavery must act to change the structures so that there can be equity. We need to see that access to the resources is given to those who have been dispossessed. We need to see that those who actually produce get an equitable return for their labor and efforts.

Second, and related to the first point, we must aid in the development of the producers. The plight of the oppressed now is often the result of development—but a development which enriches the rich and impoverishes the dispossessed. There needs to be equity in development, so that those at the bottom are not deprived by the development schemes. This again means that we must work to broaden access to the economic resources.

How can we work for structural change and aid in the development of the dispossessed? First, we can become informed about issues and become active in bringing influence to bear on those who are oppressing the poor and dispossessing them. Second, we can lobby for good development and foreign economic politics by supporting and promoting Christian lobbies like Bread for the World. Third, we can decrease our own consumption in order to shift resources to equitable development for the poor and oppressed. Several suggestions have been given for how one might do this. One is the "graduated tithe," so that the more you earn the greater percentage you give. Another would be to divide your family food budget by the number of people you feed. Take one "food unit" as a base amount for giving to development projects for the oppressed. This is in essence giving what it would cost to feed one more mouth in North America, to help someone feed several mouths in the Third World.

Problems of justice are of course structural. Here we have been able to suggest only a few simple ways in which an individual might begin to respond to these problems. Because of the complexity of the issues involved, group discussion and a conscience-sensitizing process needs to occur before concrete application can be made in specific situations.

Matthew 5:38-42

In studying Matthew 5:38-42 we saw that the principle Jesus is teaching is the reciprocity of love. We are no longer to respond to others according to human standards, but rather on the basis of love. In this passage, this way of love is contrasted with the way of normal human justice. We no longer measure an appropriate response by eye for an eye, but by going beyond this to showing love. This, of course, does not mean that we are free to act in unjust ways. Rather it is through the response of love that true justice is achieved.

The theme of acting from love is found elsewhere in the New Testament. The next antithesis in Matthew 5:43-48 teaches love for the enemy because God loves both the good and the bad. Also, if we only love our friends, we do no more than live according to normal human standards. By loving the enemy we extend the scope of our love beyond the usual social conventions.

This same lesson is taught in a negative fashion in Romans 12:17-21, where Paul exhorts Christians not to seek vengeance for wrongs done to them. Instead they are to repay evil with kindness. Again the reciprocity of love refuses to treat people on the basis of customary social norms.

In a positive way, we are taught throughout the New Testament that love is the cornerstone, the foundation, of Christian behavior. In Matthew 22:34-40 Jesus teaches that the law and the prophets hang on love for God and love for one's neighbor. The parable of the Good Samaritan in Luke further defines who the neighbor is (Luke 10:25-37). Paul in Romans 13:8-10 also sees the love of neighbor as the fulfillment of the law, the only obligation the Christian has to his fellows. Paul again stresses the obligation of love in Galatians 5:14. Here he emphasizes the limits of Christian freedom. We are limited by love for others which fulfills the law. In James the love command is called the royal law (2:8). In 1 John 4:20-21 love for the brother is a sign of a proper relationship with God. Without this love for the other we cannot legitimately claim to love God either.

From this rather brief survey we can see that the love command is found frequently in the New Testament in a wide variety of writers. We can conclude that it is a basic New Testament theme. Our passage in Matthew, then, is part of this larger core motif.

This passage is important from yet another angle. We have seen that the antitheses represent the way to greater righteousness (5:20). Yet

234   From Word to Life

before the introduction to the antithesis in 5:13-16, another passage
prepares the way for these instructions of Jesus. In 5:13-16 Jesus'
followers are exhorted to be salt and light. By acting out the way of love,
by reciprocating in ways that show love, the Christian becomes the salt
and the light. By not responding in this way, we become salt that has lost
its flavoring powers or a lamp hid under a cover. Jesus' teaching then
goes to the basis of what the Christian presence is about in the world.

At the end of the sermon Jesus again makes obedience the key to
Christian commitment—not every one who says "Lord" but those who
do God's will are the ones who will enter into the kingdom. This same
point is reinforced in Matthew 25:31-46. Those who do acts of kindness
to the poor and oppressed are those who will enter into the kingdom at
the close of the age. The context reinforces the importance of love as the
sign of Christian obedience.

Having examined the principle of the passage in the light of other
material in the New Testament (clues 2 and 3), we can now turn to applying this principle. Our situation is different than Jesus', so our applications may well be different than the ones he suggested. For
example, being struck on the right cheek or going two miles are not immediately relevant in our situation. We need to find our own relevant
practices of love.

There are, however, similarities between our times and the times of
the New Testament. Normal ideas of justice are still regarded as the
measuring stick for human behavior. We all want things to come out
even according to our measure. The plot of many television programs revolves around the culprit getting what is coming to him. The conflict is
resolved when people finally get what they deserve. We are uneasy
when someone "gets by" with something.

On the other hand, we do not want others to get something for
nothing; there has to be a match between input and results achieved.
Nothing seems to upset us more than the thought that others might be
getting something which they really don't deserve. This is especially true
if we feel that we are footing the bill. For example, the welfare program
is unpopular with many people because they feel people on welfare do
not really deserve what they are getting.

If, however, as Christians we respond to people on the basis of what
we think is fair, what we estimate they deserve, we are responding on
the basis of an "eye for an eye." Rather than trying to measure out carefully what everybody should get, we ought to respond in love. The

response of love does not necessarily mean only material aid. It might be more radical than welfare. Why should the poor pay more for substandard conditions? Love might demand structural changes, reforms, so that people could have control over their lives and be able to benefit from the economic resources as others do.

How the principle of treating the oppressed and poor on the basis of love rather than on the basis of human calculations will take shape depends on local conditions. But it does seem clear that if we would take this teaching of Jesus seriously, it would revolutionize many Christians' attitudes and would lead them to behave in different ways.

Romans 13:1-7

From our study of Romans 13:1-7 in its context, we have concluded that Paul's teaching is based on the principle of love. How the Christian relates to the officials of the state should be governed by love, just as all his interaction with others should be. Further, the Christian's relationship to the state is also supported by the principle that the state does have legitimate functions—it is to operate for good. This functioning of the state takes place within the general providence of God. (See tradition and redaction analysis above.)

From our study of tradition history we saw that this passage was not a blanket command to submit to the state. States also incurred God's judgment; therefore, the Christian must be discerning in his relationship to it. Rather, what Paul is concerned about is that in relating to state officials, love be expressed. In this particular case he is writing to those inclined to enter into a tax revolt. Paul advised against this as not in keeping with the principle of love.

The principle of love not only regulates our relationship to state officials, but also our participation or support of the state. Our submission to the state is to be an expression of our love for our fellows. But this limits our submission, because where the state no longer operates for the benefit of others, we must challenge it. This princple of cooperation based on love is supported first by the passage internally, in 13:3-4. Here the state is to promote the good and punish evil. Where it does not do this, it is negligent and not fulfilling its proper function. Second, from context, 13:8-10, we learn that we are to owe only love. This includes our obligation not only to the state personnel, but also to all our fellow human beings. When the state operates for the detriment of others so that our participation in the state is harmful, we must act to remedy this.

We also saw that it is within the church where decisions are to be made about the appropriate mode of Christian action. The state cannot do this for the church. The Christian must be constantly examining the working of the state and its officers in order to see to what extent they are in accord with the principle of love, that is to what extent they are promoting good for others. Thus the principle is, that by our submission we show love both to the officers of the state and to the public they serve.

Having expressed the principle of the passage and how it relates to other themes (clues 2, 3), we can examine what differences and similarities exist between our times and situations and those of Romans. Obviously we in North America live in a very different political context. We have ways of participating in government that were not open to Christians in the first century. We likewise have greater ability to make our wishes known to our government officials. So too we probably know a good deal more about what our government is doing than did they. This dramatic increase in the Christian's participation in government will influence how we will apply this passage.

Another difference is that in both Canada and the United States there is a strong identification between our government and Christian religion. Phrases like "Christian country" show how we have confused nationalism with Christian faith. Consequently we have confused what we perceive to be good for our country with what is good from a Christian perspective. This may put the claims of the nation ahead of the needs of people both in our and in other countries. Likewise, we have identified certain economic policies or political inclinations as being Christian. Capitalist economics are thought to be Christian while the economics of communism are not. This identification often works to the detriment of the poor and oppressed, the very ones whose interest the Christian faith, like its God, has at heart.

On the other hand, it is still true that there are conflicts between Christian convictions and the state's action. Even though Christians participate in government at all levels, the state continues to act in ways contrary to what some feel expresses the principle of love or the support of the good.

Given these differences and similarities which we have just briefly sketched, how may this passage apply to us today? First, we would continue to say that the state does have a proper function to serve within the providence of God. It is to promote the good and curb or restrain evil. For the Christian, this proper functioning of the state can be an expression of love. Where the state falls short of this goal, the Christian should work to change things. This can be done in a positive way through participation which can range all the way from voting and letter-writing to sponsoring public forums on issues, promoting Christian lobbies like Bread for the World, and participating in the government itself.

It can also be done in negative actions. Policies and laws can be challenged in the courts to see whether or not they measure up to the state's own notions of what is proper. Civil disobedience can be used as a way of resisting improper policies and practices. Here again, the attempt is to call the state to a way of acting more in keeping with its proper concern and responsibilities for others. In this way the Christian expresses love for the neighbor.

In our relationship with government officials either positively or negatively, however, we are also to express love. Our attempts to influence government because of our concern for others must never be at the expense of loving those whom we are attempting to influence.

Specifically, what might all this mean? One example would be that we as Christians ought to be concerned with shifting money from defense spending to helping people. The high defense spending in the United States is not good for its citizens. It directly contributes to inflation and our national decline in productivity. It is not good for citizens of other nations which it endangers. On the other hand, we have enormous social problems within the United States as well as around the world. While it is not necessarily true that money will solve problems, it can certainly help. More importantly such a shift in priorities would be symbolic of a shift of values: from the destruction of life, to the preservation and humanization of life.

How might Christians support this? First, they can do so by direct action as suggested above. Second, they can resist the paying of taxes for programs which express hate rather than love. Or they can protest the further proliferation of unnecessary weapons systems and the development of offensive weaponry.

This last example of tax resistance as being an application of Romans 13:1-7 illustrates the principle that the application of the text must take forms relevant to our times by applying the principle behind the biblical practices. In Paul's situation, the paying of taxes may have been an expression of Christian love to the tax official and was not inconsistent with love for all people. In our situation, the withholding of specific taxes is a way to express love for all peoples and does not express hostility toward the specific tax agent who will handle the case. In fact, the dialogue with the agent presents further opportunity for the expression of love to another. On the other hand, the continued quiet support and payment for weapons which will destroy vast numbers of people can hardly be viewed as an act of love. Thus we see again that it is the application of the principle which is so important, for in practicing the letter we may often be acting contrary to the spirit.

Notes

Chapter 1

1. See the bibliography as well as the items referred to in the following footnotes for a history of modern biblical scholarship. On the close connection between Reformation (Protestant) theology and the historical method, see G. Ebeling, "The Significance of the Critical Historical Method for Church and Theology in Protestantism," in *Word and Faith*, trans. James W. Leitch (Philadelphia: Fortress Press, 1963), pp. 17-61.

2. The Reformation was preceded and accompanied by that great intellectual revolution called the Copernican Revolution. This scientific revolution which ushered in our "scientific age" did much to discredit allegiance to tradition in the face of reason and data. These are the two major roots of modern biblical studies. They should, however, be seen as roots only. What grew from them developed into modern historical studies only during and after the Enlightenment (18th century). On these developments see the histories of biblical scholarship listed in the bibliography and in the following notes.

3. R. M. Grant, *A Short History of the Interpretation of the Bible*, rev. ed. (New York: Macmillan, 1963), p. 124.

4. Ibid., p. 119.

5. Ibid., p. 112.

6. W. G. Kümmel, *The New Testament: The History of the Investigations of Its Problems*, trans. S. McLean Gilmour and Howard C. Kee (Nashville: Abingdon Press, 1972), p. 21. See also H. J. Kraus, *Geschichte der historisch-kritischen Erforschung des Altes Testaments*, 2nd edition (Neukirchen-Vluyn: Neukirchener Verlag, 1969), pp. 6-8 on Luther's understanding of *sola scriptura*.

7. R. H. Bainton, "The Bible in the Reformation," in *The Cambridge History of the Bible*, vol. 3, ed. S. L. Greenslade (Cambridge: Cambridge University Press, 1975), p. 1.

8. Ibid., p. 28.

9. Kümmel, *History of Investigations*, p. 23.

10. Kraus, *Geschichte*, pp. 9-15 on the hermeneutics of the Reformation. J. B. Rodgers and D. K. McKim, *The Authority and Interpretation of the Bible: An Historical Approach* (New York: Harper and Row, 1979) quote Luther, "It was very difficult for me to break away from my habitual zeal for allegory. And yet I was aware that allegories were empty speculations and the froth, as it were, of the Holy Scriptures. It is the historical sense alone which supplies the true and sound doctrine" (p. 85).

11. Cf. ibid.; Grant, *Short History*, p. 131, on how Luther considered a historical understanding of the author and his times as essential. Also, Kümmel, *History of Investigations*, p. 24, and Rodgers and McKim, *Authority*, pp. 83 ff.

12. J. S. Preus, *From Shadow to Promise* (Cambridge, Mass.: Harvard University Press, 1969) traces Luther's pilgrimage in the study of the Bible against the background of medieval exegesis.

13. John Locke wrote, "Reason is natural revelation, whereby the eternal Father of light and fountain of all knowledge communicates to mankind that portion of truth which he has laid within the reach of their natural faculties; revelation is natural reason enlarged by a new set of discoveries communicated by God immediately; which reason vouches the truth of, by the testimony and proofs it gives that they come from God. So that he that takes away reason to make way for revelation puts out the light of both, and does much the same as if he would persuade a man to put out his eyes, the better to receive the remote light of an invisible star by a telescope," cited by W. Neil, "The Criticism and Theological Use of the Bible 1700-1950," in *Cambridge History of the Bible*, vol. 3, ed. S. L. Greenslade (Cambridge: Cambridge University Press, 1975), pp. 240f. For Luther's positive assessment of reason, see Kümmel, *History of Investigations*, pp. 20f. Cf. Rodgers and McKim, *Authority*, pp. 81f. Luther sees regenerated reason as a helpmate of faith, but it cannot dictate to faith.

14. T. H. L. Parker, *Calvin's New Testament Commentaries* (Grand Rapids: Eerdmans, 1971), pp. 56-58. Zwingli also stressed the plain meaning as one of his three rules of interpretation. On these rules see E. G. Kraeling, *The Old Testament Since the Reformation* (New York: Schocken, 1969), p. 22.

15. Kraus, *Geschichte*, pp. 16-18.

16. Since the human, historical dimension of Scripture was such a crucial part of the Reformation's revolution in the use of the Bible, it is worthwhile to quote two passages which give vivid testimony to the Reformers' views. Luther: "The Holy Scripture is God's Word, written, and so to say 'in-lettered,' just as Christ is the eternal Word of God incarnate in the garment of his humanity. And just as it is with Christ in the world, as he is viewed and dealt with, so it is also with the written Word of God."

Calvin: "For who even of slight intelligence does not understand that, as nurses commonly do with infants, God is wont in a measure to 'lisp' in speaking to us? Thus, such forms of speaking do not so much express clearly what God is like as accommodate the knowledge of him to our slight capacity. To do this he must descend far beneath his loftiness." Quoted in Rodgers and McKim, *Authority*, pp. 78 and 108 respectively.

17. Kümmel, *History of Investigations*, p. 26.

18. Ibid., p. 24.

19. Bainton, "Bible in the Reformation," p. 12. Luther used the imagery of a basket of reeds patched with clay and pitch which contains a beautiful boy like Moses as an analogy with Scripture which is in human form but contains God's revelation. Rodgers and McKim, *Authority*, p. 86.

20. Bainton, "Bible in the Reformation," p. 13. See Rodgers and McKim, *Authority*, pp. 109-114 for Calvin's concept of error in Scripture.

21. Bainton, "Bible in the Reformation," p. 13.

22. This principle is seen by S. Neill, *The Interpretation of the New Testament 1861-1961, The Firth Lectures*, 1962 (London: Oxford University Press, Oxford Paperbacks, 1964), p. 32, as the irreversible turning point in the rise of modern scholarship. He puts the question, "Is the Bible to be treated like any other book or not?" (p. 30). Likewise, R. P. C. Hanson sees the rise of modern biblical studies based on the assumption: "It meant that the books of the Bible were henceforward open to being treated precisely as all other ancient documents are treated by historians of the ancient world." R. P. C. Hanson, gen. ed., *The Pelican Guide to Modern Theology*, 3 vols. (Middlesex, England: Penguin Books, 1970), vol. 3: *Biblical Criticism*, by Davidson and A. R. C. Leaney with introduction by R. P. C. Hanson, p. 10.

23. Calvin argued that if the interpreter is not free, if the interpreter cannot dissent,

then it is ridiculous to even take up the exposition of Scripture. Rather it is the context of Scripture which must be studied to find its meaning. Parker, *Calvin's Commentaries*, chapter 5: "Prolegomena to Exegesis," and pp. 190ff. Cf. Rodgers and McKim, *Authority*, pp. 97f.

24. In the Enlightenment, skepticism went further when it was felt necessary to interrogate the sources—the ancient authors—rather than to accept them passively at face value. Collingwood writes about the revolution in historiography as follows:

"I call it Cartesian historiography because it was based, like the Cartesian philosophy, on systematic skepticism and thoroughgoing recognition of critical principles. The main idea of this new school was that the testimony of written authorities must not be accepted without submitting it to a process of criticism based on at least three rules of method: (1) Descarte's own implicit rule, that no authorities must induce us to believe what we know cannot have happened; (2) the rule that different authorities must be confronted with each other and harmonized; (3) the rule that written authorities must be checked by the use of non-literary evidence." R. G. Collingwood, *The Idea of History* (New York: Oxford University Press, Galaxy Books, 1956), p. 62.

This scepticism growing out of the Enlightenment went further than the Reformers' more pragmatic skepticisms discussed in the preceding paragraph. Here a shift has been made from concern with traditional interpretations and their validation to being skeptical about the contents, the information in the source itself. The concern is with the veracity of the source. This later position has heavily influenced subsequent developments in biblical scholarship.

25. For a discussion of objectivity see J. Barr, *Old and New in Interpretation: A Study of the Two Testaments* (New York: Harper and Row, 1966), pp. 186f. and G. N. Stanton, "Presuppositions in New Testament Criticism," in *New Testament Interpretation: Essays on Principles and Methods*, ed. I. H. Marshall (Exeter: Paternoster, 1977), pp. 160-174.

26. On the importance of understanding the nature of language for our understanding of the Bible and in particular on the difference between says, means, and application see my earlier book, *Toward Understanding the Bible: Hermeneutics for Lay People* (Newton, Kansas: Faith and Life Press, 1978). A helpful discussion of linguistics and interpretation is found in A. C. Thiselton, "Semantics and New Testament Interpretation," in *New Testament Interpretation*, pp. 75-104. Concerning what we call the says-means-application distinction, he writes, "Because biblical language as language can only be understood with reference to its context and extra-linguistic situation, attention to the kind of question raised in critical study of the text is seen to be necessary on purely linguistic grounds. To try to loose "propositions" in the New Testament from the specific situation in which they were uttered and to try thereby to treat them "timelessly" is not only bad theology; it is also bad linguistics. For it leads to a distortion of what the text means" (p. 79). Two recent works in particular dwell on the problems encountered in interpreting the Bible: D. Nineham, *The Use and Abuse of the Bible: A Study of the Bible in an Age of Rapid Cultural Change* (London: Macmillan Press, 1976) and J. Barr, *The Bible in the Modern World* (London: SCM Press, 1977).

27. Smart, *Modern World*, p. 61.

28. Ibid., and Nineham, *Use and Abuse*, for the problems connected with the use of the Bible in the twentieth century.

29. An even sharper illustration is in 1 Samuel 16. God commands Samuel to go to Jesse in Bethlehem to anoint a replacement for Saul. Samuel replied that Saul would kill him if he did that. God told him to take an animal and say he was going in order to sacrifice. Here God tells Samuel to deceive Saul!

30. B. Childs has stressed this point, *Biblical Theology in Crises* (Philadelphia: Westminster Press, 1970), part II. pp. 91 ff.

31. For the problems and embarrassment which disregarding these distinctions has

242   *From Word to Life*

caused the church see Willard Swartley's forthcoming Conrad Grebel Lectures on Slavery,
Sabbath, War, and Women, *Case Studies in Biblical Interpretation* (Scottdale, Pa.: Herald
Press, 1983).
        32. J. A. Sanders, "Adaptable for Life; The Nature and Function of the Canon," in
Magnalia Dei: The Mighty Acts of God, eds. F. M. Cross and W. E. Lemke (Garden City:
Doubleday, 1976), pp. 531-560.
        33. The following eight steps represent one or more areas of scholarly study and spe-
cialization. Whole monographs are written using each one of these methods of analysis. Because of the rather independent use of these methods apart from either a total method of
analysis or the commitment to exegete specific passages, these studies often form the background preparation for an understanding of the text. Consequently when these methods
are integrated as steps in a comprehensive method directed to the explicating of specific
passages, they may undergo some modifications and be pursued somewhat differently.
Some elements put together in a monograph treatment may indeed be parceled out among
several stages of study.
        There have been several attempts in the 1970s to develop a comprehensive method
out of the various methods often used individually in biblical studies. The following works
are those which I have used the most extensively in developing the sequence of steps and
their procedures as set forth below and in the following chapters where the methods of
analysis are presented in detail. Often I have simplified their presentations in order to make
them more understandable by people without scholarly knowledge, especially of the
original languages.
        K. Berger, *Exegese des Neuen Testaments: Neue Wege vom Text zur Auslegung*
(Heidelberg: Quelle und Meyer, 1977); H. Barth and O. H. Steck, *Exegese des Alten
Testaments: Leitfaden der Methodik*, 4th ed. (Neukirchen-Vluyn: Neukirchener Verlag,
1973); G. Fohrer, et. al., *Exegese des Alten Testaments: Einführung in die Methodik*, 2nd
ed. (Heidelberg: Quelle und Meyer, 1976); W. Richter, *Exegese als Literatur-wissenschaft:
Entwurf einer alttestamentlichen Literaturtheorie und Methodologie* (Göttingen:
Vandenhoeck und Ruprecht, 1971); J. Schriener, ed., *Einführung in die Methoden der
biblischen Exegese*, (Würzburg: Echter Verlag, 1971); G. M. Tucker and D. O. Via eds.,
Guides to Biblical Scholarship (Philadelphia: Fortress Press, 1969) is a series of books each
devoted to an aspect of scholarly study.
        The reader is encouraged to consult these for additional detail and perspective on the
following stages of study.
        34. If you wish to pursue the subject of textual criticism, the following works can help
get you started: R. W. Klein, *Textual Criticism of the Old Testament: From the Septuagint
to Qumran, Guides to Biblical Scholarship, Old Testament Series* (Philadelphia: Fortress
Press, 1974); E. Würthwein, *The Text of the Old Testament*, trans. P. R. Ackroyd (Oxford:
Basil Blackwell, 1957); B. M. Metzger, *The Text of the New Testament: Its Transmission,
Corruption, and Restoration*, 2nd ed. (Oxford: Clarendon Press, 1968).
        35. While this language reflects the Christian tradition, the same would also be true
of other religious traditions based on the Bible. The Jewish experience has also contributed
richly to our understanding of Scripture.
        36. Religious experience and obedience, as methodological presuppositions, may
hinder understanding as well as help. They may be necessary, but alone are not sufficient
for a correct understanding. Because claims about meaning based on the Holy Spirit or
experience are not open to testing, such claims cannot be validated. Thus they cannot be
used to show the correctness of an interpretation. Two equally religious people both claiming the Spirit can diverge in understanding. They need something else yet to arbitrate their
competing claims. This means that they also need something else to arrive at an understanding of Scripture in the first place. Religious commitment can provide presuppositions
which promote understanding. But this religious commitment and the understanding

which flows from it must also be judged by empirical data and reason. See Luther's comments above on regenerated reason as a handmaiden to understanding, but not its dictator. (Note 13.)

37. See works on the sociology of knowledge or ones written from that perspective. For example, Peter Berger's recent work on Christian faith, *The Heretical Imperative; Contemporary Possibilities of Religious Affirmation* (Garden City: Doubleday, Anchor Books, 1979).

Chapter 2

1. On finding basic units see: Fohrer, et. al., *Exegese*, pp. 44, 47f., Koch, et. al., *Amos Untersucht met den Methoden einer struckturalen Formgeschichte*, AOAT 30 (Neukirchen-Vluyn: Neukirchener Verlag, 1978), vol. 1 p. 11. An extensive discussion of coherence and how it is marked in a unit is given by Berger, *Exegese*, pp. 12-26. As part of this discussion he also notes how units typically begin and end (pp. 18-21).

2. See P. Weimer, *Untersuchungen zur Redaktionsgeschichte des Pentateuch*, BZAW 146 (Berlin: Walter de Gruyter & Co., 1977), pp. 1f. for a discussion of this phrase as a stylistic feature which marks the beginning of a unit.

3. While most scholars find here an independent narrative, there is a difference of judgment as to where to draw the boundaries of the unit. H. Gunkel, *Genesis: Übersetzt und Erklärt* Göttingen: Vanderhoeck & Ruprecht, 3rd ed., 1964), would include the transitional verses 12:9 and 13:1-4 as part of the present basic unit.

4. For further detailed instructions on finding the structure of the text consult the following items: Berger, *Exegese*, pp. 12-26; Fohrer, et al., *Exegese*, pp. 57-73, 76-80; Richter, *Exegese*, pp. 72-98, 104-112. Much of the finer detail discussed in these works has been omitted here, since these details depend on knowledge of the original languages.

5. Cf. D. L. Peterson, "A Thrice-Told Tale: Genre, Theme, and Motif," BR 18(1973) pp. 30-43.

6. R. C. Culley, *Studies in the Structure of Hebrew Narrative* (Missoula, Mont.: Scholars Press, 1976), pp. 33 ff., suggests a different outline; J. Van Seters, *Abraham in History and Tradition* (New Haven: Yale U. Press, 1975), pp. 167ff. suggests another. A critique of Van Seters' analysis is found in T. L. Thompson, "A New Attempt to Date the Patriarchal Narratives," JAOS 98 (1978) pp. 81f. C. Westermann, *Genesis*, BK (Neukirchen-Vluyn: Neukirchener Verlag, 1976), stresses the importance of the speeches in his analysis of the structure.

7. Synonymous poetry means that the second half of the line corresponds in meaning to the first half of the line. In verse 6b for example we find: "They sold the righteous for silver, the needy for a pair of shoes." One crime is being mentioned which is expressed in two similar (synonymous) ways. To indicate these relationships of meaning, we would scan the line a.b.c./b'c2'. This means "sell" in the first half of the line has no corresponding member (a') in the second half line. Needy and righteous and silver/pair of shoes are however parallel pairs. The two after "c" indicates that there are two words parallel to "c" in the first half of the line. (See IDB s.v. "Poetry" or other reference works for a description of Hebrew Poetry.)

8. While the structure of this type of prophetic speech is widely agreed upon, names for it and its parts are not. See: L. Markert, *Struktur und Bezeichnung des Scheltworts*, BZAW 140 (Berlin: Walter de Gruyter, 1977), pp. 5-43. The division of the unit into its segments is clear in Hebrew, since both Israel's sins and the statement of judgment begin with nominal sentences, setting their beginning off from the previous part.

9. K. Koch, et. al., *Amos Untersucht*, pp. 15f.

10. On this structure cf. C. E. B. Cranfield, *A Critical and Exegetical Commentary on the Epistle to the Romans*, ICC 2 vols. (Edinburgh: T&T Clark, 1975), vol. 2, pp. 651ff., especially p. 664.

11. This stage of study could include the types of analysis practiced in structuralist work. I have not attempted to do this for two reasons: (1) Analysis of this type appears to be only loosely related to the actual formal or linguistic structure of the text. For example, R. C. Culley, *Oral Transmission*, pp. 33f., begins his analysis of structure with (a)"on entering a foreign country. . . ." But in fact the problem arises before Abram's entrance. Actually the first element is the famine and the consequent journey to Egypt. His second element is (b) "The Patriarch pretends that his wife is his sister (deception)." We do not actually find this element in the structure of the text, we infer it. Omitted is what we do find in the text, the plan to deceive. Cf. R. C. Culley, "Structuralism: It is done with mirrors," *Interpretation* 28(1974) 165-181. This high level of abstraction which treats plot-patterns—because of its distance from the particulars of the text—seems to lack objectivity, repeatability, and consequently, verification. This makes it difficult to define this type of analysis operationally and thus show others how to do it. (2) The language and terms used to discuss structure are rather opaque. It would take considerable explanation to even make this type of analysis understandable (e.g., the semiotic square). For a brief introduction into this mode of study see J. Calloud, "A Few Comments on Structural Semiotics: A Brief Review of a Method and Some Explanation of Procedures," *Semeia* 15 (1979) 51-80. Also, J. Calloud, *Structural Analysis of Narrative*, trans. D. Patte, *Semeia Supplements* 4 (Philadelphia: Fortress Press, 1976), Part I, pp. 1-46.

12. J. Beekman and J. Callow, *Translating the Word of God* (Grand Rapids, Mich.: Zondervan, 1974), pp. 267ff., contains an extensive discussion of logical relationships.

13. This list of questions follows Barth and Steck, *Exegese*, pp. 27-36.

14. We have deferred compositional analysis, usually referred to as literary or source criticism, to this point because what may appear to us as inconsistencies, digressions, etc., may represent normal features of style. We should give the text the benefit of first attempting to make sense out of it. Berger, *Exegese*, writes, "Doublets, parallels, and tensions are therefore in no way already in themselves a reference to the activity of different hands. Rather the exegete has first the obligation to assume the unity of the text . . ." (p. 29). Cf. Koch, et. al., *Amos Untersucht*, vol. 1 p. 11. The focus here is on understanding the basic unit, not on source analysis in the classic sense. Cf. Richter, *Exegese*, pp. 63ff.; Fohrer, et. al. *Exegese*, pp. 46ff. This last reference is also the source of the terminology used here for the different types of units.

15. Westermann, *Genesis*, p. 189.

16. S. Tengström, *Die Hexateucherzählung: Eine literaturgeschichtliche Studie*, CBOT 7 (Lund: CWK Gleerup, 1976).

17. Weimer, *Untersuchungen*, p. 5.

18. *Ibid.*, p. 10. He argues that she asses occur with camels, not male donkeys in other lists of animals (he cites Genesis 32:15-16; Job 1:3, 14; 42:12; 1 Chronicles 27:29-31). Also slaves are usually listed either before or after animals, but not among them, animals—slaves—animals as here. (Exceptions to this he gives as Genesis 24:35; 30:43). Thus he concludes she asses and camels are an addition here. This addition created this anomalous list. If this is accepted, then the unit is an expanded one. Cf. Gunkel, *Genesis*, l.c.

19. Much of what is taken to be editorial expansion seems to depend on two rather subjective factors. First, how much tension or roughness can be tolerably assigned to a single author? In this judgment, contrary assumptions often seem to be made. The original author wrote entirely harmonious, smoothly flowing accounts. Thus any material which seems to raise tensions is due to a later hand. These later editors or redactors, however, produced out of these straightforward units, units filled with tensions and rough joints. Original authors wrote smoothly, editors roughed these units up. Certainly the opposite must have been the case in some units. The finding of tensions is also often accompanied by defining the meaning of words apart from the context of the unit. The words so defined then clash with their present context. On the importance of understanding the meaning of

words in context, see chapter four. Second, one's conception of the nature of the composition and transmission of the unit will affect this stage of analysis. If one assumed rigid transmission with the splicing in of individual words and phrases, then one can select these bits out and assign them to later editors. (Weimar, *Untersuchungen*, is a fine example of this type of analysis.) If however, one presupposes either a more oral or organic process of transmission, then repetitions and awkward spots are to be expected. Cf. B. O. Long, "Recent Field Studies in Oral Literature and Their Bearing on Old Testament Criticism," VT 26 (1976) 187-198; R. C. Culley, *Studies in the Structure of Hebrew Narrative*, Part I, "Oral Transmission."

20. See, H. W. Wolff, *Joel and Amos*, Hermeneia, ed. S. D. McBride, Jr., Trans. W. Janzen, S. D. McBride, Jr., and C. A. Muenchow (Philadelphia: Fortress Press, 1977), p. 169, who argues for these verses as an addition. Among others, T. R. Hobbs, "Amos 3:1b and 2:10," ZAW 81 (1969) 284-287, contends for their being an original part of the oracle. For a summary of the evidence see Koch, et. al., *Amos Untersucht*, Vol. 1, pp. 122f.

Chapter 3

1. Form and type of language are used here as synonyms. Since both written and spoken language have types, by using the word language, I mean to include both of them. Theoretically, the phrase literary type or type of literature would include both written and oral literature. However, by using literature, some might think that only written literature would be included. Thus language type or form seems more general.

2. What constitutes a form or genre of language has often been discussed. There seems to be no unanimity on a definition. Even the terminology used changes. At one time it seems that German "Form" and "Gattung" referred to the object of form criticism—a class of language units. More recently, the method books and others are dividing between these two terms. "Form" is the study of the individual passage's structure and style. In the United States, studies in this area have been called rhetorical criticism. See J. Muilenburg, "Form Criticism and Beyond," JBL 88(1969) 1-18, and a review of Muilenburg's contribution by R. F. Melugin, "Muilenburg, Form Criticism and Theological Exegesis," in *Encounters with the Text*, ed. M. Buss (Missoula, Mont.: Scholars Press, 1979,) pp. 91-99. Gattung becomes then the study of genre. Following this division, the last chapter is form analysis while this chapter is genre analysis. The terms structure and form analysis have been used in their stead because (1) they seem to communicate more readily, and (2) genre used in this sense is not clear. It may refer to various levels of abstraction. It may refer to a group of stories, such as etymological legends, or a broader classification such as legend or saga. As used here, form criticism refers to a group of basic units, which are classed together because they share macro-syntactic conventions. Thus the group may be large or small, depending on the type of convention selected for the purposes of classification. If parallelism is used, for example, the form class would be that of poetry, a large group. If, as in an example below, it focuses on the structure and function of an initial speech in a story, the class is much smaller. The features selected for classification are justified on their heuristic value—how they help uncover the conventions operating in the unit under study.

Form criticism has been practiced differently because different types of criteria have been used to classify units. For example, in the patriarchal narratives in Genesis, Gunkel relied heavily on content, basing his classification on what he considered the dominant feature of the content of a story. H. Gunkel, *The Legends of Genesis*, trans. H. W. Carruth (New York: Schocken, 1964), K. Koch, *The Growth of the Biblical Traditions; The Form Critical Method*, trans. S. M. Cupitt (London: Adams and Charles Black, 1969), pp. 111ff., as well as many others follow this line of analysis. However, dissatisfaction has been expressed with this procedure. First, motifs may be chosen which are not central or organic to the unit. Cf. D. Greenwood, "Rhetorical Criticism and Formgeschichte: Some Methodological Considerations," JBL 89(1970) 418-426; O. Kaiser, *Introduction to the Old*

Testament, A Presentation of Its Results and Problems, trans. J. Sturdy (Minneapolis: Augsburg Publishing House), pp. 51f.; A. Bentzen, *Introduction to the Old Testament*, 2 vols., 4th ed. (Copenhagen: G. E. C. Gad, 1958), vol. I, p. 109; C. Westermann, *Erträge der Forschung* Genesis 12-50 (Neukirchen-Vluyn: Neukirchener Verlag, 1977), pp. 21ff.; *idem, Grundfrägen zu den Erzählungen der Genesis*, pp. 40ff. Richter, *Exegese*, pp. 74ff. Second, depending on which motif was chosen, a unit could be assigned to several genres. See Gunkel, *Legends*, pp. 34f. Thus it seems to some that Gunkel and his successors have classified motifs rather than the literary type of the unit. Cf. Westermann, *Grundfrägen*, p. 41. As a result, terminological confusion seems to reign, as in the case of the terms "saga" and "legend." Cf. R. M. Hals, "Legend: A Case Study in Old Testament Form Critical Terminology," CBQ 34(1972) 166-176, and van Seters, *Abraham*, pp. 131ff. Third, the social situation was also considered normative for defining a form, but the difficulty, if not the impossibility in using this criterion has been shown on various grounds. Cf. B. O. Long, "Recent Field Studies," who bases himself on modern field studies of oral literature; Berger, *Exegese*, pp. 111ff. from the standpoint of linguistics; and H. W. Hoffman, "Form-Function-Intention," ZAW 82(1970) 341-346, on the basis of an actual example. Cf. G. Tucker, "Form Criticism," IDB(S) on "sociological determinism." Recently attempts have been made to define genre or form on formal grounds. This was called for by Bentzen, *Introduction*, p. 109; has been developed by Richter, *Exegese*, pp. 81ff. and L. Markert, *Struktur and Bezeichnung des Scheltworts*, pp. 278 ff. This development, too, has its roots in the work of Gunkel; see his "Fundamental Problems of Hebrew Literary History," in *What Remains of the Old Testament and Other Essays*, trans. A. K. Dallas (New York: Macmillan, 1928), pp. 57-68, especially pages 60f. But a narrow formal approach has not been without its critics. See K. Koch, "Reichen die formgeschichtliche Methode für die Gegenswartsaufgaben der Bibelwissensschaft zu?" TLZ 98(1973) 811f. and Tucker, "Form Criticism." The analysis presented here tries to walk something of a middle way. I rely heavily on structure, style, and content to define what is called a form of language. Units belonging to the same form thus share some macro-syntactic convention in one or more of these areas. (Cf. Koch, "Reichen," pp. 811f.) The social context, intention, and function may vary from unit to unit.

It seems clear from the history of research that genre or form is not a monothetic category—it is not defined by a single characteristic. Rather it involves a cluster of identifying properties. Some genres may rely solely on structure for identification, while others, such as a lament, may include subject matter in its identification. Yet other genres may be identified on the basis of their distinctive vocabulary or use of words. *All criteria used, however, should be evidenced in the texts used to establish the identifying keys.* This would rule out social context, intention, and function as identifying markers. (These do not belong to the macro-syntactic elements present in a text which can be used to classify it as to form.) Inference about these, however, can be made from the form, and do help in understanding the form of text. They, however, should not be relied upon to define a form. For the history of form criticism, see the works listed in the bibliography.

3. By content is meant the linguistic elements used in a text—the words selected and how they are used. This includes the type of characters present. It also refers to the mood or expectation aroused by the use of words.

4. As the story now stands in Genesis 16, scholars divide the story into two literary sources, usually titled "J" and "P." The "J" account which contains the speech and its fulfillment does not come to resolution because its ending has been replaced by "P." The course of the narrative is disturbed from verse 9 on; there is both redundancy and lack of sequence. For these reasons verses 9 and 10 are eliminated as being later additions to "J." This was done in order to harmonize chapter 16 with its duplicate account in chapter 21. See Gunkel, *Genesis*, l.c. and S. E. McEvenue,"A Comparison of Narrative Styles in the Hagar Stories," *Semeia* 3(1975) 64-80. Van Seters, *Abraham*, pp. 192ff. has argued that

verse 9 is original since it is connected both with verse 8 and the theme of affliction mentioned earlier in "J." This judgment would be supported by the structural conventions we are assuming to be at work in this unit.

5. Because of duplications in the stories and differences of style between them, scholars see Genesis as a combination of three literary strands or sources. These are given the labels J, E, and P. We will discuss sources in Chapter 5.

6. Following D. N. Freedman's suggested translation; *apud.* R. G. Boling, *Judges: Introduction, Translation and Commentary, Anchor Bible,* ed. D. N. Freedman (Garden City, New York: Doubleday and Co., 1975), p. 249.

7. C. J. Exum, "Promise and Fulfillment: Narrative Art in Judges 13," JBL 99(1980) 43-59 notes the importance of the promise and fulfillment theme in the story. She, however, sees the story structured differently than presented here.

8. On the importance of speeches for the narratives in Genesis as well as in this story in particular, see Gunkel, *Legends,* pp. 64f.; Koch, *Growth,* p. 150; Weimar, *Untersuchungen,* p. 15; and Westermann, *Genesis,* l.c. who lays great emphasis on both speeches in the passage. On classifying the narratives in Genesis as stories, see Westermann, *Grundfragen,* pp. 36ff. and idem, *Ertrage,* pp. 21ff. His basic definition of a story is a narrative which moves from tension to solution.

9. If one assumes an oral background, it may be impossible to be precise about the social situation envisioned. See B. O. Long, "Recent Field Studies," p. 198.

10. Another difference is that "thus says the Lord" rather than coming in 3 "Introduction," comes in 1 "Summons to hear."

11. This pattern has been studied extensively by C. Westermann, *Basic Forms of Prophetic Speech,* trans. H. C. White (London: Lutterworth Press, 1967), pp. 90ff. His analysis has been widely used. Koch, *Growth,* pp. 183-195 and Koch, et. al., *Amos Untersucht,* vol. 2 pp. 124-159 offers an alternative analysis. In Koch's analysis the form of prophetic speech we are studying ends at times with a concluding characterization. Perhaps we have something in that vein here in the Micah passage.

12. For a listing of the judgment speeches in the historical books, see Westermann's list, *Basic Forms,* p. 137.

13. Ibid. p. 169. For evidence regarding the messenger formula see chapter 4 below.

14. Koch, et. al., *Amos Untersucht,* p. 149.

14a. Considerable effort has been made to place the prophets as spokespersons within the cult. This attempt rests on two major presuppositions: (1) The oracles in Amos, for example, are cast in a cultic form of language, and (2) a one-to-one correspondence exists between an instance of a form and a given social situation. The first argument works, at best, for only some forms in Amos, while the second is unconvincing. See, Reventlow, *Das Amt.*

15. Koch, op. cit., among others (cf. Wolff, *Amos,* l.c.) considers the unit to extend from v. 21 to v. 27. In v. 27 we do have a pronouncement of judgment. This might then be considered a "speech of doom." Yet because of its different structure and style it would seem best to classify the unit as belonging to a different form.

16. Proposed by D. Daube, "Ye Have Heard . . . But I Say Unto You," *The New Testament and Rabbinic Judaism* (London: University of London, 1956), pp. 55-62.

17. J. P. Meier, *Law and History in Matthew's Gospel: A Redactional Study of Matthew 5:17-48* (Rome: Biblical Institute, 1976), pp. 131ff.

18. See Daube, "Ye Have Heard."

19. See S. Greengus, "Law in the O.T.," IDB(S).

20. J. D. Crossan, "Jesus and Pacifism," *No Famine in the Land: Studies in Honor of John L. McKenzie,* eds. J. W. Flanagan and A. W. Robinson (Missoula, Mont.: Scholars Press, 1975), pp. 195-208.

21. R. C. Tannehill, "Matthew 5:39b-42, Turning the Other Cheek (the 'Focal

Instance'),'' in *The Sword of His Mouth* (Philadelphia: Fortress Press, 1975), pp. 67-78.

22. Ibid., p. 72.

23. Ibid., pp. 73ff.

24. The form "exposition of Scripture by focal instance" is hypothetical because we do not have this combination of structure and content elsewhere. Presumably this form was more widely used than its present literary occurrence would indicate.

25. Cf. D. Schroeder, "Parenesis," and "Exhortation in the N.T.," IDB(S) s.v.

26. See M. Dibelius, *James: A Commentary on the Epistle of James*, trans. M. A. Williams, revised by H. Greeven (Philadelphia: Fortress Press, 1976), p. 38.

27. Ibid., pp. 1, 124ff.

28. See H. W. Hoffman, "Form-Function-Intention."

29. For source analysis and the probability that this was the ending now missing in J see footnote 4 above.

30. C. J. Exum, "Promise and Fulfillment," p. 59, notes how the ending of the story in its focus on Samson is a bridge to the following chapters which recount Samson's exploits.

31. For these earlier speeches of judgment to individuals see Westermann, *Basic Forms*, pp. 141ff.

32. On this see Westermann, *Basic Forms*, pp. 129ff. and 169ff. The basis of Amos's message will be analyzed in chapter 5.

33. As we shall see below in tradition analysis, some scholars divide the antithesis into two groups. The first set, which strengthens the law, being earlier than those which abrogate the law. If this position is assumed, then we would have development, but as the later group are literarily dependent on the earlier, this would not be evidence of a conventional form of language developing.

Chapter 4

1. This axiom of linguistics was acutely brought to the attention of biblical scholars by J. Barr, *The Semantics of Biblical Language* (Oxford: University Press, 1961).

2. We have discussed the ambiguous nature of language in 1.30.

3. Barr, *Semantics*, attacked a biblical scholarship which studied words apart from context under the guise of studying concepts or ideas.

4. This widely accepted notion that the meaning of a word is derived from seeing the way it is used is attributed to the philosopher Wittgenstein. J. Lyons states, "What words and sentences mean is theoretically inexplicable and empirically unverifiable except in terms of what speakers of that language mean by their use of these words and sentences." *Semantics*, 2 vols. (Cambridge: Cambridge University Press, 1977), vol. 1, p. 4.

5. This method of finding the meaning of words is based on structural semantics. The basic text to this analysis is J. Lyons, *Structural Semantics*, (Oxford: Basil Blackwell, 1963). A survey of the development of structural semantics is given by S. Öhman, "Theories of 'Linguistic Field,' " *Word* 9(1953) 123-134 and L. M. Vassilyev, "The Theory of Semantic Fields: A Survey," *Linguistics* 137(1974) 79-93. This method of analysis has been applied to biblical studies by J. Beekman and J. Callow, *Translating the Word of God* (Grand Rapids, Michigan: Zondervan, 1974) and J. F. A. Sawyer, *Semantics in Biblical Research: New Methods of Defining Hebrew Words for Salvation, Studies in Biblical Theology*, second series, 24 (Naperville, Ill.; Alec R. Allenson, 1972). The concepts and techniques of field theory and structural semantics have been widely adopted by linguists. For an application of "semantic field" theory to biblical exegesis see Berger, *Exegese*, pp. 137-159. In the following discussion both linguistic and semantic field ideas are combined to some extent, since both paradigmatic and syntagmatic relationships are analyzed. Indeed in the literature they are not carefully distinguished one from another.

6. For the various ways in which the meaning of words and language has been

understood, see the items in the bibliography on semantics and philosophy of language. R. M. Kempson, *Semantic Theory* (Cambridge: Cambridge University Press, 1977), attempts to integrate linguistic theory with the philosophy of language.

7. The combination of "green dreams" is an anomaly, but not necessarily meaningless. That is, it breaks the conventions, but in a certain context (fantasy writing) it might make sense. On anomaly in language see D. L. F. Nilsen and A. P. Nilsen, *Semantic Theory: A Linguistic Perspective* (Rowley, Mass.: Newbury House Publishers, 1975), pp. 38-41.

8. J. Lyons, *Structural Semantics*, p. 59, defines meanings as, "The set of (paradigmatic) relations that the unit in question contracts with other units of the language (in the context or contexts in which it occurs). . . ." He places the primary emphasis on the vertical (paradigmatic) relationship.

9. J. Lyons, *Structural Semantics*, p. 59ff. discusses and illustrates the varieties of relationships within a word group. Cf. J. Lyons, *Introduction to Theoretical Linguistics* (Cambridge: Cambridge University Press, 1968), pp. 446ff. and idem, *Semantics*, vol. 1, pp. 230-335.

10. This is done by using a concordance which allows you to find the occurrences of the Greek or Hebrew word, not the English word used to translate it in your passage. An example of such a concordance would be R. Young, *Analytical Concordance to the Bible* (New York: Funk and Wagnalls Co., N.D.).

11. This type of analysis of word meaning is called componential analysis. For greater detail and precision consult Kempson, *Semantics*, and Lyons, *Semantics*.

12. The evidence for "thus says the Lord" as a messenger formula and the prophets as the messengers of God is presented in Westermann, *Basic Forms*. This view has been widely accepted. Against this view see Koch, *Growth*, p. 191. Ordinarily the study of such set phrases has been seen as part of form analysis. However, where we have a separate step devoted to lexical study, it seemed best to include this study here. The results, insofar as they are applicable to or supplement the findings of form analysis, can be transferred back to that stage of study.

13. Study of the word "needy" and other words for poor is found in P. D. Miscall, *The Concept of the Poor in the Old Testament* (PhD dissertation, Harvard University, 1972); G. J. Botterweck, *Theological Dictionary of the Old Testament*, under *ebyon;* and E. Gerstenberger, *Theologische Handworterbuch*, under 'bh. Consult Miscall for the history of research on these words.

14. Not all uses in the Psalms are "religious" uses, since there are various types of psalms. Psalm 72, for example, is a royal psalm. In it the word '*ebyon* occurs several times and refers to the oppressed (secular usage). For a more precise lexical analysis we would not lump the psalms together as we have done here.

15. These conclusions are similar to Miscall, *Concept of the Poor*, pp. 71ff., who clearly distinguishes the '*ebyon* from orphan, widow, and alien in legal texts. Cf. K. Koch, "Die Entstehung der sozialen Kritik bei den Profeten," in *Probleme biblischer Theologie*, ed. H. W. Wolff (Munchen: C. Kaiser, 1971), pp. 236-257.

16. H. Strack and P. Billerbeck, *Kommentar zum Neun Testament aus Talmud und Midrasch*, 5 vols., 5th ed. (Munich: Beck Verlag, 1969), s.v. Matthew 5:38ff.

17. D. Daube, "Eye for an Eye," in *The New Testament and Rabbinic Judaism* (London: University of London, 1956), pp. 55-62.

18. Ibid.

19. Strack and Billerbeck, *Kommentar*, at Matthew 5:38ff.

20. C. G. Montefiore, *Rabbinic Literature and Gospel Teachings* (reprinted, New York: Ktav Publishing House, 1970, originally published in 1930) at Matthew 5:42, interprets this verse as giving to the needy. The rabbis emphasized this on the basis of Deuteronomy 15:7-11. This would make this case an illustration of law as well.

21. A. Strobel, "Zum Verständnis von Rm 13," ZNTW 47(1956) 67-93; J. Friedrich, W. Pöhlmann, and P. Stuhlmacher, "Zur historischen Situation und Intention von Rom 13, 1-7," ZThK 73(1976) 131-166, especially p. 135ff.

22. C. K. Barrett, *A Commentary on the Epistle to the Romans*, 7(New York: Harper & Row, 1973), in commenting on 13:4; Cf. H. Schlier, *Der Römerbrief*, HTKNT (Freiburg: Herder & Herder, 1977), l.c.

23. Friedrich, Pöhlmann, and Stuhlmacher, "Situation," pp. 141ff.

24. Ibid.

25. Cranfield, *Romans*, vol. 2, pp. 661-663; J. H. Yoder, *The Politics of Jesus* (Grand Rapids, Mich.: Eerdmans, 1972), p. 212; cf. W. Schrage, *Die Christian und der Stadt nach dem Neuen Testament* (Gutersloh: Mohn, 1971), p. 59.

26. Schlier, *Der Römerbrief* at 13.1; O. Michel, *Der Brief an die Römer* (Göttingen: Vanderhoeck & Ruprecht, 1955, 5th ed. 1977) at 13.1; and Cranfield, *Romans*, vol. 2 p. 660. Cf. E. Käsemann, "Principles of Interpretation of Rom. 13," in *New Testament Questions of Today* (Philadelphia: Fortress Press, 1969), p. 215.

27. O. Cullman, *Christ and Time* (Philadelphia: Westminster, 1964), pp. 191-210; idem, *The State in the New Testament* (New York: Scribner, 1956), Excurses: "On the Most Recent Discussion of the Exousia in Romans 13:1," pp. 100-113; C. D. Morrison, *The Powers That Be* (London: SCM, 1960) gives a survey of the debate.

28. Morrison, *Powers*, pp. 17-20.

29. Ibid., pp. 21-25; for additional arguments for this position see pp. 25-39.

30. For the negative reaction to Cullman's arguments (following K. L. Schmidt) see ibid., pp. 40-55; Also Strobel, "Verständnis," pp. 67-71. Cranfield, *Romans*, vol. 2, pp. 664-659 explains why he has changed his judgment from Cullman's position to that of the opposition. The balance of contemporary scholarship seems to be against construing Romans 13:1 as Cullman and his followers would.

31. Strobel, "Verständnis," pp. 75-79; Friedrich, Pöhlmann, and Stuhlmacher, "Situation," p. 135.

Chapter 5

1. The next two stages of study, tradition analysis, and transmission and redaction analysis are conceptually hazy. Different scholars understand these phases of study quite differently. As J. Scharbert noted in his review of several works on method, these methods of analysis are marked by a chaos of terminology, tasks, and methods ("Zu den Methoden der alttestamentlichen Exegese," ThR 70(1974) p. 8.). D. Knight, *The Traditions of Israel* (Missoula, Mont.: Society of Biblical Literature, 1973), gives a historical survey of how tradition analysis has been understood and practiced. For some it refers to the intellectual traditions upon which a text draws or the history of ideas (Barth and Steck, *Exegese*, pp. 70-80; cf. Kaiser and Kümmel, *Exegetical Method*, "Tradition Criticism"). Related to this, Berger, *Exegese*, pp. 137ff., visualizes tradition analysis as the study of semantic fields: the particular configuration or association of words through which a certain idea or understanding is expressed. For others tradition analysis studies the oral forerunners of written texts. W. E. Rast, *Tradition History and the Old Testament*, (Philadelphia: Fortress Press, 1972). For others this stage of study includes everything between form or genre analysis and redaction analysis or even everything between genre analysis and the present text as we find it in the Bible. (See the reviews of methodology by H. Ringgren, "Literarkritik, Formgeschichte, Überlieferungsgeschichte," TLZ 91(1966) 641-650; R. Rendtorff, "Literarkritik und Traditionsgeschichte," EvTh 27(1967) 138-153; cf. C. Rylaarsdam, "Introduction," to Rast, *Tradition*, and the scholars surveyed in Knight, *Traditions of Israel*.) In this chapter, tradition analysis has two basic focuses: (1) the conceptual or social background of the words, phrases, themes, motifs, etc. found in a passage. This analysis is akin to intellectual history. (2) The use of literary sources. We are thus construing tradition

analysis broadly as including the intellectual, social, and literary roots and relationships of a passage. Cf. G. W. Coats, "Tradition Criticism, OT," IDB(S). We distinguish this state of study from the next, transmission and redaction by the following criteria: (1) Transmission analysis concerns the transmission of the basic unit, tradition analysis has to do with its compositional roots and relationships. Transmission analysis is marked by a relatively fixed text. Additions are supplemental to the function and intention of the text; there is no change in the basic genre of the text. (2) Redaction analysis concerns the present place of the basic unit in the literary work and changes made in the unit to fit it to its present place and function. In this latter respect redaction analysis can be looked upon as the last step in the transmission of the basic unit.

2. It is sometimes customary to speak of schools or circles of tradition which passed on material and to which the origins of the material can be traced. However, in looking at tradition analysis from the standpoint of understanding the basic unit, we are seeking to understand the dynamics of its particular composition. Thus the word "author" in the general sense would seem to be appropriate. Here we have a tension between sociological determinism and the creation of individual, unique material. If our task is to explain the individual unit, then our emphasis falls on the "author" and the dynamics of composition. If our task is constructing a history of ideas, motifs, traits, etc., then our emphasis falls on the generic and the sociological forces at work over time. Explanation of the individual is carried out in this tension between the particular and the generic.

3. Whether or not Gnosticism was already a visible, viable phenomenon at the time of the composition of the Fourth Gospel is debated. Bultmann, *Primitive Christianity in Its Contemporary Setting*, trans. R. H. Fuller (Cleveland: The World Publishing Co., Meridian Books, 1956), pp. 162-171, argues in favor of such a view. R. E. Brown, *The Gospel According to John (i-xii)*, The Anchor Bible, eds., W. F. A. Albright and D. N. Freedman (Garden City, New York: Doubleday & Co., 1966), LII-LVI, argues against such a view. He understands John's language against the background of Jewish wisdom tradition and sectarian views like those of the Dead Sea Scrolls community. Cf., E. Pagels, "Gnosticism" IDB(S).

4. The idea of the prophet as messenger of God is discussed by J. Ross, "The Prophet as Yahweh's Messenger," in *Israel's Prophetic Heritage*, B. W. Anderson and W. Harrelson eds. (New York: Harper and Row, 1962), pp. 99-107. Cf. K. Baltzer, "Considerations Regarding the Office and Calling of the Prophet," HTR 61(1968) 567-581. Y. Kaufmann, *The Religion of Israel: From Its Beginning to the Babylonian Exile*, trans. and abridged by M. Greenberg (Chicago: University of Chicago Press, 1960), pp. 212-216, discusses the significance of apostolic prophecy for Israelite religion.

5. See below in the discussion of Amos's tradition.

6. For Paul's use of hymns and traditional material see M. Barth, *Ephesians: Introduction, Translation, and Commentary on Chapters 1-3, Anchor Bible*, eds. W. F. A. Albright and D. N. Freedman vol. 34 (Garden City, New York: Doubleday & Co., 1974), pp. 6-10.

7. For a discussion of the terms theme, trait, plot, etc., see the exegetical handbooks under tradition analysis, especially Fohrer, et al., *Exegese*, and Knight *Traditions of Israel*, pp. 114ff.

8. On hymnic style see Barth, *Ephesians*, pp. 6-10.

9. It often appears that the reconstruction of earlier developmental phases of the material is done more in order to gain insight for the writing of history than it is to gain insight into the present text unit.

10. See end note 1. We want to distinguish traditional material used in composing a unit from material added to a unit during its transmission and redaction.

11. There are many different hypotheses concerning the relationship of the three stories in Genesis 12, 20, and 26. Gunkel aruges that 12 was the earliest on the basis of traits

found in the story, e.g., in 12 Pharaoh takes Sarai as wife, in 20 she is taken but no consummation, and in 26 she is not taken. Thus 12 is morally the most primitive. (Gunkel, *Genesis*, pp. 225-226); Koch, *Growth*, pp. 122ff. supports this chronological order, but Genesis 12 is not the direct ancestor of the other two—they go back to a hypothetically reconstructed older version (p. 126). Van Seters, *Abraham*, also keeps this order, but sees chapter 20 as a variant of 12 while 26 used both 12 and 20 in its composition. Cf. Westermann, *Genesis*, at 12.10-20 for the range of views. Weimar, *Untersuchungen*, has argued the other major point of view—that 26:1-11 is the oldest (pp. 102ff.). Chapters 26 and 20 arose independently, while 12 is related to both 26 and 20. This point of view is based on an extremely rigid literary critical view of the individual stories and phrases shared between them. If one is inclined to see here mountains made of molehills, then suspicion is also cast on his conclusions. Finally others see these stories as variants of a tradition (R. Polzin, "The Ancestress of Israel in Danger," *Semeia* 3 (1975) 81-98; R. C. Cully, "Oral Transmission and Biblical Texts," in *Studies in the Structure of Hebrew Narrative*, pp. 33ff.; C. A. Keller, "Die Gefährdung der Ahnfrau: Ein Beiträge zur gattungs-und motivgeschtlichen Erforschung alttestamentlicher Erzählungen," ZAW 66(1954) pp. 184 f.

12. Arguments for literary dependency are given by van Seters, *Abraham*, pp. 161-180; Weimar, *Untersuchungen*, pp. 102-110. They come to opposite conclusions however. Van Seters sees the sequence 12, 20 and 26, with 26 being a combination of 12 and 20. Weimar has 26 as the oldest followed by 20, with 12 being a combination of 26 and 20! The evidence of dependency not only seems to be ambiguous, but also in my judgment not sufficient to show direct literary dependency. Neither author takes into account the different forms of the stories.

13. Weimar, *Untersuchungen*, pp. 23-26.

14. Gunkel, *Genesis*, l.c.

15. Weimar, *Untersuchungen*, pp. 17-20.

16. Other reconstructions have been offered. See for example, van Seters, *Abraham*, pp. 167f; Koch, *Growth*, pp. 125f.

17. The time of the patriarchs is a matter of dispute. That the stories can be dated at all, at least by the usual means used, has been challenged by Thompson, *Historicity*. Indeed this is for him the wrong question to ask the material since it does not have a historical intention. Van Seters, *Abraham*, would place the stories toward the end of Israel's history rather than at the beginning. There are a variety of views between the traditional one and these two extremes on the continuum. Westermann, *Genesis*, takes a more moderate view.

18. According to Noth, these stories circulated as independent cycles around the major themes of the Pentateuch before the sources like J organized them into a continuous narrative. This organization in fact antedates J, going back to premonarchy times in Israel. See also Tengström, *Die Hexateuch*.

19. The division of Genesis into "sources" or strands of material is an often told story. Since there are many variations as well as problems with this division of the material and assignment to the sources, the reader is referred to the standard introductions and commentaries. Three of the major topics of discussion in this regard may be simply mentioned: (1) The age of the cycles of material, including the problem of whether J and E go back to a common source. (2) The integrity and history of J—is it a combination of more than one cycle of material? Is it a cycle with additions and redactions? (3) The scope of the source—where do the strands begin and end?

20. Those who see J as an amalgamation which has gone through several editions see this story as originally non-J material now incorporated into J. See Gunkel, *Genesis*, l.c.; Eissfeldt, *Introduction*, paragraphs 27 and 28, Weimar, *Untersuchungen*, p. 43, and Tengström, *Die Hexateuch*, pp. 25ff.

21. For the prophets taking up the law see for example: E. Würthwein, "Der

Ursprung der Prophetischen Gerichtsrede," ZThK 49(1952) 1-16; R. Bach, "Gottesrecht und weltliches Recht in der Verkündigung des Propfeten Amos," in *Festschrift für Günther Dehn*, Ed. W. Schneemelcher, Neukirchen: Neukirchener Verlag, 1957, pp. 23-34 and R. V. Bergren, *The Prophet and the Law* (PhD diss. Hebrew Union College, 1972). These scholars see Amos and the other prophets basing their censure of Israel on the apodictic law. This view is based on two major premises: (1) That Amos and other prophets were associated with the cult and spoke as covenant law spokespersons. (Cf. H. G. Reventlow, *Das Amt des Propheten bei Amos*, FRLANT 80 (Göttingen: Vandenhoeck & Ruprecht, 1962). (2) Their accusations are based on the regulations of the law. Both of these arguments have been contested. H. H. Schmid, "Zur Frage nach der geistigen Heimat des propheten Amos," *Wort und Dienst* 10(1969) 85-103 has summarized the objections of the above view. (1) That Amos was a cult prophet has not been shown; (2) Parallels to the law in Amos are material only, never verbal; (3) If Amos's intent is to charge the people with breaking covenant law, why doesn't he mention covenant, Moses, or Sinai? (4) The core vocabulary of Amos is not legal; see Amos 3:8-11 and words like good (tob), evil (ra'). Schmid concludes that parallels exist between Amos and ancient Israelite law, but it cannot be said that Amos measured the behavior of the people directly or indirectly on concrete amphictyonic covenant law (p. 91). Cf. H. W. Wolff, *Amos the Prophet: The Man and His Background*, trans, F. R. McCurley (Philadelphia: Fortress Press, 1973), pp. 1ff.; R. E. Clements, *Prophecy and Tradition*, (Atlanta: John Knox, 1975), especially pages 27-44.

A more general hypothesis holds that the prophet argued not from specific laws but from his role as prophet, Yahweh's messenger who keeps alive the pre-king covenant-amphictyony traditions in Israel. Covenant influence is seen in their use of the covenant lawsuit form. For this view which is widely held, see H. B. Huffmon, "The Covenant Lawsuit in the Prophets," *JBL* 78(1959) 285-95; idem, "The Origin of Prophecy," in *Magnalia Dei; The Mighty Acts of God*, eds. F. M. Cross, W. E. Lemke, and P. D. Miller (Garden City, New York: Doubleday, 1976), pp. 171-186.; G. E. Wright, "The Law Suit of God: A Form-Critical Study of Deuteronomy 32," in *Israel's Prophetic Heritage: Essays in Honor of James Muilenburg*, eds. B. W. Anderson and W. Harrelson (New York: Harper and Brothers, 1962), pp. 26-67; cf. R. Rendtorff, "Reflections on the Early History of Prophecy in Israel," *Journal for Theology and Church* 4(1967) 14-34. Against this view of the rooting of prophecy in Israel's early covenant tradition see H. C. Schmitt, "Prophetie und Tradition: Beobachtungen zu Frühgeshichte des israelitischen Nabitums," *ZThK* 74(1977) 255-272 and R. E. Clements, *Prophecy and Tradition*, pp. 8-23.

22. See H. W. Wolff, *Amos the Prophet*, and S. Terrien, "Amos and Wisdom," in *Israel's Prophetic Heritage: Essays in Honor of James Muilenburg*, eds. B. W. Anderson and W. Harrelson (New York: Harper and Brothers, 1962), 108-115. Cf. J. W. Whedbee, *Isaiah and Wisdom* (Nashville: Abingdon Press, 1971).

23. Against reading Amos's message too specifically against a wisdom background, see Schmid, "Heimat," pp. 92-101, and J. L. Crenshaw, "The Influence of the Wise upon Amos," ZAW 79(1967) 42-52.

24. On "righteousness" see H. H. Schmid, *Gerechtigkeit als Weltordnung: Hintergrund und Geschichte des alttestamentlichen Gerechtigkeitsbegriffes*, BHTh 40 (Tübingen: J. C. B. Mohr, 1968) and K. Koch, "sedeq," *THAT*, vol. 2 pp. 507-530.

25. For a general view of kingship of the ancient Near East see H. H. Frankfort, *Kingship and the Gods: A Study of Ancient Near Eastern Religion as the Integration of Society and Nature* (Chicago: University of Chicago Press, 1948) and J. de Fraine, *L'aspect Religieux de la Royauté Israelite, L'institution monarchique dans L'Ancien Testament et dans les textes mesopotamiens*, Analecta Biblica 3 (Rome: Pontifical Biblical Institute, 1954). On righteousness in the ancient Near East see Schmid, *Gerechtigkeit*.

26. Quoted in Frankfort, *Kingship*, p. 237. Translation by Thorkild Jacobson.

27. Quoted by G. Pettinato, *Das altorientalische Menschenbild und die sumerischen und akkadischen Schöpfungsmythen, Abhandlungen der Heidelberger Akademie der Wissenschaften* (Heidelberg: Carl Winter, 1971) from *uš* and *ashnan* (p. 32).

28. Quoted by ibid., p. 88 line 17 from *uš* and *ashnan*.

29. *Quoted by* S. N. Kramer, *The Sumerians: Their History, Culture, and Character* (Chicago: University of Chicago Press, 1963), p. 318.

30. Ibid., p. 336.

31. ANET, p. 164 lines 22ff.

32. G. R. Driver and J. C. Miles, *The Babylonian Laws*, vol. 2 (Oxford: Clarendon Press, 1955), p. 97 lines 59ff.

33. Kramer, *Sumerians*, 319.

34. Ibid., pp. 336, 339.

35. See E. A. Speiser, "Early Law and Civilization," in *Oriental and Biblical Studies: Collected Writings of E. A. Speiser*, eds. J. J. Finkelstein and M. Greenberg (Philadelphia: University of Pennsylvania Press, 1967), pp. 534-555, especially pp. 552ff.; ibid., "Authority and Law in Mesopotamia," pp. 313-323; idem, "Cuneiform Law and the History of Civilization," *Proceedings of the American Philological Society* 107(1963) pp. 536-541; also the items mentioned in note 17 above and the bibliography cited in them. Cf. S. Paul, *Studies in the Book of the Covenant in the Light of Cuneiform and Biblical Law* (Leiden: E. J. Brill, 1970), pp. 3-10.

36. G. R. Driver, *Canaanite Myths and Legends*, Old Testament Studies vol. 3 (Edinburg: T & T Clark, 1956), pp. 46-47 (Keret II, vi, 39-54).

37. Ibid., pp. 52-53 (Aqhat II, ii, 3-7).

38. Cf. E. Hammershaimb, "On the Ethics of the Old Testament Prophets," VTS 7(1960) pp. 75-101; F. C. Fensham, "Widow, Orphan and the Poor in Ancient Near Eastern Legal and Wisdom Literature," *JNES* 21(1962), 129-139.

39. F. R. Krause, "Ein zentrale probleme des altmesopotamischen Rechts: Was ist der Codex Hammu-rabi?" *Geneva* 8(1960), 283-296; J. J. Finkelstein, "Ammisaduqa's Edict and the Babylonian Law Codes," *JCS* 15 (1961), pp. 91ff. and idem, "Gesetze" in *RLA*, l.c.; S. Paul, *Studies*, pp. 11-26.

40. This was partly the reason for J. Wellhausen's late dating of the laws in the Pentateuch; *Prolegomena to the History of Ancient Israel*, trans. Menzies and Black (Cleveland: World Publishing Co., Meridian Books, 1957).

41. See items in note 31 above.

42. G. C. Macholz, "Die Stellung des Königs in der israelitischen Gerichtsverfassung," *ZAW* 84(1972) 157-181, and idem, "Zur Geschichte der Justizorganization in Judah," *ZAW* (1972) 314-340.

43. On ancient Near Eastern reform acts see: F. R. Kraus, *Ein Edikt des Königs Ammi-Saduqa von Babylon, Studia et Documenta*, vol. 5 (Leiden: E. J. Brill, 1958); J. J. Finkelstein, "Some New *Misharum* Material and Its Implications," in *Studies in Honor of Benno Landsberger on His Seventy-Fifth Birthday, April 21, 1965*, eds. H. G. Güterbock and T. Jacobsen, *Assyriological Studies* 16(Chicago: University of Chicago Press, 1965), pp. 233-246; F. R. Kraus, "Ein Edikt des Königs Samsu-Iluna von Babylon," in ibid, pp. 225-232; J. J. Finkelstein, "Ammisaduqa's Edict," Cf. the entries for "*anduraru*" and "*misharum*" in *CAD* and *AHwb*.

44. M. Weinfeld, *Deuteronomy and the Deuteronomic School* (Oxford: Clarendon Press, 1972), pp. 146ff. Contra Weinfeld see the items mentioned in the following footnotes.

45. On the relationship of the reform legislation in the ancient Near East and the biblical materials see: N. P. Lemche, "Andurārum and Mīšarum: Comments on the Problem of Social Edicts and Their Application in the Ancient Near East," *JNES* 38(1979) 11-22; idem, "The Manumission of Slaves—The Fallow Year—The Sabbatical Year—The

Jobel Year," VT 26(1976) 38-59; on the Jubilee law see R. North, *Sociology of the Biblical Jubilee, Analecta Biblica* 4 (Rome: Pontifical Biblical Institute, 1954).

46. In the Psalms, Psalm 72 links kingship with the concepts of justice and righteousness in a prayer for the king.

47. Seeing Amos as calling for reforms based on justice and righteousness explains why he does not mention the breaking of specific law, but rather more general social injustices. While both the reform legislation and law collections were to bring about the proper order, reform acts were a more *ad hoc* social reform to deal with specific abuses or inequities in the society. Amos by pointing out the injustices and calling for justice and righteousness is calling for action—to institute the necessary reforms. This also explains why Amos does not call for a revolution against the oppressors. Built into the system was to be a system of checks to social inequality.

48. See chapter 2, page 59f.

49. On Q consult the introductions to the New Testament listed in the bibliography; D. Lührmann, *Die Redaktion der Logienquelle, WMANT* 33 (Neukirchen-Vluyn: Neukirchener Verlag, 1969); H. T. Wrege, *Die Überlieferungsgeschicte der Bergpredigt, WUNT* 9 (Tübingen: J. C. B. Mohr, 1968) argues that Matthew and Luke do not go back to a common source (p. 79).

50. See: R. Bultmann, *History of Synoptic Tradition*, pp. 79, 83, 91-93, and especially pp. 101-106; Wrege, *Überlieferungsgeschichte*, p. 80.

51. Bultmann, *History of the Synoptic Tradition*, pp. 79, 83, 91-93, and 101-106.

52. It is widely assumed that Jesus is teaching against revenge rather than against *lex talionis*. Strecker, who sees here the principle of *talionis* claims Matthew understood it as revenge: G. Strecker, "Die Antithesen der Bergpredigt (Mt. 5:21-48 par)," *ZNW* 69(1978), p. 63. Cf. Wrege, *Überlieferungsgeschichte*, who sees the antithesis developed from parenesis against revenge (p. 80).

53. See the commentaries.

54. Bultmann, *History of the Synoptic Tradition*, p. 137; E. Schweizer, *Matthew*, pp. 110f.

55. Bultmann, ibid., p. 137.

56. Ibid., p. 137.

57. J. M. Suggs, "The Antithesis as Redactional Products," in *Jesus Christus in Historie und Theologie*, ed. Georg Strecker (Tübingen: J. C. B. Mohr, 1975), pp. 433-444. While Suggs argues that both types of antitheses are Matthew's composition, Wrege argues that the antithesis in 5:38-39a cannot be due to Matthew, but he took it up from his tradition. So also Luhrmann following a careful study of "verily I say to you" passages in Matthew (*Redaction*, p. 118).

58. G. Strecker, "Die Antithesen," examines the criteria listed above and concludes that the antitheses 1, 2, 4 are pre-Matthean; 3, 5, 6 formed from Q material (pp. 47 and 63f).

59. See: C. D. Morrison, *The Powers That Be*, SBT 29 (London: SCM, 1960) pp. 48ff.; Friedrich, Pöhlmann, and Stuhlmacher, "Zu historischen Situation," pp. 145ff.; J. B. Caird, *Principalities and Powers* (Oxford: Clarendon Press, 1956), pp. 1-13.

60. See the items in note 59 and the commentaries by Cranfield and Michel.

61. See Morrison's discussion, *The Powers That Be*, pp. 17-20, 55ff.

62. See, A. J. Bandstra, *The Law and the Elements of the World: An Exegetical Study in Aspects of Paul's Teaching* (Grand Rapids, Mich.: Eerdman's, 1964) for a discussion of the elements.

63. See Morrison, *The Powers That Be*, pp. 21-29; O. Cullmann, *Christ and Time*, trans. F. V. Filson (Philadelphia: Westminster, 1964), pp. 191-210; idem, *The State in the New Testament*, "Excurses on the most recent discussion of the exousia in Romans 13:1" (New York: Scribner, 1956), pp. 95-114, for a more positive evaluation of the powers in the

New Testament. This positive assessment is based on the argument that the powers have been recommissioned to serve Christ. There is little evidence, seemingly, to support this view.

64. This argument for conditionality rests on putting the passage as a whole in its proper theological setting. On internal grounds as well submission may be conditional: as long as the state promotes good and punishes evil. This internal argument would hold that if the reasons Paul gives for submitting to the state are not found—if a particular government does not rule according to Divine providence by not promoting good or punishing evil, then Christians are no longer obligated to submit. For different variations of this type of argument, see E. Käsemann, "Principles in the Interpretation of Romans 13"; Cranfield, *Romans* at Romans 13:1-7, and J. H. Yoder, *The Politics of Jesus* (Grand Rapids, Mich.: Eerdman's, 1972), pp. 193-214, especially pp. 207 ff.

Chapter 6

1. E. Güttgemanns, *Candid Questions of Gospel Form Criticism: A Methodological Sketch of the Fundamental Problematics of Form and Redaction Criticism*, Pittsburgh Theological Mongraph Series, 26, general ed. D. Y. Hadidian (Pittsburgh: Pickwick Press, 1979) discusses the tension between the study of individual units and their present function as part of a larger whole.

1a. See G. Tucker, "Prophetic Superscriptions and the Growth of a Canon," in *Canon and Authority: Essays in Old Testament Religion and Theology*, Burke O. Long and George W. Coats (Philadelphia: Fortress Press, 1977), pp. 56-70.

2. Cf. Jeremiah 30:1-3; 36:1-32.

3. In the Pentateuch where a unit functions as part of a source like "J," "J's" transmission is studied.

4. The following general criteria can be used in order to determine whether an analysis belongs to transmission study rather than tradition study: (1) The relative fixedness of the text—e.g., the Lord's Prayer. (2) No change in the genre or type. J's use of oral tradition to compose Genesis 12:10-20 was placed under tradition analysis because the assumption was made that the present form of the text is due to J: he cast traditional material into a . . . speech fulfilling story is due to J. (3) The changes made are supplemental to the function or intention of the text. In Amos 2:6-16 verses 9-12 do not change the basic form, function, or intention of the passage; they strengthen the motivation for the judgment. They will consequently be studied under transmission. (4) Finally, for transmission analysis the composer of the unit must be different than the author of the work. If they are the same, then the study of sources belongs to tradition anaylsis.

5. See tradition analysis for references to source analysis.

6. See the introductions and commentaries for the details of this process.

7. Some find significant editorial additions and reworking; see Weimar, *Untersuchungen*, pp. 102ff.

8. On the hypothesis that J set the agenda for the Pentateuch see below under redaction analysis and the references cited there.

9. For differing views on the transmission of the material in Amos see the commentaries by Wolff and Mays. A summary of views is presented in Koch, et al., *Amos Untersucht*, pp. 124ff. Wolff sees 2:6-16 as going back to Amos.

10. It is in seeking these literary and ideological connections with other material in a book or books that we discover either a source used in composing a book (such as J in Genesis) or a stage in the transmission of the material. That is, these modifications from a common viewpoint point to a certain circle, time, or function through which the material passed. The difference is: did the author of the unit use sources to compose the unit, or is this material a later expansion of the unit. If a later expansion, then it is studied under

transmission. If a source used in composing, under tradition.

11. On Deuteronomic additions see: W. H. Schmidt, "Die deuteronomistische Redaktion des Amos Buches"; Wolff, *Amos*, l.c.; J. Vollmer, *Geschichtliche Rückblicke und Motive in des Prophetie des Amos, Hosea, und Jesaja*, BZAW 119 (Berlin, Walter de Gruter, 1971), pp. 20ff. Cautions and counterarguments by S. Wagner, "Überlegung zur Frage nach den Beziehungen des Propheten Amos zum Sudreich," *TLZ* 96(1971) 653-70, and T. R. Hobbs, "Amos 3.1b and 2.10," *ZAW* 81(1969) 184-187. Summary of those for and against in Koch, et al. *Amos Untersucht*, at 2.9-12.

12. Wolff, *Amos*, l.c.

13. On the Deuteronomistic literature and theology see the introduction of Eisfeldt, Fohrer, Soggin, and Kaiser.

14. See items in note 11 above.

15. G. Von Rad, "The Deuteronomic Theology of History in I and II Kings," in *The Problem of the Hexateuch and Other Essays*, trans. E. W. T. Dicken (London: Oliver and Boyd, 1966), pp. 205-221.

16. Cf. Güttgemanns, Candid Questions; H. Frankenmölle, "Evangelist und Gemeinde: Ein methodenkritische Besinnung mit Beispielen aus dem Mattäusevangelium," *Biblica* 60(1979) 153-190.

17. Check the footnotes of a Bible which gives cross references.

18. Gunkel, *Genesis*, includes verse 9 as part of the basic unit which he sees as extending to 13.4. He also does not consider the story as originally belonging to J. It was placed here to explain Abraham's wealth which is the reason for the division between Lot and Abraham in chapter 13.

19. On redactional studies of this material, besides the commentaries, see: R. Polzin, "The Ancestress of Israel in Danger," *Semeia* 3 (1975) 81-98; Tengström, *Die Hexateuherzählung*, especially pp. 28f.; Weimar, *Untersuchungen*, pp. 44ff. for the boundaries of the unit, pp. 102ff for redaction history.

20. Tengström, *Die Hexateuherzählung*, following Fissfeldt, stresses the distinction between the smallest unit and the smallest literary composition. A story which is relatively self-contained may have its literary form as part of a larger literary whole. This understanding underlines the necessity of using the broader narrative context in interperting a story.

21. On the importance of the theme of promise to the J narration see, C. Westermann, *Die Verheissungen; Idem*, "Promises to the Patriarchs," *IBD(S)*; Wolff, "The Kerygma of the Jahwist," in *The Vitality of the Old Testament Traditions*; pp. 46-63.

22. Genesis 12:1-3 is pivotal in J's history. It not only binds the three parts of J together (primeval history, patriarchs, and nation) but it relates J's material to his time. For the role of 12:1-3 in J's history see: Ruprecht, "Vorgegebene Tradition und theologische Gestaltung in Genesis xii 1-3," *VT* 29(1979) 171-188; idem, "Der traditionsgeschichtliche Hintergrund der einzelnen Elemente von Genesis xii 2-3," *VT* 29 (1979) 444-464; Wolff, "Kerygma"; W. Brueggemann, "Yahwist," *IBD(S)*; Westermann, *Die Verheissungen*, p. 39.; idem, "Genesis," *IBD(S)*.

23. Gunkel, *Genesis*, explains the location of this account differently; see note 18 above.

24. Genesis 12:10-20 could also be treated from the standpoint of the final redaction of the book of Genesis. If we were to do this the function of the unit would change little. Since below in chapter 7, we will discuss the historical background for J, it seems appropriate to end the illustration here. This type of redaction study will form a complementary example to the study of the redaction of Matthew where the final stage of the book is the point of departure.

For a different understanding of the redactional relationship between 12, 20, and 26, see Polzin, "The Ancestress."

25. An exception is the fact that all the oracles against the foreign nations come at the

beginning of the book.

26. K. Koch, "Die Rolle der hymnischen Abschnitte des Amos-Buches," ZAW 86 (1974) 505-535 sees a definite literary function of these hymns in the redaction of the book.

27. On the structure of Amos 1:3—2:3 see: S. Paul, "Amos 1.3-2.3: A Concatenous Literary Pattern," JBL 90(1971) 397-403.

28. Y Kaufmann, Toldot Haemunah Hayisraelit, 8 vols. (Tel Aviv: Mosad Bialik-Dvir, 1937-1956), vol. 3, pp. 61ff.

29. For a treatment of the structure of the book see: Koch, et al., Amos Untersucht, pp. 105ff.; W. A. Smalley, "Recursion Patterns and the Sectioning of Amos," The Bible Translator, 30 (1979) 118-127.

30. G. Barth, "Matthew's Understanding of the Law," in Tradition and Interpretation in Matthew, G. Bornkamm, G. Barth, and H. Held, trans. P. Scott (Philadelphia: Westminster Press, 1963), p. 60 on the relationship of 5:17-20 to the antithesis. See also: Meier, Law and History, U. Luz, "Die Erfüllung des Gesetzes bei Matthäus (Mt. 5:17-20)," ZThK 75(1978) 398-435.

31. That the whole discussion of the law and the antithesis are preceded by the light and salt statements would also seem to be significant. These teachings on the law are part of what it means to be salt and light and they have a missionary motive.

32. For a rebuttal of Bacon's five divisions see: J. Kingsbury, Matthew: Structure, Christology, Kingdom (Philadelphia: Fortress Press, 1975), pp. 4ff.; R. G. Hammerton-Kelly, "Matthew, Gospel of," IDB(S); W. D. Davies, Sermon on the Mount (Cambridge: University Press, 1966), pp. 14-25.

33. Kingsbury, Matthew.

34. See the New Testament introductions listed in the bibliography for information on Matthew's use of Mark and Q and the design of the work.

35. Besides the structure of the Gospel, that Jesus' teachings are central to the Gospel can also be seen from Matthew's stress on judgment and obedience (Barth, "Matthew's Understanding" pp. 58ff.). Likewise it is the only Gospel which demands righteousness of the disciples (Kümmel, Introduction, p. 80.). Matthew's presentation of Jesus' activity also stresses his teaching function—Matthew is the only Gospel linking together proclamation and teaching (Bornkamm, "End-Expectation," p. 38 fn. 1). Indeed, the stress on Jesus' teaching in Matthew is so great that the book has been seen as a catechism for the church (Bultmann, Synoptic Tradition, p. 356.).

36. On these two contrary themes in Matthew see: Luz, "Erfüllung," especially pp. 399ff.; Barth, "Matthew's Understanding."

37. See Schweitzer, Matthew, pp. 110f.; also works listed in the next note for a variety of explanations of what appears to be the annulment of certain laws.

38. That it is Jesus and his interpretation of the law which is normative is widely held. Because of who he was he could give the greater principles whereby to interpret the law. See: G. Bornkamm, "End-Expectation and Church in Matthew," in Bornkamm, Barth, and Held, Tradition and Interpretation in Matthew, pp. 15-45; Barth, "Matthew's Understanding"; J. M. Suggs, Wisdom, Christology and Law in Matthew's Gospel (Cambridge, Mass.: Harvard University Press, 1970); idem, "The Antithesis as Redactional Products"; J. P. Meier, Law and History. For Christology as central to Matthew see also W. Schenk, "Das Präsens Historicum als makrosyntaktisches Gliederungssignal im Mathäusevangelium," NTS 22(1976) 464-475; R. G. Hammerton-Kelly, "Matthew."

39. See K. Stendhall, The School of St. Matthew, and Its Use of the Old Testament (Lund: CWK Gleerup, 2nd ed. 1968).

40. Bornkamm, "End-Expectation," p. 41.

41. Barth, "Matthew's Understanding," pp. 58ff. pp. 159ff.

42. Following Suggs, Wisdom, Christology and Law; cf. Hammerton-Kelly, "Matthew"; Strecker, "Antithesis," p. 71. Caution to this understanding is expressed by Luz,

"Erfüllung," p. 427, note 116. That Jesus is a teacher of the Torah is denied by Frankenmölle, "Evangel und Gemeinde," p. 171. Because of the redactional significance of 6:10b he sees Jesus as God's eschatological messenger.

43. Bornkamm, "End-Expectation," p. 31; Barth, "Matthew's Understanding," pp. 75-85; Schweitzer, *Matthew*, l.c.; Suggs, *Wisdom*, pp. 117ff. For problems with this view see Luz, "Erfüllung," p. 400, who also accepts love as a key to Matthew's understanding of Jesus' teachings.

44. Bornkamm, "End-Expectation," p. 26.

45. The genitive, "your righteousness," is usually taken to be an objective genitive; the righteousness which accrues to you. It can also be seen as a subjective genitive: the righteousness which results from your actions. The emphasis on Jesus' teachings can also be seen in Matthew's stress on judgment and obedience (Barth, "Matthew's Understanding," pp. 58ff.). It is also the only Gospel which demands righteousness of the disciples (Kümmel, *Introduction*, p. 80).

46. V. P. Furnish, *Theology and Ethics in Paul* (Nashville: Abingdon Press, 1968), pp. 101ff.

47. For various divisions of these chapters see: Furnish, *Theology and Ethics in Paul*, p. 100; Cranfield, *Romans*, p. 652; the division here is that of Friedrich, Pöhlmann, and Stuhlmacher, "Zu historischen Situation," pp. 150-153.

48. Käsemann, "Principles," p. 216.

49. 13.1-7 is commonly linked to the heading in 12:1-2. See the commentaries.

50. G. B. Caird, *Principalities and Powers*, pp. 91ff., especially pp. 97ff.

Chapter 7

1. For the use of anachronisms to set the date before which J could not have been composed as well as the dating of J in general see the introductions listed in the bibliography. Cf. H. H. Rowley, *The Growth of the Old Testament* (New York: Harper and Row, 1963) and S. R. Driver, *Introduction to the Literature of the Old Testament* Edinburgh, T & T Clark, 9th ed., 1913).

2. See the items in the preceding note.

3. For a discussion of evidence on the dating of J to this time see items in note 1 and Wolff, "Kerygma," pp. 43-45.

4. For a comparison of these narratives and the J material see P. E. Ellis, *The Yahwist: The Bible's First Theologian* (Notre Dame, Ind.: Fides Publishers, 1968), pp. 67ff.

5. For this historical context as a suitable environment for the composition of J besides the items mentioned in the above notes cf. W. Brueggemann, "David and His Theologian," *CBQ* 30(1968) 156-181; idem, "Yahwist"; Ruprecht, "Der Traditionsgeschichte." Others would date J or its redaction later. Weimar, *Untersuchungen*, argues for a date late in the eighth century for the composition of what we are calling the J material (which he sees as a combination of J material with other material added by the redactor Je). He sees this material emanating from wisdom royal circles, and speaking to the royal circle. His setting is similar to that presumed here, only about 200 years later. Van Seters would date the material yet later (*Abraham*). Thompson holds that the material cannot be dated at present. See Thompson, *The Historicity of the Patriarchal Narratives: The Quest for the Historical Abraham*, BZAW 133 (Berlin: Walter de Gruyter, 1974); idem, "Conflict Themes in the Jacob Narratives," *Semeia* 15 (1979) 5-23.

6. On J's theology see specially Wolff, "Kerygma"; Brueggemann, "Yahwist"; Ellis, "Yahwist"; and G. von Rad, "The Form-Critical Problem of the Hexateuch," in *The Problem of the Hexateuch and other Essays*, trans. E. W. Trueman (Edinburgh: Oliver and Boyd, 1960), pp. 1-78.

7. For the following cf. Wolff, "Kerygma"; Brueggemann, "Yahwist"; Ruprecht,

"Vorgegebene Tradition"; idem, "Traditionsgeschichtliche."

    8. Ruprecht, ibid., argues in a detailed examination of the elements of the promise in Genesis 12:1-3 that the elements of promise have their closest parallel in the promise of blessing for the king. Genesis 12:1-3 can thus be seen as royal language whose real fulfillment comes with a rise of kingship. Brueggemann, "David and His Theologian," relates the J material in Genesis 1—11 to events in the time of David.

    9. Ibid.

    10. See the items in note 7. In fact, from David's subjugation and harsh treatment of Israel's neighbors it might appear that Israel was a negative factor rather than a positive one. Ruprecht sees a line extending from Genesis 12:1-3 to Isaiah 2:2-4 and Zechariah 9:9-10 in which Israel is a benefactor in all nations ("Traditions geschichtliche," p. 463).

    11. Weimar, *Untersuchungen*, sees Genesis 12:10-20 taken up by Je, a redactor, because it relates to his theological perspective and events of the years 705-701. Here under Assyrian pressure Israel seeks security under Egyptian hegemony. Similar intent is expressed in Isaiah 30:2 and 31:1 which also denounce the allegiance with Egypt. Instead, Je and Isaiah call for trust in God (see pages 40-43, 51-55, and 108-110).

    We could also study the historical situation of the final redaction of Genesis to see how this story also spoke to that situation. Here again, as in chapter 6, (see note 24) this example should be seen as complementary to the study of Matthew where the historical setting for the final redaction is discussed. Taken together these two examples illustrate the value of studying both the historical situation of the original composition of the material and its final setting in the work (Genesis or Matthew). In a full treatment both historical settings may be given, or only the latter. Here, due to shortage of space, we have divided our discussion between the two passages, although this shortchanges our study of the Genesis material, since the final form is what we set out to understand.

    12. For the historical setting of Amos see the commentaries on Amos by Wolff and Mays; J. A. Soggins, "Amos VI: 13-14 und I:3 auf dem Hintergrund der Beziehungen zwischen Israels und Damaskus in 9. und 8. Jahrhundert," in *Near Eastern Studies in Honor of W. F. Albright*, ed. H. Goedicke (Baltimore: Johns Hopkins Press, 1971), pp. 433-441; J. Bright, *A History of Israel*, 2nd ed. (London: SCM, 1972); and S. Herrmann, *A History of Israel in Old Testament Times*, trans. J. Bowden (Philadelphia: Fortress Press, 1975).

    13. See the sources in note 12 for this historical sketch.

    14. For this basis of Amos's social critique cf.: K. Koch, "Die Entstehung der sozialen Kritik bei den Profeten," in *Probleme biblischer Theologie*, ed. H. W. Wolff (München: C. Kaiser Verlag, 1971) pp. 236-257; W. H. Schmidt, *Zukunftsgewissheit und Gegenwartskritik: Grundzuge prophetischer Verkündigung* (Neukirchen-Vluyn: Neukirchener Verlag, 1973), pp. 67f; M. Fendler, "Zu Socialkritik des Amos," *EvTh* 33(1973) 32-53; G. Wanke, "Zu Grundlegen und Absicht prophetischer Socialkritik," *KD* 18(1972) 2-17; H. Donner, "Die sozial Botschaft der propheten im Lichte der Gesellschaftsordnung im Israel," *OR* 2(1963) 229-245; and G. J. Botterweck, "Sie Verkaufen den Unschuldigen um Geld," *Bibel und Leben* 12(1971) 215-231. There is in these sources the notion that the oppression is due to the rise of kingship with its necessity for taxation. This was coupled with a borrowing of Canaanite economic principles. On the other hand, the problem may have naturally developed as a result of urbanization and social differentiation.

    15. Koch, "sozialen Kritik," argues against Amos basing his critique on justice and righteousness—otherwise he would have addressed himself to the king (pp. 23ff).

    16. J. S. Holladay, Jr., "Assyrian Statecraft and the Prophets," HTR 63 (1970) 29-51.

    17. See Stendhal, *The School of St. Matthew*.

    18. Kümmel, *Introduction*, p. 80.

    19. Ibid., pp. 80ff.

20. For these arguments see: Meier, *Law and History*, pp. 9 ff.; Luz, "Die Erfüllung," sees the gospel as written at the beginning of a Christian mission to the Gentiles by a Jewish church, before it had faced all the problems that it would face once the mission was actually underway. It is to show the continuation of the Old Testament and the church after the break with Judaism (pp. 426ff.). E. Schwitzer, "Christianity of the Circumcized and Judaism of the Uncircumcized—The Background of Matthew and Colossians," in *Jews, Greeks, and Christians*, eds. R. Hammerton-Kelly and R. Scroggs (Leiden: Brill, 1976), argues for an itinerent, ascetic Jewish Christian setting. Against this see J. D. Kingsbury, "The Verb Akolouthein ("to follow") as an Index of Matthew's View of His Community," *JBL* 97(1978) p. 62.

21. In fact, Bultmann saw the antithesis as "debating sayings" which would have been used by the church against its Jewish opponents (*Synoptic Tradition*, p. 146).

22. Barth, "Matthew's Understanding," pp. 159-162.

23. Kümmel, *Introduction*, p. 84. Another view of Matthew's background is to set it against an assumed antinomian enthusiasm. Cf. Barth, "Matthew's Understanding," pp. 159ff.

24. See, Schlier, *Der Römerbrief;* M. Black, *Romans*, NCB (Greenwood, S.C., The Attic Press, 1973); C. K. Barrett, *II Corinthians* (New York: Harper and Row, 1973).

25. Note the Gentile representatives who traveled along with Paul to Jerusalem (Acts 20:1-6; 21:27ff.). (This was brought to my attention by D. Garber.)

26. See A. J. M. Wedderburn, "The Purpose and Occasion of Romans Again," *ET* 90(1979) 137-141.

27. See Black, *Romans*, p. 20.

28. P. Minear, *The Obedience of Faith: The Purpose of Paul in the Epistle to the Romans* (London: SCM, 1971).

29. Friedrich, Pöhlmann, Stuhlmacher, "Zu historischen Situation," pp. 156ff.

30. For Roman taxation practices see: A. H. M. Jones, "Taxation in Antiquity," in *The Roman Economy*, ed. P. A. Brunt (Oxford: Blackwell, 1974), pp. 151-186; idem, "Over-Taxation and the Decline of the Roman Empire," ibid., pp. 82-89.

31. Friedrich, Pöhlmann, Stuhlmacher, "Zu historischen Situation," tie this advice of Paul to both the general missionary motive, which is intensified in 1 Peter 2.15 and the theme of conquering through love. In this situation of oppressive taxation, paying taxes, was a chance to return good for evil (p. 161).

Bibliography

Abarbanel, Isaac, *Perush n^{e}bi'im uke-tubim.* Tel Aviv: Abarbanel Books, 1933.

Albrektson, Bertil, "Prophecy and Politics in the Old Testament," in *The Myth of the State.* Ed. by H. Biezais, *Script. Inst. Donneriani Abrensis* 6(1972) 45-56.

Alston, William P., *Philosophy of Language.* Englewood Cliffs, N.J.: Prentice-Hall, 1964.

Alonso-Schökel, A., "Hermeneutical Problems of a Literary Study of the Bible," *VTS* 18(1974) 1-15.

Bach, Robert, "Gottesrecht und weltliches Recht in der Verkündigung des Propheten Amos," in *Festschrift fur Günther Dehn.* Ed.¹Wilhelm Schneemelcher, Neukirchen: Neukirchener Verlag, 1957, pp. 23-34.

Bainton, Roland A., "The Bible in the Reformation," in *The Cambridge History of the Bible,* Vol. III. Ed. S. L. Greenslade, Cambridge: Cambridge University Press, 1975, pp. 1-37.

Baltzer, Klaus, "Considerations Regarding the Office and Calling of the Prophet," *HTR* 61(1968) 567-581.

Bandstra, A. J., *The Law and the Elements of the World: An Exegetical Study in Aspects of Paul's Teaching.* Grand Rapids: Eerdman's, 1964.

Barr, James, *The Bible in the Modern World.* London: SCM Press, 1977.

——————, *Comparative Philology and the Text of the Old Testament.* London: Oxford at the Clarendon Press, 1968.

——————, *Old and New in Interpretation: A Study of the Two Testaments.* New York: Harper & Row, 1966.

——————, *The Semantics of Biblical Language.* Oxford: University Press, 1961.

Barrett, Charles K., *A Commentary on the Epistle to the Romans.* New York: Harper & Row, 1958.

——————, *The Second Epistle to the Corinthians.* New York: Harper & Row. 1973.

Barth, Gerhard, "Matthew's Understanding of the Law," in *Tradition and Interpretation in Matthew.* Trans. Percy Scott, Philadelphia: Westminster Press, 1963, pp. 58-164.

Barth, Hermann & Steck, Odil Hannes, *Exegese des Alten Testaments: Leitfaden der Methodik,* 4th ed. Neukirchen: Neukirchener Verlag, 1973.

Barth, Markus, *Ephesians: Introduction, Translation, and Commentary on Chapters 1-3, Anchor Bible.* Ed. W. F. Albright and D. N. Freedman, Garden City, N.Y.: Doubleday, 1974.

Beachy, Alvin, "The Bible as Witness to Revelation," unpublished paper.

263

Beegle, Dewey M., *Scripture, Tradition and Infallibility.* Grand Rapids, Mich.: Eerdman's, 1973.

Beek, M. A., "The Religious Background of Amos II:6-8," *OTS* 5(1948) 132-141.

Beekman, John and Callow, John, *Translating the Word of God.* Grand Rapids, Mich.: Zondervan, 1974.

Bellert, Irena, "On a Condition of the Coherence of Texts," *Semiotica* 2(1970) 335-363.

Ben-Amos, Dan, "Themes, Forms, and Meanings: Critical Comments," *Semeia* 3(1975) 128-132.

Bentzen, A., "The Ritual Background of Amos 1:2—2:16," *OTS* 8(1950) 85-99.

——————————, *Introduction to the Old Testament,* 7th Edition. Copenhagen: G. E. C. Gad Publisher, 1967.

Berger, Klaus, *Exegese des Neuen Testaments: Neue Wege vom Text zur Auslegung,* Heidelberg, Quelle & Meyer: Uni-Taschenbücher 658, 1977.

Berger, Peter L., *The Heretical Imperative: Contemporary Possibilities of Religious Affirmation.* Garden City, N.Y.: Doubleday, 1979.

Bergren, Richard V., *The Prophets and the Law, Monograph of the Hebrew Union College.* Cincinnati: Hebrew Union College-Jewish Institute of Religion, 1974.

Betz, O., "Might, Authority, Throne," *DNTT,* Vol. 2. Ed. Collin Brown, Grand Rapids, Mich.: Zondervan, 1975, pp. 601-616.

Birger, Olsson, *Structure and Meaning in the Fourth Gospel: A Text-Linguistic Analysis of John 2:1-11 and 4:1-12.* Gleerup: Lund, Sweden; CWK, 1974.

Bjetenhard, H., "Beginning, Origin, Rule, Ruler, Originator," *DNTT,* Vol. 1. Ed. Collin Brown, Grand Rapids, Mich.: Zondervan, 1975, pp. 164-169.

Black, Matthew, *Romans, New Century*

Bible, Greenwood, S.C.: The Attic Press, Inc., 1973.

Black, Max, *The Labyrinth of Language.* New York: Praeger, 1968.

Blass, F., Debrunner, A., *A Greek Grammar of the New Testament and Other Early Christian Literature.* Ed. Robert W. Funk, Chicago: University of Chicago Press, 1961.

Boas, Marie, *The Scientific Renaissance 1450-1630.* New York: Harper & Row, 1962.

Boecker, H. J., *Redeformen des Rechtslebens im Alten Testament,* WMANT 14 Neukirchen-Vluyn: Neukirchener Verlag, 1964.

Boling, R. G., *Judges: Introduction, Translation and Commentary,* Anchor Bible. Ed. D. N. Freedman, Garden City, New York: Doubleday, 1975.

Bonelli, M. G. R. and Shea, William R., ed., *Reason, Experiment, & Mysticism in the Scientific Revolution.* Science Hist. Publ., New York, 1975.

Bornkamm, G., "End-Expectation and Church in Matthew," in *Tradition and Interpretation in Matthew.* Trans. Percy Scott, Philadelphia: Westminster Press, 1963, pp. 15-57.

Botterweck, G. J., "Sie verkaufen den Unschuldigen um Gelt," *Bibel und Leben* 12(1971) 215-231.

——————————, "אֶבְיוֹן," *TDOT,* ed. G. Johannes Botterweck and Helmer Ringgren, Grand Rapids: Eerdman's, 1974.

Bright, J., *A History of Israel.* London: SCM, 2nd ed., 1972.

Brown, R. E., *The Gospel According to John (i-xii),* The Anchor Bible. Ed. W. F. Albright and D. N. Freedman, Garden City, N.Y.: Doubleday, 1966.

Brueggeman, Walter, "Yahwist," *IDB(S).* Ed. Keith Crim, Nashville: Abingdon, 1976.

——————————, "David and His Theologian," *CBQ* 30(1968) 156-181.

—————— & Wolff, H. W., *The Vitality of Old Testament Tradition*. Atlanta: John Knox, 1975.

Bultmann, Rudolf, *Primitive Christianity in Its Contemporary Setting*. Trans. R. H. Fuller, Cleveland: World Publishing Co., 1956. Meridian Books.

——————, *History of the Synoptic Tradition*. Trans. John Marsh, London: Basil Blackwell, 1972.

Buss, Martin J., "Appropriate and Not-so-appropriate Ways of Relating Historical and Functional Methods: A Draft," in *SBL Seminar papers*, Philadelphia: Fortress Press, 1979, pp. 445-474.

——————, "Understanding Communication," in *Encounters with the Text: Form and History in the Hebrew Bible*. Ed. M. J. Buss, Missoula: Scholars Press, 1979, pp. 3-44.

Caird, George, *Principalities and Powers*. Oxford: Clarendon Press, 1956.

Calloud, Jean, "A Few Comments on Structural Semiotics: A Brief Review of a Method and Some Explanation of Procedures," *Semeia* 15(1979)51-83.

——————, *Structural Analysis of Narrative*, Semeia Supplements 4. Translated by Daniel Patte, Missoula Mont.: Scholars Press, 1976.

Callow, Kathleen, *Translating the Word of God: Discourse Consideration*. Grand Rapids: Zondervan, 1974.

Carlston, C. E., "Form Criticism, N.T.," *IDB(S)*. Ed. Keith Crim, Nashville: Abingdon, 1976.

Cazelles, H., "Biblical Criticism, O.T.," *IDB(S)*. Ed. Keith Crim, Nashville: Abingdon, 1976.

Childs, B., *Biblical Theology in Crises*. Philadelphia: Westminster Press, 1970.

——————, "The Etiological Tale Re-examined," *VT* 24(1974) 387-397.

Chomsky, Noam, *Aspects of the Theory of Syntax*. Cambridge: MIT Press, 1965.

Clements, R. E., *Prophecy and Covenant*. *SBT* 43, London, 1965.

——————, *Prophecy and Tradition*. Atlanta: John Knox, 1975.

Coats, G. W., "Tradition Criticism, O.T.," *IDB(S)*. Ed. Keith Crim, Nashville: Abingdon, 1976.

Cohen, S., "Political Background of the Words of Amos," *HUCA* 36(1965)153-160.

Collingwood, R. G., *The Idea of History*. New York: Oxford, 1956.

Colwell, E. C., *The Study of the Bible*. Chicago: University of Chicago, 1964.

Conzelmann, H., "Literaturbericht zu synoptischen Evangelien," *ThR*. 43(1978) pp. 35-43.

Cragan, John F., "The Prophet Amos in Recent Literature," *Biblical Theology Bulletin* 2(1972) 242-261.

Cranfield, C. E. B., *A Commentary: Romans 12-13*, SJT occasional papers 12(1965), London: Cambridge University Press.

——————, *The Epistle to the Romans*, 2 vols. International Critical Commentary. Edinburgh: T&T Clark Ltd., 1975, 1979.

Crenshaw, "Influence of Wise on Amos," ZAW 79(1967)42-52.

Crossan, John D., "Jesus and Pacifism," in *No Famine in the Land: Studies in Honor of John L. McKenzie*. Ed. James W. Flanagan and Anita Weisbrod Robinson, Missoula, Mont.: Scholars Press, 1975, pp. 195-208.

Crüsemann, Frank, *Der Widerstand gegen des Königtum: Die antikönglichen Texte des Alten Testaments und der Kampf um den frühen israelitischen Stadt*. Neukirchen-Vluyn: Neukirchener Verlag, 1978.

Culley, Robert C., "Structural Analysis: Is It Done with Mirrors?" *Interpretation* 28(1974)165-181.

—————, *Studies in the Structure of Hebrew Narrative.* Missoula, Mont.: Scholars Press, 1976.

Culmann, O., *Christ and Time.* Trans. Floyd V. Filson, Philadelphia: Westminster, 1964.

—————, *The State in the New Testament.* New York: Scribner, 1956.

Daube, David, "Eye for Eye," in *The NT & Rabbinic Judaism.* London: University of London, Athione Press, 1956, pp. 254-265.

—————, "Ye Have Heard ... But I Say Unto You," in *The NT & Rabbinic Judaism.* London: University of London, Athione Press, 1956, pp. 55-62.

Davies, William David, *Sermon on the Mount.* Cambridge: University Press. 1966.

Delling, Gerhard, " στοιχειον ," *TDNT,* Vol. 7. Ed. Gerhard Kittel, Grand Rapids: Eerdman's, 1964, pp. 666-686.

—————, " αρχη ," *TDNT,* Vol. 1. Ed. Gerhard Kittel, Grand Rapids: Eerdman's, 1964, pp. 479-484.

—————, "άρχων," *TDNT,* Vol. 1. Ed. Gerhard Kittel, Grand Rapids: Eerdman's, 1964, pp. 488-489.

—————, " ὑποτάσσω ," *TDNT,* Vol. 8. Ed. Gerhard Kittel, Grand Rapids: Eerdman's, 1964, pp. 39-46.

—————, "τάσσω," *TDNT,* Vol. 8. Ed. Gerhard Kittel, Grand Rapids: Eerdman's, 1964, pp. 27-31.

Dibelius, Martin, *James, Hermenia.* Philadelphia: Fortress Press, 1976.

Dijk, Teun A., *Some Aspects of Text Grammars: A Study in Theoretical Linguistics and Poetics, Janua linguarum Ser. Major* No. 63. The Hague: Mouton, 1972.

Dion, Hyacinthe M., "The Patriarchal Traditions and the Literary Form of the 'Oracle of Salvation,'" *CBQ* 29(1967)198-206.

Donner, H., "Die soziale Botschaft der propheten im lichte der Gesellschafts Ordnung in Israel," *Oriens Antiquus* 2(1963)229-245.

Doty, William G., "The Concept of Genre in Literary Analysis," *SBL Seminar Papers,* 1972, Vol. ii, pp. 413-448.

—————, *Contemporary New Testament Interpretation.* Prentice Hall, 1972.

—————, "The Discipline and Literature of New Testament Form Criticism," *Anglican Theological Review* 51(1969)257-321.

—————, "Linguistics and Biblical Criticism," *JAAR* 41(1973)114-121.

Driver, G. R., *Canaanite Myths and Legends, Old Testament Studies.* Edinburgh: T & T Clark, 1956.

Driver, G. R. and Miles, J. C., *The Babylonian Laws.* Oxford: Clarendon Press, 1955.

Driver, S. R., *Introduction to the Literature of the Old Testament.* Edinburgh, T & T Clark, 9th ed., 1913.

Dürr, L., "Altorientalisches Recht bei den Propheten Amos und Hosea," *BZ* 23(1935)150-157.

Ebeling, Gerhard, "The Significance of the Critical Historical Method for Church and Theology in Protestantism," in *Word & Faith,* trans. James W. Leitch. Philadelphia: Fortress Press, 1963, pp. 17-61.

Eissfeldt, Otto, *The Old Testament: An Introduction.* Oxford: Basil Blackwell, 1965.

Elon, Menachem, "Pledge," *Encyclopedia Judaica,* Vol. 13. Jerusalem: Keters Publishing House, 1972, pp. 635-644.

Ellis, Peter F., *The Yahwist: The Bible's First Theologian.* Notre Dame, Ind.: Fides Publishing, 1968.

Exum, Cheryl J., "Promise and Fulfillment: Narrative Art in Judges 13," *JBL* 99(1980)43-59.

Farmer, William R., "The Present State of the Synoptic Problem," *Perkins Journal* 32(1978)1-7.

Fendler, Marlene, "Zur Sozialkritik des Amos: Versuch einer wirtschaft und sozialgeschichtlichen Interpretation alttestamentlicher Texte," *Evangelische Theologie* (München), 33(1973)32-53.

Fensham, Charles F., "Common Trends in Curses of the Near Eastern Treaties and KUDURRU-inscriptions Compared with Maledictions of Amos and Isaiah," *ZAW* 75(1963)155-175.

——————, "Widow, Orphan and the Poor in Ancient Near Eastern Legal & Wisdom Literature," *JNES* 21(1962)129-139.

Finkelstein, J. J., "Ammisaduqa's Edict and the Babylonian Law Codes," *JCS* 15(1961)91ff.

——————, "Gesetze," RLA, ed. Ernst Weidner and Wolfram von Sodon, Berlin: Walter de Gruyter, 1957-71.

——————, "Some New *Misharum* material and its Implications," in *Studies in Honor of Benno Landsberger on his Seventy-Fifth Birthday, April 21, 1965.* Ed. H. G. Güterbock and T. Jacobsen, *Assyriological Studies*, 16 Chicago: University of Chicago Press, 1965.

Foerster, Werner, " ἐξουσία," *TDNT*, Vol. 2. Ed. Gerhard Kittel, Grand Rapids: Eerdman's, 1964, pp. 560-574.

Fohrer, G., et. al., *Exegese des Alten Testaments: Einführung in die Methodik*, 2nd ed. Heidelberg: Quelle & Meyer, 1976.

——————, *The History of Israelite Religion.* Trans. by D. E. Green. Nashville: Abingdon, 1972.

Fokkelman, J. P., *Narrative Art in Genesis: Specimens of Stylistic and Structural Analysis.* Assen: Van Gorcum, 1975.

Fortna, R. T., "Redaction Criticism, N.T." in *IDB(S)*. Ed. Keith Crim, Nashville: Abingdon, 1976.

de Fraine, J., *L'aspect Religieux de la Royauté Israelite: L'institution monarchique dans L'Ancien Testament et dans les textes mesopotamiens, Analecta Biblica 3.* Rome: Pontificio Instituto Biblico, 1954.

Frankenmölle, H., "Evangelist und Gemeinde, Ein Methodkritische Besinnung mit Beispielen aus dem Mattäusevon gelium," *Biblica* 60 (1979)153-190.

——————, "Exegese und linguistik-Methoden: Probleme Neuer exegetischer Veröffentlichen," *ThR* 71(1975)1-12.

Frankfort, Henri, *Kingship and the Gods: A Study of Ancient Near Eastern Religion on the Integration of Society and Nature.* Chicago: University of Chicago Press, 1948.

Fretheim, T. E., "The Jacob Traditions Theology and Hermeneutic," *Interpretation* 26(1972)419-436.

——————, "Source Criticism," *IDB(S)*. Ed. Keith Crim, Nashville: Abingdon, 1976.

Friedrich, J., Pöhlmann, W., Stuhlmacher, P., "Zu historischen Situation und Intention von Rom 13, 1-7," *ZThK* 73(1976)131-166.

Funk, Robert W., "The Significance of Discourse Structure for the Study of the New Testament," in *No Famine in the Land: Studies in Honor of J. L. McKenzie.* Ed. James W. Flanagan and Anita Weisbrod Robinson, Missoula: Scholars Press, 1975, pp. 209-221.

Furnish, V. P., *Theology and Ethics in Paul.* Nashville: Abingdon Press, 1968.

Gammie, John G., "Theological Interpretation by Way of Literary and Tradition Analysis: Genesis 25-36," in *Encounters with the Text: Form & History in the Hebrew Bible.* Ed. M. J. Buss, Missoula: Scholars Press, 1979, pp. 117-134.

Gerstenberger, E., " אבה ," *Theologisches Handwörterbuch zum Alten Testament.* Ed. Ernst Jenni & Claus Westermann, München: Chr. Kaiser Verlag, 1976, pp. 20-25.

Ginsberg, H. L., "Ugaritic Studies and the Bible," in *The Biblical Archaeological Reader.* Ed. David Noel Freedman and Edward F. Campbell, Jr., New York: Doubleday & Co., 1964, Anchor Books, pp. 34-50.

Golka, Friedman, W., "The Aeteologies in the Old Testament, Part 1," *VT* 26(1976)410-428.

Gottwald, N., *All the Kingdoms of the Earth.* New York: Harper & Row, 1964.

Grant, Robert M., "The Sermon on the Mount in Early Christianity," *Semeia* 12(1978)215-231.

—————, *A Short History of the Interpretation of the Bible.* New York: Macmillan, 1963.

Greengus, S., "Law in the O.T.," *IDB(S).* Ed. Keith Crim, Nashville: Abingdon, 1976.

Greenwood, David, "Rhetorical Criticism and Formgeschichte: Some Methodological Considerations," *JBL* 89(1970)418-426.

Gunkel, H., "Fundamental Problems of Hebrew Literary History," in *What Remains of the Old Testament and Other Essays.* Trans. A. K. Dallas, New York: Macmillan, 1928, pp. 57-68.

—————, *Genesis übersetzt und erklärt von Hermann Gunkel.* Göttingen: Vandenhoeck & Ruprecht, 3rd ed., 1964.

—————, *The Legends of Genesis.* Trans. H. W. Carruth, New York: Schocken Books, 1964.

Gunneweg, A. H. J., *Understanding the Old Testament.* Trans. J. Bowden, London: SCM Press, 1978.

Güttgemanns, Erhardt, *Candid Questions Concerning Gospel Form Criticism: A Methodological Sketch of the Fundamental Problematics of Form and Redaction Criticism.* Trans. William G. Doty, *Pittsburgh Theological Monograph Series 26,* General editor Dikron Y. Hadidian, Pittsburgh: Pickwick Press, 1978.

—————, "What is 'Generative Poetics'?" *Semeia* 6(1976)1-21.

Habel, Norman C., *Literary Criticism of the Old Testament.* Philadelphia: Fortress Press, 1971.

Hahn, H. C., "Conscience," *DNTT,* Vol. 1. Ed. Collin Brown, Grand Rapids: Zondervan, 1975, pp. 348-353.

Hals, Ronald M., "Legend: A Case Study in Old Testament Form Critical Terminology," *CBQ* 34(1972)166-176.

Hammershaimb, E., "On the Ethics of the Old Testament Prophets," *VTS* 7(1960)75-101.

Hammerton-Kelly, R. G., "Matthew, Gospel of," *IDB(S).* Ed. Keith Crim, Nashville: Abingdon, 1976.

—————, "Sermon on the Mount," *IDB(S).* Ed. Keith Crim, Nashville: Abingdon, 1976.

Hanson, Paul D., "The Theological Significance of Contradictions Within the Book of the Covenant," in *Canon & Authority.* Ed. G. W. Coats and B. O. Long, Philadelphia: Fortress Press, 1977, pp. 110-131.

Hanson, R. P. C., "Introduction to Volume iii," *The Pelican Guide to Modern Theology,* Vol. 3. Baltimore: Penguin Books, 1970, pp. 9-21.

Haran, M., "From Early to Classical Prophecy: Continuity and Change," *VT* 27(1977)385-397.

———————, "Observations on the Historical Background of Amos 1:2— 2:6," *IEJ* 18(1968)201-212.

Harder, Günther, "πονηρός," *TDNT*, Vol. 6. Ed. Gerhard Kittel. Grand Rapids: Eerdman's 1964, pp. 546-565.

Harrington, Daniel J., "Matthean Studies Since Joachim Rohde," *Heyth J* 16(1975)375-388.

Herrmann, Siegfried, *A History of Israel in O.T. Times*. Trans. John Bowden, Philadelphia: Fortress Press, 1975.

Hirsch, Eric, *The Aims of Interpretation*. Chicago: University of Chicago, 1976.

Hobbs, T. R., "Amos 3:16 and 2:10," *ZAW* 81(1969) 384-386.

Hoffmann, Hans, "Form-Function-Intention," *ZAW* 82(1970) 341-346.

Holladay, John S., Jr., "Assyrian Statecraft and the Prophets," *HTR* 63(1970)29-51.

Hooker, Morna, "In His Own Image," in *What About the New Testament? Essays in Honor of Christopher Evans*, ed. Morna Hooker and Colin Hickling. London: SCM Press, 1975.

Howington, N. D., "Towards an Ethical Understanding of Amos," *Review and Expositor* 58(1966)405-412.

Huffman, H. B., "The Covenant Lawsuit in the Prophets," *JBL* 78(1959) 285-295.

———————, "The Origins of Prophecy," in *Magnalia Dei: The Mighty Acts of God*. Ed. Frank Moore Cross, Werner E. Lemke, and Patrick D. Miller, Garden City, N.Y.: Doubleday, 1976, pp. 171-186.

Jackendoff, Ray S., *Semantic Interpretation in Generative Grammar*. Cambridge: MIT Press, 1972.

Jepsen, Alfred, "Israel und das Gesetz," *TLZ* 93(1968)88-94.

Jones, A. H. M., "Over-Taxation & the Decline of the Roman Empire," in *The Roman Economy*. London: Blackwell's, 1974, pp. 82-89.

———————, "Taxation in Antiquity," in *The Roman Economy*. London: Blackwell's, 1974, pp. 151-186.

Kahan, Arcadius, "Economic History," *Encyclopedia Judaica*, Vol. 16, Supplement, pp. 1266-1323.

Kaiser, Otto and Kümmel, Werner G., *Exegetical Method*. Trans. E. V. N. Goetchius, New York: Seabury Press, 1963.

———————, *Introduction to the Old Testament: A Presentation of its Results & Problems*. Trans. John Sturdy, Minneapolis: Augsburg Publishing House, 1975.

Kapelrud, A. S., *Central Ideas in Amos*. Oslo: Oslo University Press, 1961.

———————, "New Ideas in Amos," *VTS* 15(1966)193-206.

Käsemann, Ernest, "Principles of the Interpretation of Rom 13," in *New Testament Questions of Today*. Philadelphia: Fortress Press, 1969, pp. 196-216.

Kaufmann, Y., *The Religion of Israel: From Its Beginnings to the Babylonian Exile*. Trans. & abridged by Moshe Greenberg, Chicago: University of Chicago Press, 1960.

———————, *Toldot haemunah hayrsraelit*, Eight Volumes. Tel Aviv: Mosad Bialik: Dvir, 1937-1956.

Kearney, Hugh, *Science and Change 1500-1700*. New York: McGraw Hill, 1971, World University Library.

Keck, Leander, *Taking the Bible Seriously*. New York: Association Press, 1962.

Kee, H. C., "Biblical Criticism, N.T.," *IDB(S)*. Ed. Keith Crim, Nashville: Abingdon, 1976.

Keller, Carl A., "Die Gefährdung der Ahnfrau: Ein Beiträge zur gattungs-und motivgeschichtlichen Erforschung altestamentlicher Erzählungen," *ZAW* (1954)181-191.

Kempson, R. M., *Semantic Theory*. Cambridge: Cambridge University Press, 1977.

Kingsbury, Matthew: *Structure, Christology, Kingdom*. Philadelphia: Fortress Press, 1975.

_____, "The Verb Akolouthein ('to follow') as An Index of Matthew's View of His Community," *JBL* 97(1978)56-73.

Klassen, William, "Anabaptist Hermeneutics: The Letter and the Spirit," *MQR* 40(1966)83-96.

_____, "The Bern Debate of 1538: Christ the Center of Scripture," *MQR* 40(1966)148-156.

Klein, R. W., *Textual Criticism of the Old Testament: From the Septuagint to Qumran, Guides to Biblical Scholarship, Old Testament Series*. Philadelphia: Fortress Press, 1974.

Knierim, Rolf, P., " 'I Will Not Cause It to Return' in Amos 1 & 2," in *Canon and Authority*. Ed. George C. Coats and Burke O. Long, Philadelphia: Fortress Press, 1977, pp. 163-175.

Knight, D., *The Traditions of Israel. Society of Biblical Literature Dissertation Series 9*. Missoula, Mont.: Society of Biblical Literature, 1973.

Koch, Klaus et al., *Amos untersucht mit den methoden einer strukturalen Formgeschichte. AOAT 30*, Neukirchen-Vluyn: Neukirchener Verlag, 1976.

_____, "Die Entstehung der sozialen Kritik bei den Profeten," in *Probleme biblischer Theologie*. Ed. H. W. Wolff, München: C. Kaiser, 1971, pp. 236-257.

_____, *The Growth of the Biblical Tradition: The Form Critical Method*. Trans. S. M. Cupitt, 2nd ed. London: Adams and Charles Black, 1969.

_____, "Reichen die formgeschichtlichen Methoden für die Gegenwarts Aufgaben der Bibelwissenschaft zu?" *TLZ* 98(1973)801-814.

_____, "Die Rolle der hymnischen Abschnitte des Amos-Buches," *ZAW* 86(1974)504-537.

Koyre, Alexandre, *The Astronomical Revolution*. Trans. R. E. W. Maddison, Paris: Hermann, 1973.

Kraeling, Emil G., *The Old Testament Since the Reformation*. New York: Schocken Books, 1955.

Kramer, S. N., *The Sumerians: Their History, Culture, and Character*. Chicago: University of Chicago Press, 1963.

Kraus, F. R., *Ein Edikt des Königs Ammi-Saduqa von Babylon, Studia et Documenta*. Vol. 5. Leiden: E. J. Brill, 1958.

_____, "Ein Edikt des Königs Samsu-Iluna von Babylon," in *Studies in Honor of Benno Landsberger on his Seventy-Fifth Birthday, April 21, 1965*, eds. H. G. Güterbock and T. Jacobsen, *Assyriological Studies 16*, Chicago: University of Chicago Press, 1965, pp. 225-232.

_____, "Ein zentrale probleme des altmesopotamischen Rechts: Was ist der Codex Hammurabi?" *Geneva* 8(1960)283-296.

Kraus, Hans-Joachim, *Geschichte der historisch-kritischen Erforschung des Alten Testaments*, 2nd ed. Neukirchener Verlag, 1969.

Kümmel, Werner G., *Introduction to the New Testament*. London: SCM Press, 1965.

_____, *The New Testament: The History of the Investigation of Its Problems*. Trans. McLean Gilmour and Howard C. Kee, New York: Abingdon Press, 1970.

Labuschagne, C. J., "Amos' Conception of God and the Popular Theology of His Time," in *Papers read at the 7th & 8th*

Meetings of Die O.T. Werkgemeenskap in Suid-Afrika, Potchefstrom: Pro Regepers Beperk, 1964-1965, pp. 122-133.

Leaney, A. R. C. and Davidson, Robert, *Biblical Criticism. The Pelican Guide to Modern Theology*, Vol. iii. Baltimore: Penguin Books, 1970.

Leenhardt, Franz J., *The Epistle to the Romans. Commentaire du Nouveau Testament*. Trans. Harold Knight, London: Lutterworth Press, 1961.

Lehming, Sigo, "Erwägugen zu Amos," *ZThK* 55(1958)145-169.

Lehrer, A., *Semantic Fields and Lexical Structure. North-Holland Linguistic Series No. 11*. Ed. S. C. Dik and J. G. Kooij, Amsterdam: North-Holland Publishing Co., 1974.

Lemche, Nils P., "Andurārum and mīšarum: Comments on the Problems of Social Edicts and their Application in the Ancient Near East," *JNES* 38(1979)11-22.

——————, "The Manumission of Slaves—The Fallow Year—The Sabbatical Year—The Jubilee Year," *VT* 26(1976)38-59.

Lenski, Richard C. H., *The Interpretation of St. Paul's Epistle to the Romans*. Columbus, Ohio: Lutheran Book Concern, 1936.

Lohfink, Gerhard, *Jetzt Verstehe ich die Bibel: Ein Sachbuch zur Formkritik*. Stuttgart: Verlag Katholisches Bibelwerk, 1973.

Long, Burke O., *The Problem of Etiological Narrative in the Old Testament, BZAW* 108, Berlin: Walter de Gruyter, 1968.

——————, "Recent Field Studies in Oral Literature and Their Bearing on O.T. Criticism," *VT* 26(1976)187-198.

——————, and Coates, George W., "Prophetic Superscriptions and the Growth of a Canon," in *Canon and Authority: Essays in Old Testament Reli-*

gion and Theology. Philadelphia: Fortress Press, 1977, pp. 56-70.

Longyear, Christopher R., *Linguistically Determined Categories of Meaning. Janua Linguarim Ser. Practica No. 92*, Mouton, 1972.

Lührmann, D., *Die Redaktion der Logienquelle. WMANT* 33. Neukirchen-Vluyn: Neukirchener Verlag, 1969.

Luz, Ulrich, "Die Erfühlung des Gesetzes bei Matthäus (Mt. 5:17-20)," *ZThK* 75(1978)498-535.

Lyons, J., *Introduction to Theoretical Linguistics*. Cambridge University Press, 1968.

——————, *Semantics*, 2 vols. Cambridge: Cambridge University Press, 1977.

——————, *Structural Semantics*. Oxford: Blockwell, 1963.

McEvenue, Sean E., "A Comparison of Narrative Styles in the Hagar Stories," *Semeia* 3(1975)64-80.

Maag, V., *Text, Wortschatz, und Begriffswelt des Buches Amos*. Leiden, 1951.

Macholz, Georg C., "Die Stellung des Königs in der israelitischen Gerichtsverfassung," *ZAW* 84(1972)157-181.

——————, "Zur Geschichte der Justizorganization in Judah," *ZAW* (1972)314-340.

March, Eugene, "Prophets," in *Form Criticism*, ed. John H. Hayes, San Antonio: Trinity University Press, 1974, pp. 141-177.

Markert, Ludwig, *Struktur und Bezeichnung des Scheltworts*. Berlin: Walter de Gruyter, 1977.

Markert, Ludwig and Gunther Wanke, "Die Propheten Interpretations: Anfragen und Überlegungen," *KD* 22(1976)191-220.

Marle, Rene, *Introduction to Herme-*

neutics. New York: Herder & Herder, 1967.

Martin, William J., "Special Revelation as Objective," in *Revelation & the Bible*. Ed. Carl F. H. Henry, Grand Rapids, Mich.: Baker Book House, 1959.

Mauchline, John, "Implicit Signs of a Persistent Belief in the Davidic Empire," *VT* 20(1970)287-303.

Maurer, Christian, " οὐνοιδα ," *TDNT*, Vol. 7. Grand Rapids, Mich.: Eerdman's, 1964, pp. 899-918.

Meier, John P., *Law and History in Matthew's Gospel*. Rome: Biblical Institute Press, 1976.

Melugin, Roy F., "Form Criticism and Theological Exegesis," in *Encounter with the Text*. Ed. M. J. Buss, Missoula, Mont.: Scholar's Press, 1979, pp. 91-99.

Merwe, "A Few Remarks on the Religious Terminology in Amos and Hosea," in *Papers Read at the 7th and 8th Meetings of Die OT Werkgemeenskap in Suid-Afrika*, Potchefstrom: Pro Regepers Beperk, 1964-1965, pp. 134-142.

Metzger, B. M., *The Text of the New Testament: Its Transmission. Corruption, and Restoration*. Oxford: Clarendon Press, 2nd ed., 1968.

Michel, Otto, *Der Brief an die Römer*. Göttingen: Vandenhoeck & Ruprecht, 1966.

Minear, Paul, *The Obedience of Faith: The Purposes of Paul in the Epistle to the Romans*. SBT 2nd ser. 19, London: SCM Press, 1971.

Miscall, P. D., "The Concept of the Poor in the Old Testament." PhD diss., Harvard University, 1972.

Montague, George T., "Hermeneutics and the Teaching of Scripture," *CBQ* 41 (1979)1-17.

Montefiore, C. G., *Rabbinic Literature and Gospel Teachings*. New York: Ktav Publishing House, 1970.

Morrison, Clinton, *The Powers That Be*. London: SCM Press, 1960.

Muilenburg, James, "Form Criticism and Beyond," *JBL* 88(1969)1-18.

Muntingh, "The Political and International Relations of Israel's Neighbouring Peoples According to the Oracles of Amos," in *Papers Read at the 7th & 8th Meetings of Die O.T. Werkgemeenskap in Suid-Afrika*, Potchefstrom: Pro Regepers Beperk, 1964-1965, pp. 134-142.

Neil, W., "The Criticism and Theological Use of the Bible 1700-1950," in *Cambridge History of the Bible*, Vol. iii. Ed. S. L. Greenslade, Cambridge: Cambridge University Press, 1975, pp. 238-293.

Neill, Stephen, *The Interpretation of the New Testament, 1861-1961*. London: Oxford, 1964.

Nida, Eugene A., *Toward a Science of Translating*. Leiden: E. J. Brill, 1964.

Nineham, Dennis, *The Use and Abuse of the Bible*. London: Unwin Bros. Ltd., 1976.

Nilsen, Don L. F. and Alleen Pace Nilsen, *Semantic Theory, A Linguistic Perspective*. Rowley, Mass.: Newbury House Publishers, 1975.

North, R., *Sociology of the Biblical Jubilee*, Analecta Biblica, Vol. 4, 1954, Rome: Pontifical Biblical Institute.

Noth, M., *A History of Pentateuchal Tradition*. Trans. Bernhard W. Anderson, Englewood Cliffs, N.J.: Prentice-Hall, 1972.

O'Neill, J. C., *Paul's Letter to the Romans*. Baltimore, Md.: Penguin Books, 1975.

Ohler, Anne Marie, *Gattungen in Alten Testament*. Dusseldorf: Patmos-Verlag, 1972-1973.

Öhman, Suzanne, "Theories of the 'Linguistic Field,' " *Word* 9(1953)123-134.

Palmer, F. R., *Semantics: A New Outline*. Cambridge: Cambridge University Press, 1976.

Palmer, Richard E., *Hermeneutics*. Evanston: Northwestern University Press, 1969.

Parker, Thomas Henry Louts, *Calvin's New Testament Commentaries*. Grand Rapids: Eerdman's, 1971.

Patrick, Dale, "Political Exegesis," in *Encounters with the Text*. Ed. M. J. Buss, Missoula, Mont.: Scholars Press, 1979, pp. 139-152.

Paul, Shalom, "Amos 1:3—2:3 A Concatenous Literary Pattern," *JBL* 90(1971)397-403.

—————, *Studies in the Book of the Covenant in the Light of Cuneiform and Biblical Law*. VTS 18, Leiden: E. J. Brill, 1970.

Perrin, Norman, *What Is Redaction Criticism?* Philadelphia: Fortress Press, 1969.

Peterson, David L., "A Thrice Told Tale: Genre, Theme, and Motif," *Biblical Research* 18(1973)30-43.

Pettinato, G., *Das Altorientalische Menschenbild und die sumerischen und akkadischen Schöpfungsmythen*, Abhandlungen der Heidelberger Akademie der Wissenschaften. Heidelberg: Carl Winter, 1971.

Poettcker, Henry, "Bible, Inner & Outer Word, *ME* Vol. I, p. 326b.

—————, "Biblical Controversy on Several Fronts," *MQR* 40(1966)127-138.

—————, "The Hermeneutics of Menno Simons," PhD diss., Princeton, 1961.

—————, "Menno Simons' Encounter with the Bible," *MQR* 40(1966), pp. 112-126.

Polzin, R., "The Ancestress of Israel in Danger," *Semeia* 3(1975)81-98.

Porteous, Norman W., "The Basis of the Ethical Teachings of the Prophets," in *Studies in Old Testament Prophecy*. Edinburgh: T and T Clark, 1950.

Preus, James Samuel, *From Shadow to Promise*. Cambridge: Belknap Press of Harvard University Press, 1969.

Rad, Gerhard von, "The Deuteronomic Theology of History in I and II Kings" in *The Problem of the Hexateuch and Other Essays*. Trans. E. W. Trueman Dicken, London: Oliver & Boyd, 1966, pp. 205-221.

—————, *Old Testament Theology*, 2 vols. Trans. D. M. G. Stalker, New York: Harper & Row, 1965.

Rast, Walter E., *Tradition History and the Old Testament*. Philadelphia: Fortress Press, 1972.

Rentorff, Rolff, "Literarkritik und Traditionsgeschichte," *Ev. Th.* 27(1967)138-153.

—————, "Reflections on the Early History of Prophecy in Israel," *Journal for Theology & Church* 4(1967)14-34.

Reumann, John, "The Lutheran 'Hermeneutics Study': An Overview and Personal Appraisal," in *Studies in Lutheran Hermeneutics*. Ed. John Reumann, Samuel H. Nafzger, and Harold H. Ditmanson, Philadelphia: Fortress Press, 1979, pp. 1-76.

—————, "Methods in Studying the Biblical Text Today," *Concordia Theological Monthly* 40(1969) 655-681.

Reventlow, H. Graf, *Das Amt des Propheten bei Amos* FRLANT 80. Göttingen: Vandenhoeck & Ruprecht, 1962.

Richards, Lawrence O., *Creative Bible Study*. Grand Rapids: Zondervan, 1971.

Richter, W., *Exegese als Literaturwissenschaft: Entwurf einer alttestamentlichen Literatur Theorie und Methodologie*. Göttingen: Vandenhoeck & Ruprecht, 1971.

Ridderbos, Herman, *Paul: An Outline of His Theology.* Trans. John DeWitt, Grand Rapids: Eerdman's, 1975.

Ringgren, Helmer, "Literarkritik, Formgeschichte, Überlieferungsgeschichte," *TLZ,* 91(1966)641-650.

Robertson, David, *The Old Testament and the Literary Critic.* Philadelphia: Fortress Press, 1977.

Rogers, Jack B. and Donald K. McKim, *The Authority and Interpretation of the Bible: An Historical Approach.* New York: Harper & Row, 1979.

Rohde, Joachim, *Rediscovering the Teaching of the Evangelists.* Philadelphia: Westminster, 1968.

Rohrbaugh, Richard L., *The Biblical Interpreter.* Philadelphia: Fortress Press, 1978.

Rohrmann, Charles Albert, "Copernicus," *Encyclopaedia Britannica,* Vol. 5, London: William Benton, 1969, pp. 145-146.

Ross, James, "The Prophet as Yahweh's Messenger," in *Israel's Prophetic Heritage.* Ed. B. W. Anderson and W. Harrelson, New York: Harper & Row, 1962, pp. 99-107.

Roth, Wolfgang M. W., "The Text Is the Medium: An Interpretation of the Jacob Stories in Genesis," in *Encounters with the Text.* Ed. M. J. Buss, Missoula, Mont.: Scholars Press, 1979, pp. 103-115.

Rowley, H. H., *The Growth of the Old Testament.* New York: Harper & Row, 1963.

——————, ed., *The Old Testament and Modern Study.* London: Oxford, 1961.

Ruprecht, Eberhard, "Der traditionsgeschichtliche Hintergrund der einzelnen Elemente von Genesis xii 2-3," *VT* 19(1979)444-464.

——————, "Vorgebene Tradition und theologische Gestaltung in Genesis xii 1-3," *VT* 29(1979)171-188.

Sanders, J. A., "Adaptable for Life; The Nature and Function of Canon," in *Magnalia Dei: The Mighty Acts of God.* Ed. Frank Moore Cross and Werner E. Lemke, Garden City, New York: Doubleday, 1976, pp. 531-560.

Sawyer, John F. A., *Semantics in Biblical Research: New Methods of Defining Hebrew Words for Salvation.* SBT 24. Naperville, Ill.: Alec R. Allenson, 1972.

Scharbert, Josef, "Zu den Methoden der alttestamentlichen Exegese," *ThR* 70(1974)Col. 1-16.

Schenk, Wolfgang, "Die Aufgaben der Exegese und die Mittel der Linguistik," *TLZ* 98(1973)881-894.

——————, "Das Präsens Historicum als Makrosyntaktisches Gliederungssignal in Matthäusevangelium," *NTS* 22(1975)464-475.

Schicklberger, Franz, "Biblische Literarkritik und Linguistische Texttheorie," *TZ* 34(1978)65-81.

Schlier, H., *Der Römerbrief. Herder's Theologische Kommentar zum Neuen Testament.* Frieburg: Herder & Herder, 1977.

Schmid, H. H., *Gerechtigkeit als Weltordnung: Hintergrund und Geschichte des alttestamentlichen Gerechtigkeitsbegriffes.* BHTh 40. Tübingen: J. C. B. Mohr, 1968.

——————, "Zur Frage nach der geistigen Heimet des Propheten," *Wort und Dienst* 10(1969)85-103.

Schmidt, Werner H., "Die deuteronomische Redaktion des Amos Buches," *ZAW* 77(1965)168-193.

——————, *Zukunftsgewissheit und Gegenwartskritik: Grundzüge prophetischer Verkündigung. Biblische Studien* 64, Neukirchen-Vluyn: Neukirchener Verlag, 1973.

Schmitt, H.-Chr., "Prophetie und Tradition: Beobachtungen zur Frühgeschichte des Israelitischen Nabitums," *ZThK* 74(1977)255-272.

Schrage, W., *Die Christen und der Staat nach dem Neuen Testament.* Gütersloh: Hohn, 1971.

Schreiner, J., ed., "Der Hermeneutische Horizont," in *Einführung in die Methoden der biblischen Exegese.* Würzburg: Echter Verlag, 1971, pp. 40-80.

Schroeder, D., "Exhortation in the N.T.," *IDB(S).* Ed. Keith Crim, Nashville: Abingdon, 1976.

_____, "Parenesis," *IDB(S),* Ed. Keith Crim, Nashville: Abingdon, 1976.

_____, *Learning to Know the Bible.* Newton, Kan.: Faith & Life Press, 1966.

Schweitzer, Eduard, "Christianity of the Circumcized and Judaism of the Uncircumcized: The Background of Matthew & Colossians," in *Jews, Greeks, & Christians.* Ed. Robert Hamerton-Kelly and Robin Scroggs, Leiden: E. J. Brill, 1976, pp. 245-260.

_____, *The Good News According to Matthew.* Trans. David E. Green, Atlanta: John Knox, 1975.

Scroggs, Robin, "Beyond Criticism to Encounter: The Bible in the Post-Critical Age," *The Chicago Theological Seminary Register* 68(1978)1-11.

Searle, John R., *Speech Acts.* Cambridge: Cambridge University Press, 1969.

Selms, V., "Amos' Geographical Horizon," in *Papers Read at the 7th & 8th Meetings of Die OT Werkgemeenskap in Suid-Afrika.* Potchefstrom: Pro Regepers Beperk, 1964-1965, pp. 166-169.

_____, "Isaac in Amos," in *Papers Read at the 7th & 8th Meetings of Die OT Werkgemeenskap in Suid-Afrika.* Potchefstrom: Pro Regepers Beperk, 1964-1965, pp. 157-165.

Shea, William R., *Galileo's Intellectual Revolution: Middle Period 1610-1632.* Science History Publications, New York: Neale Watson Academic Publications, 1972.

Smalley, William A., "Recursion Patterns and the Sectioning of Amos," *The Bible Translator* 30(1979)118-127.

Smith, Alan G. R., *Science and Society.* London: Thames & Hudson, 1972.

Smitmans, A., "Ein Beispiel aus dem Neuen Test," in *Einführung in die Methoden der Biblischen Exegese.* Ed. J. Schreiner, Würzburg: Echter Verlag, 1971, pp. 149-193.

Soggins, J. Alberto, "Amos VI:13-14 und I:3 aus den Hintergrund der Bezichungen zwischen Israels und Damaskus in 9. und 8. Jahrhundret," in *Near Eastern Studies in Honor of W. F. Albright.* Ed. Hans Goedicke, Baltimore: Johns Hopkins Press, 1971, pp. 433-441.

_____, *Introduction to the Old Testament.* Trans. J. Bowden, London: SCM Press, 1976, pp. 94-98.

Speiser, E. A., "Early Law and Civilization," in *Oriental & Biblical Studies.* Ed. J. J. Finkelstein and M. Greenberg, Philadelphia: University of Pennsylvania Press, 1967, pp. 534-555.

_____, "Authority and Law in Mesopotamia," Ibid., pp. 313-323.

_____, "Of Shoes and Shekels," in *BASOR* 77(1940)15-20.

_____, "Cuneiform Law and the History of Civilization," *Proceedings of the American Philosophical Society,* 107 (1963), pp. 536-541.

Stanton, G. N., "Presuppositions in New Testament Criticism," in *New Testament Interpretation: Essays on Principles and Methods.* Ed. I. H. Marshall, Exeter: Paternoster, 1977.

Stein, R. H., "What Is Redaktionsgeschichte?" *JBL* 88(1969)45-56.

Stendhal, Krister, *The School of St. Matthew and Its Use of the Old Testament.* Lund: Gleerup, 1968, 2nd ed.

Strack, Herman and Billerbeck, Paul, *Commentar zum Neuen Testament aus*

Talmud und Midrasch, 5th ed. Münich: Beck Verlag, 1969.

Strecker, Georg, "Die Antithesis der Bergpredigt," *ZNW* 69(1978)36-72.

Strobel, A., "Zum Verständnis von Rom. 13," *ZNW* 47(1956)67-93.

Stuhlmacher, Peter, *Historical Criticism & Theological Interpretation of Scripture.* Philadelphia: Fortress Press, 1977. Trans. Roy A. Harrisville.

Suggs, M. Jack, "The Antithesis as Redactional Products," in *Jesus Christus in Historie und Theologie Fs. für H. Conzelmann zum 60.* Ed. G. Strecker, Tübingen: Mohr, 1975, pp. 433-444.

——————, *Wisdom, Christology and Law in Matthew's Gospel.* Cambridge: Harvard University Press, 1970.

Tannehill, Robert C., "Matthew 5:39b-42. Turning the Other Cheek ("The Focal Instance")," in *The Sword of His Mouth.* Philadelphia: Fortress Press, 1975, pp. 67-78.

Tengström, Sven, *Die Hexateucherzählung: Eine Literaturgeschichtliche Studie.* Lund: Gleerup, 1976.

Terrien, S., "Amos & Wisdom," in *Israel's Prophetic Heritage: Essays in Honor of James Muilenburg.* Ed. Bernard W. Anderson and Walter Harrelson, New York: Harper & Brothers, 1962, pp. 108-115.

Thiselton, Anthony C., "Semantics and New Testament Interpretation," in *New Testament Interpretation: Essays on Principles and Methods.* Ed. I. Marshall, Exeter, England: Pater Noster Press, 1977, pp. 75-104.

Thompson, T. L., "A New Attempt to Date the Patriarchal Narratives," *JAOS* 98(1978)76-84.

——————, "Conflict Themes in the Jacob Narratives," *Semeia* 15(1979)5-23.

——————, *The Historicity of the Patriarchal Narratives: The Quest for the*

Historical Abraham. Berlin: Walter de Gruyter, 1974.

Tucker, Gene, "Form Criticism, OT," *IDB(S).* Ed. Keith Crim, Nashville: Abingdon, 1976.

——————, *Form Criticism of the Old Testament.* Philadelphia: Fortress Press, 1971.

Tucker, G. M. and Via, D. O., eds., *Guides to Biblical Scholarship.* Philadelphia: Fortress Press, 1969.

Van Seters, John, *Abraham in History and Tradition.* New Haven, Conn.: Yale University Press, 1975.

Vassilyev, L. M., "The Theory of Semantic Fields: A Survey," *Linguistics* 137(1974)79-93.

Vater, Ann M., "Story Patterns for a Sitz: A Form—or Literary—Critical Concern?" *JSOT* 11(1979)47-56.

Vollmer, Jochen, *Geschichtiche Rückblicke und Motive in des Prophetie des Amos, Hosea und Jesaja.* Berlin: Walter de Gruyter, 1971.

de Vries, S. J., "Biblical Criticism," *IDB(S).* Ed. Keith Crim, Nashville: Abingdon, 1976.

Wagner, Siegfried, "Überlegungen zur Frage nach den Beziehungen des Propheten Amos zum Sudreich," *TLZ* 96(1971) 653-670.

Wagner, V., "Zur Systematik in dem Codex Ex. 21:2—22:16", *ZAW* 81(1969)176-182.

Waldow, H. E., *Der Traditionsgeschichtliche Hintergrund der Prophetischen Gerichtsreden. BZAW* 85(1963), Berlin: Walter de Gruyter & Co.

——————, "Some Thoughts on Old Testament Form Criticism," in *SBL Seminar Papers,* Vol. 2, 1971, pp. 587-600.

Wallis, Gerhard, "Die Tradition von den drei Ahnvätern," *ZAW* 81(1969)18-40.

Wanke, Gunther, "Zu Grundlegen und Absicht prophetischer sozial Kritik," *KD* 18(1972)2-17.

Warner, S. T. "Primitive Saga Men," *VT* 29(1979)325-335.

Watts, J. D. W., "Amos the Man," *Review and Expositor* 58(1966)387-392.

Wedderburn, A. J. M., "The Purpose and Occasion of Romans Again," *ET* 90(1979)137-141.

Weimar, Peter *Untersuchungen zur Redaktionsgeschichte des Pentateuch.* New York: Walter de Gruyter, 1977.

Weinfeld, M., *Deuteronomy and the Deuteronomic School.* Oxford: Clarendon Press, 1972.

Weiss, M., "The Pattern of 'Execration Texts' in the Prophetic Literature," ISrEJ 19(1969)150-157.

Wellhausen, J., *Prolegomena to the History of Ancient Israel.* Trans. Menzies and Black, Cleveland: World Publishing Co., Meridian Books, 1957.

Westermann, C., *Basic Forms of Prophetic Speech.* Trans. Hugh Clayton White, London: Lutterworth Press, 1967.

—————, *Erträge der Forschung Genesis 12-50.* Neukirchen-Vluyn: Neukirchener Verlag, 1977.

—————, "Genesis," *IDB(S).* Ed. Keith Crim, Nashville: Abingdon, 1976.

—————, *Genesis Biblischer Kommentar: Altes Testament.* Neukirchen-Vluyn: Neukirchener Verlag, 1966.

—————, "Promises to the Patriarchs," *IDB(S).* Ed. Keith Crim, Nashville: Abingdon, 1976.

—————, *Die Verheissungen an die Väter, FRLANT,* Vol. 116. Göttingen: Vandenhoeck & Ruprecht, 1976.

Wharton, J. A., "Redaction Criticism, O.T.," *IDB(S).* Ed. Keith Crim, Nashville: Abingdon, 1976.

White, Andrew D., *A History of the Warfare of Science with Theology in Christendom.* New York: D. Appleton & Co., 1917.

White, Hugh C., "Structural Analysis of the Old Testament," in *Encounters with the Text.* Ed. M. J. Buss, Missoula, Mont.: Scholars Press, 1979, pp. 45-68.

Whedbee, J. William, *Isaiah and Wisdom.* Nashville: Abingdon Press, 1971.

Wilcoxen, Jay A., "Narrative," in *Old Testament Form Criticism.* Ed. John H. Hayes, San Antonio: Trinity University Press, 1974, pp. 57-98.

Willi-Plein, Ina, *Vorformen der Schriftexegese innerhalb des Alten Testaments* in *BZAW* 123 Berlin: de Gruyter, 1971.

Willis, John T., "Redaction Criticism and Historical Reconstruction," in *Encounters with the Text.* Ed. M. J. Buss, Missoula, Mont.: Scholars Press, 1979, pp. 83-89.

Wolff, H. W., *Amos' geistige Heimat.* *WMANT* 18, 1964.

—————, *Amos the Prophet: The Man and His Background.* Trans. F. R. McCurley, Philadelphia: Fortress Press, 1973.

—————, *Joel & Amos, Hermeneia,* Philadelphia: Fortress Press, 1977.

—————, "The Kerygma of the Yahwist," *EvTh* 24(1964)73-98.

Wrege, Hans-Theo, *Die Überlieferungsgeschichte der Bergpredigt, WUNT* 9, 1968 Tübingen: J. C. B. Mohr.

Wright, George Ernest, "The Lawsuit of God—A Form-Critical Study of Dt. 32," in *Israel's Prophetic Heritage.* Ed. Bernard Anderson and Walter Harrelson, New York: Harper & Row, 1962, pp. 26-678.

Würthwein, Ernst, *The Text of the Old Testament.* Trans. P. R. Ackroyd, Oxford: Basil Blackwell, 1957.

——————————, "Kultpolemik oder Kultbescheid," in *Tradition und Situation: Studien zur alttestamentlichen Prophetie Festschrift für Artur Weiser*, Ed. E. Würthwein and Otto Kaiser, Göttingen: Vandenhoeck and Ruprecht, 1963, pp. 115-131.

——————————, "Der Ursprung der prophetischen Gerichtsrede," *ZThK* 1(1952)1-16.

Yoder, John Howard, *The Politics of Jesus*. Grand Rapids: Ecrdman's, 1972.

Yoder, P. B., *Toward Understanding the Bible: Hermeneutics for Lay People*. Newton, Kan.: Faith and Life Press, 1978.

Young, Robert, *Analytical Concordance to the Bible*. New York: Funk & Wagnalls Co., no date.

Zenger, E., "Ein Beispiel exegetischer Methoden aus dem Alten Testament," in *Einführung in die Methoden der Biblischen Exegese*. Ed. J. Schreiner, Würzburg: Echter Verlag, 1971, pp. 97-148.

Name and Subject Index

279

Scripture Index

The Conrad Grebel Lectures

The Conrad Grebel Lectureship was set up in 1950 to make possible an annual study by a Mennonite scholar of some topic of interest and value to the Mennonite Church and to other Christian people. It is administered by the Conrad Grebel Projects Committee appointed by and responsible to the Mennonite Board of Education. The committee appoints the lecturers, approves their subjects, counsels them during their studies, and arranges for the delivery of the lectures at one or more places.

Conrad Grebel was an influential leader in the sixteenth-century Swiss Anabaptist movement and is honored as one of the founders of the Mennonite Church.

The lectures are published by Herald Press, Scottdale, Pa. 15683, and Kitchener, Ont. N2G 4M5, as soon as feasible after the delivery of the lectures. The date of publication by Herald Press is indicated by parenthesis.

Lectures thus far delivered are as follows:

1952—*Foundations of Christian Education*
by Paul Mininger

1953—*The Challenge of Christian Stewardship* (1955),
by Milo Kauffman

1954—*The Way of the Cross in Human Relations* (1958),
by Guy F. Hershberger

1955—*The Alpha and the Omega* (1955),
by Paul Erb

1956—*The Nurture and Evangelism of Children* (1959),
by Gideon G. Yoder

1957—*The Holy Spirit and the Holy Life* (1959),
by Chester K. Lehman

1959—*The Church Apostolic* (1960),
by J. D. Graber

1960—*These Are My People* (1962),
by Harold S. Bender

1963—*Servant of God's Servants* (1964).
by Paul M. Miller

1964—*The Resurrected Life* (1965),
by John R. Mumaw

1965—*Creating Christian Personality* (1966),
by A. Don Augsburger

1966—*God's Word Written* (1966),
by J. C. Wenger

1967—*The Christian and Revolution* (1968),
by Melvin Gingerich

1968-1969—*The Discerning Community: Church Renewal,*
by J. Lawrence Burkholder

1970—*Woman Liberated* (1971),
by Lois Gunden Clemens

1971—*Christianity and Culture: An African Context,*
by Donald R. Jacobs

1973—*In Praise of Leisure* (1974),
by Harold D. Lehman

1977—*Integrity: Let Your Yea Be Yea* (1978),
by J. Daniel Hess

1979—*The Christian Entrepreneur* (1980),
by Carl Kreider

1980—*From Word to Life* (1982)
by Perry Yoder

1980—*Case Studies in Biblical Interpretation* (1983)
by Willard M. Swartley

1981—*Christians in Families* (1982)
by Ross T. Bender

Perry Yoder has taught Bible and religion at Bethel College, North Newton, Kansas, since 1977. Earlier he was on the faculty of Bluffton College, Bluffton, Ohio.

He studied Semitic languages and literature with E. A. Speiser and Moshe Greenberg in the department of Near East studies at the University of Pennsylvania. He wrote his doctoral dissertation on A-B pairings in Hebrew poetry, receiving his degree in 1970.

Yoder attended Hesston College and Goshen College (BA, 1962). He studied at Hebrew University in Jerusalem in 1964-65 and participated in excavations with the French Archaeological Mission at Munhata in 1965.

He spent two years in a Voluntary Service project, "People's Teachers of the Word," itinerating through Mennonite churches in North America.

Perry and Elizabeth (Gingerich) Yoder are members of Jubilee Mennonite Church, North Newton, Kansas, and the parents of twin sons, Joel and Joshua.